Dreams in Analysis

Nathan Schwartz-Salant and Murray Stein, editors

Chiron Publications • Wilmette, Illinois

The Chiron Clinical Series
ISBN 0-933029-20-9

© 1990 by Chiron Publications. All rights reserved. No part of this publication may be reproduced, stored in a retrieval system, or transmitted in any form, by any means, electronic, mechanical, photocopying, recording, or otherwise, without the prior written permission of the publisher, Chiron Publications, 400 Linden Avenue, Wilmette, Illinois 60091.

Printed in the United States of America.

Book design by Elaine Hill.

Library of Congress Cataloging-in-Publication Data

Dreams in analysis / Nathan Schwartz-Salant and Murray Stein, editors.
    p. cm. — (The Chiron clinical series)
    ISBN 0-933029-20-9 : $15.95
    1. Dreams. 2. Psychoanalysis. I. Schwartz-Salant, Nathan, 1938-
II. Stein, Murray, 1943- . III. Series.
    [DNLM: 1. Dreams. 2. Psychoanalysis. WM 460.5D8 D7718]
RC506.D74 1989
616.89'17—dc20
DNLM/DLC
for Library of Congress

89-22104
CIP

Contents

The Chiron Clinical Series
Policy on capitalizing the term "Self"

Jung's understanding of the Self is significantly different from
how this term is often used in other contemporary psychoanalytic
literature. The difference hinges primarily on the understanding of
archetypes: the Jungian conceptualization of the Self sees it as rooted
in the transpersonal dimension. Hence the frequent capitalization of
this term. Since the clinical concern with the Self often relates more
narrowly to the sphere of ego-consciousness, however, it can be more
mystifying than edifying always to allude to the archetypal level in
the literature. Consequently the editors of *Chiron* have chosen to
allow authors to exercise an option on the question of capitalization.
They may choose to capitalize Self and thereby to emphasize its
transpersonal, archetypal base; or, they may choose to employ the
lower case, signifying by this that they are discussing issues that have
to do principally with ego-identity and the personal relation to this
central factor of psychic life, which may be less precisely articulated
by reference to the archetypal substratum.

On Dreams and Dreaming

Edward C. Whitmont

Why do we dream? What is the natural function of the dream and dreaming? People have been dreaming since time immemorial. Children and babies — even in utero — dream and, to all appearances, even animals seem to dream. They have no psychotherapists to interpret their dreams and, unlike Pharaoh who called on Joseph, not even soothsayers. Nor, for that matter, would a therapist's or soothsayer's service be of much avail to dreaming babies or dogs. Although up until the time of the Enlightenment there had been a sense of the prophetic nature of some dreams, the overwhelming majority of dreams have been and are only inadequately understood by most people. Hence, more often than not, most dreams, particularly the "trivial" ones, have been dismissed as meaningless. It is only now, owing to Freud's and, particularly, Jung's epochal discoveries, that we are beginning to develop some sort of rational understanding of the dream's vast possible implications and ways to approach them.

From our present vantage point we can see that in past times

Edward C. Whitmont, M.D., is a member of the C. G. Jung Training Center of New York and maintains a private practice in New York City and Irvington, N.Y. He is the author of *The Symbolic Quest, Psyche and Substance: Essays on Homeopathy in the Light of Jungian Psychology, The Return of the Goddess: Desire, Aggression and the Evolution of Consciousness,* and co-author of *Dreams: A Portal to the Source.*

dreams frequently have been misunderstood, owing to insufficient psychological understanding and awareness of unconscious dynamics.

Take, for example, Hannibal's dream before the second Punic war (von Franz 1960). He dreamed that he was admitted to the council of the gods and that Jupiter Capitolinus invited or challenged him to make war on Rome. This he did subsequently, encouraged as he was by what he regarded the good omen of the dream. Yet, obeying what he thought was the dream's meaning, he was thoroughly and decisively defeated. He had failed to consider that Jupiter Capitolinus represented the guardian power of Rome, not Hannibal or Carthage. The dream offered him not a felicitous omen, but was what we today would consider a confrontation with his own unconscious motivation: his ambition and envious urge to challenge Rome's power. It foretold nothing, neither defeat nor, least of all, victory. It simply showed him where he was, psychologically. A similar experience, we have been told, occurred to Hitler in the form of a waking dream or vision. Standing at the balcony of the Viennese Hofburg and receiving the ovations of the crowd after the accomplished occupation of Austria, he had a vision of Odin, the ancient Germanic war god, appearing in the clouds and pointing to the east. This Hitler took as an omen, invitation, and favorable confirmation of his plans to invade Russian, the outcome of which was even more catastrophical for him than Hannibal's venture.

In another example, President Lincoln dreamt the night before his assassination that he came to the White House to find it all draped in black and mourning, with honor guards before a bier. When he asked what had happened, he was told that "the president was killed by an assassin" (Brook 1987). Lincoln's comment upon waking and recounting the dream to his wife was apparently something in the order of "See, there is no reason to worry; the president was supposed to be dead, but I was alive." And yet, strangely, that might indeed be the dream's implied but not clearly understood message: the temporal entity, the president, was to die, but the core of selfness is unaffected by death.

But also in our work as therapists we tend to meet with dreams that puzzle us in respect to their implications and do not seem to fit into any of our categories of clinical usefulness. Here I recall a dream brought during the first few months in the course of working upon a patient's mother complex. In that dream a huge horse bit the dream ego from behind in the right shoulder. Concerning the injuriousness of the mother complex in respect to his outgoing activity (shoulder, arm), this dream did not seem to offer any information not already available.

An amplification in terms of Pelops offering his child to the gods and Demeter eating the shoulder did not feel relevant at this point.

However, within a few days the dreamer developed a serious case of very painful and disabling bursitis in that shoulder. The dream may be viewed as showing the imminent, somatizing "attack" of the life force upon that shoulder. But, we may ask, of what value would it have been to know this beforehand, even had the dream been so understood at the time? Theoretically it may be considered as presenting synchronicity dynamics. But, to what? No new insight was mediated or even emphasized. And, assuming the possibility that the dream's "intent" had been to foretell or forewarn, why would it not render its message in more understandable terms? Why stage a horse rather than offer a simple message concerning a shoulder affliction?

To be sure, Hannibal, Hitler or Lincoln might have been helped had they been able to understand their dreams. But the fact is that they were not and could not possibly have been able to understand, given the limitations of person, time, and culture. Nevertheless the dreams presented themselves to them in puzzling dramatization.

The assumption that dreams occur "in order" to help us increase our awareness and to compensate for conscious positions does not seem sustained by the evidence any more than the classical assumption of psychoanalysis that dreams defend sleep by censoring and modifying unacceptable wishes. Such deliberate "intentionality" or "purposefulness" of that explanation seems too simplistic in view of the average dream's overt incomprehensibility to the average dreamer. Dreams do not represent wishes or wish fulfillments, as the above examples clearly show; neither do they necessarily represent compensations of one-sided conscious positions. (The above horse dream did not compensate any conscious position.) In his seminar on *Kinderträume* Jung speaks of a category of dreams that do not seem to have any relevance to anything currently going on.

Then why do we dream? What is the point of dreaming? What may be the role or function of dreams in a world apart from, or prior to the advent of psychoanalysis?

The most helpful characterization is probably Jung's; he described the dream as

> an expression or involuntary, unconscious psychic process beyond the control of the conscious mind. It shows the inner truth and reality of the patient as it really is; not as I conjecture it to be, and not as he would like it to be, but *as it is*. . . . The dream rectifies the situation. It contributes the material that was lacking. . . . (Jung 1934, par. 304; 1948, par. 482)

But here a further clarification may be needed. What is the nature of that "inner truth" or "reality" relative to the "situation" that is to be rectified, and how are we to account for the (more often than not) incomprehensible, or at least, hard to decipher way in which that rectification is presented? I should like to deal with the second question first.

It would seem that dreams have a tendency to play and dramatize — indeed, at times even to overdramatize. They do not offer "simple" or rational statements but present allegorical stories, sometimes quite weird, and even fragments or wholes of almost stage-worthy plays. They play with endless variations of "central" themes and forms in expectation-tension, creation-destruction-recreation, or lyrical modes that remind us of dramatic art. They almost seem to take pleasure in exaggerating, embellishing, or at times grotesquely distorting their themes. It would appear as though the intent were to have an idea or archetype incarnated by using the artist's ways of calling forth an experience that involves embodied emotion and dramatic meaning.

In Hannibal's dream envy was represented not as envy simply, but as the dramatically impressive stage performance of a council of the gods and a summons by Jupiter. Hitler was confronted not with a factual message of his dangerously overweening lust of conquest but with the dramatic Wagnerian image of the mythological god of warring heroes, shining forth from the clouds; more poignantly even, a god who in Norse mythology is notorious for leading his followers to victory first and abandoning them to defeat and death ultimately, which point was, fortunately for us, completely lost on the receiver of the "message." Lincoln's dream did not speak of death per se but dramatized it into the impressive spectacle of mourning, with catafalque, honor guards, and a veiled implication of survival of the dreamer's individuality. A prosaic case of rheumatism was dramatized into an attack by a horse-demon.

We are so used to this dramatizing or play-acting tendency that we even utilize it for interpretation. We organize dreams structurally into exposition, peripeteia, crisis and lysis. But we have not stopped to give too much thought to the significance of the dramatizing performance tendency as such and to where this may place the dream in the overall pattern of natural dynamics.

Yet, it is this dramatizing play tendency that shows the dream to be a special instance of a general trend of the life process to present itself to our perceptions through endless arrays of seemingly arbitrary, often capricious forms which do not necessarily have any practical survival value or purpose. In biology, what formerly was considered a result of random selection, based on survival of the fittest qualities, is now seen as *lusus naturae*, a play of nature, as though "intentionally" bent upon a representational performance of artistic forms, akin to a staging of a play for an onlooking or listening audience.

The biologist Portmann has coined the term "representation value"—or "exhibition value" (*Darstellungswert*)—of forms for the characterization of what biology calls "unaddressed" phenomena of living beings, namely forms, colorings, markings, etc., that are obviously devoid of any overt life-supporting function in that they serve neither adaptation, nor mimicry nor as a signal to identify the species. Because they could not be explained in terms of natural selection, the tendency has been to disregard and dismiss them as "merely esthetic" (Portmann 1965). For a particularly instructive example, Portmann cites the descent of the testicles. As they gain in importance in the ascending development from fish to mammal, the testicles descend from the anterior rump to the pelvis and finally, in what Portmann (1956) calls "a directly paradoxical situation," are placed outside of the abdominal cavity in a scrotal bag. Portmann emphasizes that there is no way whatsoever in which this process could be explained by natural selection. It places those organs, so highly important for the preservation of species, into a most dangerously exposed position, for which they even have to readapt themselves to temperatures lower than inside the abdominal cavity. Only in terms of "artistic" exhibition value, namely exhibition and ornamental decoration of the genital pole, analogous to the color exhibition of male animals and the development of impressive (albeit not necessarily useful) horn formations, does the phenomenon seem to make sense. Portmann also points to analogous representations in heraldic representations of the ram as well as other artistic or imaginal demonstrations or exhibitions of maleness, such as 16th- and 17th-century paintings of mercenaries. Other examples are codpieces, sepicuris or penisholders, New Guinea penis horns, or the ornate horns or long hairy manes of some animals useless, indeed even hindrances, for fighting, but decorative.

While some of such ornamental exhibitions indeed also have life supportive value, those functions could also be supplied in other, more simple ways and would not require such grandiose and picturesque exhibitions as the windings of the antelope's horns, the beard of the wild goat, the paunch of the bull's neck, the coloring of the zebra, or the frequent dramatic ritual performances (courtship, fighting rituals, belling of stags, etc.) of animals, rationally quite "useless" but nevertheless, by virtue of their "performance" value and drama, exerting hormonal and CNS effects upon participants and audience (Portmann 1956, p. 189) and thus serving life and life's expressions.

The dramatic sense is also intrinsic to our own human experiencing. We get an intuitive sense of the "characters" that we feel expressed in the forms and shapes of trees and flowers, the soft sensitivity of a birch or the ruggedness of the oak, the loveliness of the rose or the soothing smell of the chamomile, the "feel" of a place, the personality of an animal (evil wolf, crazy bat, proud lion, etc.), all of which we have been taught to explain away, positivistically, as anthropomorphic projection. Our clothing fashions express and dramatize attitudes: the exhibitionistic showing off of the beginning "me, me" in roccoco, the "working morality" expressed in 19th-century garments, or the discreetly dignified wrapping of self in the Roman toga.

In the same way, dreams play the performance game even when, regardless of understanding or even capacity to remember them such as in REM state, they serve a learning and adaptive function. They do not simply present facts for learning; they present dramatic exhibits — like ornamental horns. Thus we can say that organismic expression of form seems not so much bent upon survival but upon play, enhanced and made more dramatic, by survival need and threat to it, by difficulties, obstacles, challenges and crises to be overcome, creation and destruction, conflict and cooperation, succeeding and failing, and the interaction of protagonist and antagonist.

Winnicott's thesis is that "Health is the ability to play" (Winnicott 1971). Huizinga (1950, p. 1) describes play as a significant function — that is, there is some sense to it. In play, there is something "at play" that transcends the immediate needs of life and imparts meaning to the action. "In acknowledging play, you acknowledge *mind*, for whatever else playing is, it is not matter. . . . From the point of view of a world wholly determined by blind forces, play would be altogether superfluous. Play only becomes possible, thinkable, and understandable when an influx of mind breaks down the absolute determinism of the cosmos" (Huizinga 1950, p. 3).

We meet here with a particular manifestation of spirit in life, with an exhibition of what we may call the expression of existential fullness or wholeness of life, not intended for a practical purpose in the narrower sense of the word, but certainly not necessarily devoid of meaning. Artistic exhibition rather than or in addition to survival purposefulness seems to be nature's way of creation and manifestation.

This exhibitional significance of "unaddressed" forms and images, expressions and revealers of intrinsic meaning and significance—a physiognomy of natural shapes—may well be a truly hieroglyphic text in which life, spirit and nature within and without ourselves create functions and meanings that our one-sided utilitarian bias has, until now, prevented us from deciphering. "Through its colorfully reflected splendor do we grasp life" ("*Am farbigen Abglanz haben wir das Leben,*" Goethe, *Faust*, 4727).

Such colorful splendor in sequences of dramatic pictures, a "world theater" or dramatic "exhibition" of life's hidden dynamic, we encounter also in our dreams. Like flowers and trees, or poems, songs, plays, or stories, they grow, expand, and differentiate the life process. Sometimes, they can be readily deciphered and translated into our ordinary rational frame of reference; then we call them metaphors or allegories. When they intimate a dynamic or meaning that can only be intuited or dimly felt because it transcends our rational capacities, we speak of symbols.

We can now also understand and value the archetypal, representational significance of actual theater, movie, television, of stories, myths and legends, as well as the significance of their appearance in dreams, such as a dream in a dream, or watching a play, movie, etc., in a dream. These may be assumed to confront the dreamer with core issues of his or her life drama, with fundamental existential significance, vignettes of basic leitmotifs of his or her life. Likewise it becomes understandable that the dream also is structured essentially dramatically, in terms of exposition, development, crisis and lysis (resolution). It is as though, in the life play of color, sound, and forms, a transpersonal or suprapersonal playwright were groping for an evolving self-awareness and creative development.

Every drama presents to its audience a fantasy, an "inner truth" as it is perceived by the playwright; it has moved the playwright, who feels it to be significant for others also. With what kind of inner truth that would "rectify the situation" is the dream's playwright concerned, and who might that playwright be? Clearly, that playwright is not our conscious, rational ego or reasoning mind.

Since no rational answer is possible, we may want to consider what symbolic hints we might get from the mythopoetic stratum of the unconscious psyche.

According to legend (Ginzberg 1961, pp. 29–31), upon conception, the angel carries the soul to the mother's womb and sets a light above her, "whereby the soul can see from one end of the world to the other." The angel carries the soul around and shows her heaven and hell and "where she will live and where she will die . . . and he takes her through the whole world, and points out the just and the sinners and all things." But upon birth "the angel fillips the babe on the nose, extinguishes the light at his head . . . Immediately the child forgets all his soul has seen and learnt, and he comes into the world crying, for he loses a place of shelter and security and rest." Yet, once having entered life on earth, "the soul escapes from the body every night, rises up to heaven and fetches new life, thence, for man."

This imagery points to a pleromatic (heavenly, intrauterine) level of being and experiencing in which an awareness of a scope of selfness exists that is lost at birth. We now know that the recuperation through sleep which the legend ascribes to "entering heaven" and fetching new life, depends not only upon undisturbed rest but also upon dreaming. Interference with dreaming can create psychic and physical pathology. Moreover, accumulated experimental experience with LSD as well as other trance experiences has acquainted us with the fact that such regressions not only are of "heaven or hell" character, but also quite similar to dream imagery and, like ordinary dreams, can lead to insights into deeply unconscious material, some even of prebirth and even preconception character.

The legend, thus, points to a dynamic of dreaming that symbolically is akin to a "remembering" of smaller or larger pieces of what the soul has "known" prior to birth about its life on earth, a dipping back into a prebirth pleroma, a space–time relative "extrane knowing of" or "being with" basic existential patterns or archetypal motives that underlie its individual life. We may presume that every dream dips back into such a prior knowing which strives toward a grounded "here and now" fulfillment through individual waking and conscious living.

In a way, the dream activity may be compared to an equivalent counterpart that Jung deduced from dreams, his own and those of patients prior to their death, as an expectation that after death, but also during sleep, their experiences of living on earth would be brought back to the "other" side, to be shared with other entities for the mutual benefit of all. The same idea is expressed by Goethe in the last scene of his Faust drama. It is also intimated in a dream of one of Edinger's patients (1972, pp. 218–19). Prior to his death, this man dreamed that he had to carve a pattern through a piece of hard and heavy wood, to be preserved at any cost and, along with a tape recording, to be given to a public library that would know how to prevent the tape from deteriorating. This dream also suggests that the fruits of earthly experiencing are to be brought back in order to be deposited and added to the accumulated "knowing" at the pleromatic level.

Hence, dreams are not necessarily in the character of Hades, the underworld, or death (Hillman 1979). We may equally justifiably place them in paradise, heaven, Valhalla, Elysium, or eternal life. All of these are symbolic fantasies about an unrepresentable dimension. This dimension is neither "under" nor "upper" but is "other" world, pleroma, fullness and emptiness in one (*sunyata*), a world of nondimensionality, beyond the opposites, comparable to a globe (rather than a circle) whose center is everywhere and whose circumference is nowhere. To this nondimensional or archaic (Gebser 1985) level, the dream constitutes a connecting bridge.

Yet, while this activity has been going on in animals, babies, children, and adults, for untold numbers of years, as an unrealized basis for the organizing of information, growth adaptation, and learning, a quantum leap has occurred in our time that is akin to the invention of the wheel, of the jet plane, and the splitting of the atom. We are beginning to understand consciously the information offered to us by the image-producing agency of the dream and to utilize this information not only for unconscious and automatic adaptation, but also for conscious understanding and differentiation. We are about to enter a new phase as more conscious witness/participants of the life play.

In the dream world itself, magical one-dimensionality prevails. Everything would seem to merge with and become everything, the here is also there, the now is yesterday and tomorrow, the part can stand for the whole and the affect results in effect.

Yet, when consciousness relates to the dream by attempting to extract insight or guidance, or even by mere remembering or observing, something new happens: as everywhere in nature, also here, the conscious position, its outlooks and expectations, polarize and modify the area of observation. In part at least, the object of observation orients itself and reacts to the observer, to his affects and intentionality. As our rational three-dimensional position meets this zero- or one-dimensional "magical" world, it creates the two-dimensional mythological level of polarity as the "meeting ground." What, in the dream, usually occurs almost simultaneously, we perceive in time extensions as stories organized around a dramatic play of opposites. This play we then interpret in terms of causality and meaning.

Meaning is established by our confronting "interference" with the impersonal self-revelation of the "play of nature." Bipolarity and relationship are established and primordial, merged identity begins to dissolve. It is now dream versus dreamer, dream or storyteller toward listener, analysand in relation to analyst. No longer merely a *lusus naturae*, the dream becomes also a reactive dynamic relative to the dreamer's consciousness. The more we turn to them, observe and try to understand them, the more the dreams "speak" to us. The more our ego dynamic is at odds with their world, the flow of our *Tao*, the more the dream level's reaction becomes polarized into complementation, compensation or even "attack" of the conscious position.

Thus, while the dream dimension orients itself toward us, it also remains true to itself and to its otherworldly nature. Hence, at times our comprehensional vessel may be too limited to do justice to the dream. Fortunately, most dream elements can be made accessible to the ego's rational comprehension. Others are approachable only dimly, through symbolic intuition, "through a glass darkly." Most dream contents are relevant and even vitally important to the ego's understanding and to current problems. Others may be beyond the ego's reach, "musings" of that other dimension to itself, musings about what to us would appear as past or future, collective or cosmic realities, possibilities or stories that, at best, speak to heart, feeling, and intuition rather than to mental understanding.

There are practical conclusions to be drawn from these theoretical considerations.

Stories are at their best unfolding between a teller and a listener. Likewise, dreams are "constellated" and more likely to be called forth when they are attended to by the dreamer and, even better, described to another person. Since they arise from the undivided pleromatic "emptiness" that encompasses both parties of an interpersonal encounter, they may be presumed to pertain also to the dynamic of that mutual encounter rather than solely to the psyche of the dreamer. In the analytic encounter they flow out of and, to varying degrees, also reflect relationship patterns, transference, countertransference, and reactions to past sessions. They may be responses to the therapy process proper or to the therapist's psychology, particularly when the therapist himself appears in the dream; or they may deal with the dreamer's psyche or other subject matter and, secondarily, include and reflect also upon the transference or mutual relationship. No firm or final rule should be attempted here, or anywhere in dream work. The playful spirit cannot be nailed down. One has to wait and see patiently where understanding, and interpretation if called for, seem to fit best and can evoke the dreamer's fiat.

But no matter what aspect of mutual relating the dream may touch upon, the very fact that it did arise in a relationship context will focus its views upon the very blind spots (see below) that the relationship manages to call forth in its partners—as every relationship invariably is wont to do. Hence, solo dream work is usually as unproductive as an attempt at solipsistic and unrelated living. Dream and analytic work need a vis-à-vis for optimal functioning. And the inner world of the therapist or listener is as relevant to what will be called forth as is the dreamer's—as we well know from our clinical experience.

Since the dream's dynamic resulting in the perception of a story flows from the pleromatic infiniteness into our limited ego world, the dream ego does not necessarily represent the dreamer as he or she knows himself or herself, as has been generally taken for granted. In the dream, the dreamer does not necessarily stand for the ego. More often, the dream ego stands for a view of the dreamer's personality as either intended or seen from the vista of the superordinated guiding eye, the Self. The dream ego may embody positive or negative shadow attitudes or sometimes even the Self's own position, such as when, in the dream, we express or realize a wisdom to which in waking life have no access.

Since the viewpoints of the dream present themselves to us as aspects of a polarization process, they will always represent non-ego views; that is, they will touch blind spots as far as consciousness is concerned. Not random blind spots, but those which are relevant to the "intended" development and realization, the "memory" with which the ego position connects by turning to the dream. In this sense, the dream always completes, complements or compensates the conscious position relative to the individuating "karma." An interpretation that does not bring to awareness any hitherto unrealized facts is, therefore, to be considered inadequate. But these new revelations need not necessarily always be *compensatory* in the sense of showing *opposite* positions, such as opposing or balancing a too high by a low. Lincoln's dream does not compensate by opposites but adds the possibility of realization, both of the mortality of the president and of the witnessing capacity of the Self core beyond death. Hannibal's dream and Hitler's vision mirror unconscious motivations. The dream *completes.* The completing may at times take the form of compensation. But the realizations called for may also come through mirroring, variations, extensions, additions—analogic or symbolic—to the conscious view, such as showing the existence of an unrealized conflict or a wish or danger. It may show the way out of a precarious situation or it may reveal transpersonal dynamics.

Exposed to the pleromatic replay of life "memories" of past, present, and future possibilities, it is up to the ego whether and to what extent it wants or is able to avail itself of the dream's revelations. While these revelations have to be gleaned from the frame of reference of magical and mythological dynamics, they aim at life in the here and now. And every, seemingly most insignificant, detail of the seemingly most insignificant dream can be found to pertain to some here and now fact, when carefully worked through, even though, clinically, this is not always necessary. But, aiming toward incarnation, the dream's dynamic also aims at being put into living reality, to be realized, that is, made real in one's personal life.

Fantasy and imagination are vital to psychic well-being. But they are means to it, not ends in themselves. They are bridges to a reality not otherwise accessible; they are not that reality in themselves. Only by means of symbolic, actual *living* experience can that reality be made real in the here and now. A fantasy activity that dissociates itself from being put into the service of personal living and its concrete problems is as uninteresting and irrelevant as aetheticism for its own sake, or the notion of a godhead that has nothing to do with human life and its concrete problems. We must steer clear, therefore, from any amplifying or fantasizing that would lead away from or be used as a defense against testing the reality of life.

Equally so we must beware of simply applying standardized or traditional mythological "answers" to individual life situations. Rather than assuming that, "because the myth says so," a situation has to be seen in a particular way—say, the hero must kill the dragon—it is a question in every instance of what particular version or variant of a motif, collective-traditional or personally created ad hoc, happens to be presented for reality testing in what particular form in that particular person's particular situation. In the Niblung version, the dragon is indeed to be killed and the hero himself slain, owing to his lack of relatedness to the anima dimension. In a poem by Schiller ("Der Kampf mit dem Drachen") about the dragon killer, the issue relates to obedience to law and the willingness to self-abnegation. There the dragon represents the ravage of heroic ambition which is not to be killed but to be disciplined. In the Chinese context, the dragon is the power of the Yang principle itself which may have to be related to in, as yet, unforseeable ways. (The dragon Yang hexagram, number one of the I Ching, describes at least six variants and their combinations.) And in some other dreamer's version of a dragon tale, it might turn out that the dragon needs to be fed. Rather than assuming that we know (from our own favored myth) where the dramatic action wants to go, we must always discover this anew, by sensitive attention to the dream's own dynamic or, when not enough of the dream action is remembered, by amplifying through active or guided imagination.

Since the dream arises from an as yet undivided prerational motivational level (in Latin, *movere* means to move, motivation is what moves us), a "realizing" linking up with this motivating source ground calls for more than mere rational and intellectual understanding. Motivation needs to be "felt" and "embodied." Here the techniques of guided or active imagination (guided imagination can restrain the patient's use of the imagery for the sake of avoiding rather than facing the problematic area), gestalt, psychodramatic enactment, and body awareness can be often helpful and at times even indispensable for grounding the dream's experience. They may be needed not in spite of their leading away from fantasy and the image (Hillman) but precisely *because and in order* to lead into a grounded experience. At such times the therapist's directive help and intervention may be called for as much as the necessity for his or her interpretation. However, just as with interpretation, in the use of guided imagination or the various body or gestalt techniques, the dreamer's resistance is to be respected (but also analyzed) and an approach is to be found that can receive his or her assent. And no more or less than by interpretive activity, the transference will be modified by the direct intervention of the therapist in proposing and directing gestalt or guided imagination. A certain degree of mana projection is bound to occur as in any and every analytic modality. This projection may or may not delay or inhibit the development of a negative transference. But obviously, this is no different from the transferential awe and "wisdom" projected upon the merely interpreting therapist, seen as the "knower" of the psyche's and dream's secrets.

The dream never tells us what we "ought" to do. That is up to us. It allows us to have a glimpse, simply, at what "is." It allows us to see "through a glass darkly." Only our own capacity to feel, understand, and judge can tell us how to relate to and utilize the information we may believe to have gained. In discovering how to apply it in life, we express our own creative activity, we "discover" rather than "make" our soul and the "intents" of our life's will.

What Herakleitos was supposed to have said about the Delphic Oracle ("The God does not reveal, neither does he conceal: He intimates"), applies to the dream as well. Perhaps those "intimations" trickling down to our waking awareness from the pleromatic realm want to be considered like *prima materia* for the development of our own feelings and judgments and meaningful understanding of the directions of our life's course.

For that reason premature interpretations ought to be avoided. Prematurity, in this context, is determined not by the length of time the analysis has run, but by the possible discrepancy between the therapist's vision and the dreamer's ability or readiness to grasp and assimilate the message and the capacity, or lack of it, to bring his or her own feeling and judgment to bear upon the validity of the interpretation.

When the therapist preempts this activity through interpretations that run ahead of the dreamer's readiness for insight, such development may be hindered rather than helped.

As long as his or her feeling or judgment capacity happens to be relatively inadequate or lacking, the "message" of the dream cannot be utilized by the dreamer. The inadequate ego functioning of the borderline person may be no more capable of being widened by the dream than that of a baby or little child. Adequate ego functioning and some measure of self-introspective capacity as well as of responsibility have to be established first, before dream work can be useful. Sometimes, even in those instances, the dreams themselves will point out that fact and initiate ways of furthering ego development. But other dreams may be reverberations of a pleromatic "knowing" which not only is inaccessible to conscious assimilation, but may also encourage confusion, loss of reality sense, or inflation, and, hence, needs to be moved away from for the sake of first achieving an adequate limited ego vessel that can utilize such "extrane" knowing for its evolution and development. In these instances, the dreams serve and are to be reserved for the therapist's own orientation as to the nature and stage of the dynamics at hand.

Finally, whenever we listen to or work with a dream we need to remember that we are witnesses to a partial unfolding of a mystery; thus an attitude of reverential humbleness and awareness of our relative ignorance is called for. We ought to beware of easy or theoretical "understandings." Jung once said to me, "Never, never assume that you know what a dream means!" He certainly did not intend this as an invitation to renounce understanding, but as a warning against a priori assumptions that are but attempts to fit the infinite possibilities of the unfolding numen into our own ideas or theoretical assumptions. It is a reminder that

The analyst who wishes to rule out conscious suggestion must . . . consider every dream interpretation invalid until such time as a formula is found which wins the assent of the patient. (Jung 1934, par. 316)

References

Brook, Stephen. 1987. *The Oxford Book of Dreams*. Oxford University Press.

Edinger, Edward F. 1972. *Ego and Archetype*. New York: G. P. Putnam's Sons.

von Franz, M. L. 1960. Dreams of Themistocles and Hannibal. *London Guild of Pastoral Psychology* (August), p. 16.

Gebser, J. 1985. *The Ever Present Origin*. Ohio University Press.

Ginzberg, Louis. 1961. *The Legends of the Jews*. New York: Simon and Schuster.

Hillman, James. 1979. *Dreams and the Underworld*. New York: Harper and Row.

Huizinga, J. 1950. *Homo Ludens*. New York: Roy Publications.

Jung, C. G. 1934. The practical use of dream analysis. In *Collected Works* 16:139–161. Princeton, N.J.: Princeton University Press, 1954.

_____. 1948. General aspects of dream psychology. In *CW* 8:235–280. Princeton, N.J.: Princeton University Press, 1969.

Portmann, Adolf. 1956. *Biologie und Geist*. Zürich: Rhein Verlag.

_____. 1965. Neue Fronten der biologischen Arbeit. In *Transparente Welt*, G. Schultz, ed. Bern: Hans Huber.

Winnicott, D. W. 1971. *Playing and Reality*. London: Penguin Books.

On Dreams and History in Analysis

Murray Stein

There is a history in all men's lives,
Figuring the nature of the times deceased. . . .
                    Shakespeare, *Henry IV*, Pt. II

When Jung was breaking with Freud, he announced in his Fordham University lectures of 1912 (Jung 1955) that in his opinion the cause of neurosis lay in the present and not in the past. It was useless for the analyst to follow a neurotic into endless ruminations about past slights, injuries, and possible traumas, he argued. What the neurotic needed to do was, in so many words, to pull up his socks and face the challenge of present life, to quit shirking (1955, pars. 373–381).

Anyone who has tried following the neurotic into the twisted trails of past miseries can sympathize with Jung's Jovian impatience. His view around 1913 had an unusually strong Adlerian tone to it and may also have resulted from the internal dynamics of the psychoanalytic group at that time. It is a remarkable ahistorical and pragmatic position for Jung to have taken precisely at a time when he was beginning to investigate

Murray Stein, Ph.D., is a member of the Chicago Society of Jungian Analysts and has a private practice in Wilmette, Ill. He is the editor of *Jungian Analysis*, co-editor of *Jung's Challenge to Contemporary Religion*, and author of *In Midlife* and *Jung's Treatment of Christianity: The Psychotherapy of a Religious Tradition*.

the greater depths of the unconscious psyche. Yet it was also the case that in investigating the deeper meanings of Miss Miller's fantasies in *Symbols of Transformation* (1952) he gave little attention to her personal history; indeed, he knew almost nothing about it. His focus was on mythic parallels and themes in the fantasy material, a focus that he was to repeat again in the 1930s when he commented on a lengthy dream series using alchemical imagery and ideas (Jung 1944, pars. 44–331). Again, in that later work, he neglected personal history and associations in favor of a symbolic/archetypal interpretation.

It must be pointed out that both of these texts were meant to represent scientific investigations of the unconscious psyche, not to serve as models for therapeutic analysis. When it came to analytic treatment of individuals, Jung was not quite so unambiguously nonhistorical (Stein 1985, pp. 30–35; 1987, pp. 62–64). And, from a theoretical point of view, he could not be. Psychoanalysis deals with complexes, and what are complexes but personal history recorded in the unconscious?

The theory of complexes insists on the practical necessity for historical reconstruction in analysis. According to Jung's formulations both early and late, complexes are basic building blocks of personal psyche and make up the contents of the personal unconscious. These are the emotional factors that disturb waking life with their autonomous vagaries and populate our dreams with their images. The dream is the theater in which the complexes, dressed up in a multitude of guises from everyday life, express themselves. According to the subjective approach of dream interpretation, dream figures are to be read as recurrent complexes: mother, father, sister (anima), brother (shadow), grandparent (wise old one, self). It is impossible, therefore, for a Jungian analysis, based as it is on Jung's theory and emphasizing the importance of dreams, to avoid the issue of personal history. Dream figures bring history trailing after them.

If one is a consistent Jungian analyst, then the rule should be that historical reconstruction would play a central role in analysis precisely because dream interpretation is so central a feature of it. Why is this not always, or perhaps even typically, the case?

As Jung separated from Freud, he developed what he came to call the symbolic and teleological view of the psyche. This view holds that expressions of the unconscious must be interpreted symbolically and teleologically, not reductively and historically. A historical view, or a developmental approach, came to be regarded as overly reductive, while the symbolical view was associated with *telos*. Instead of reflecting the past, dreams were seen to anticipate the future. From this arose the notion, for example, that the first important dream in analysis is an "initial dream" that forecasts important developments and issues that are likely to arise in the course of the analysis ahead.

This does not necessarily mean, of course, that a future as presaged by the unconscious is discontinuous with the past. It may be held, indeed, that the unconscious is able to lay out the future because it contains the complexes as formed in the past and because, furthermore, there is a strong tendency for complexes to repeat the past in the present and future. The repetition compulsion, seen through Jungian eyes, is simply the complexes discharging themselves over and over again upon the passive ego from out of their own inner necessity to repeat. So, on the assumption that dreams are based on complexes and on their internal relations with one another, and that psychological patterns of repetition are formed by complexes, which behave mostly autonomously and require a discharge of energy time and time again, one could argue that dreams do indeed have a prospective, forward-looking agenda: namely, to repeat the past. The task of analysis would be to strengthen a tendency in the psyche to produce an *opus contra naturam*, which would free the individual from these historical patterns and help to dissolve the complexes through interpretation and working through the emotional issues housed in the complexes.

Yet, because dreams have been taken as symbolic in another sense, this analytic task of psychological deconstruction has often taken a secondary position. In Jung's later theorizing, the complex was seen to have an archetypal core. And archetypes are ahistorical, at least to some degree; that is, they are not produced by personal experience but are rather inborn potentials for experiencing. Thus the mother complex is a mixture of one's personal experiences with one's own mother, plus the innate potential for receiving and relating to a mother. When one comes to interpret the mother complex, both of these elements are taken into account. On the one hand there is mom, on the other there is the Great Mother. When the accent falls on the Great Mother, the interpreter tends to look away from personal history to a collective history of the race or, even further, to the idea of Mothering Itself. This leads to the meaning of Mothering, to the inner Mother as She impinges on the psyche here and now. This naturally draws attention away from historical concerns, from interpreting the mother–child relationship and its ramifications in the particular case at hand. In this way, dream interpretation runs exactly counter to historical reconstruction and to working out personal issues with childhood and/or projection of childhood into present situations such as in transference.

The dichotomy between symbolic/archetypal interpretations of dreams and historical/personal interpretations has lead the field of analytical psychology into one of its central dilemmas (cf. Dieckmann 1986). Questions such as: Should one take a symbolic view of case material, or should one be "clinical," i.e., reductive and historical? Should one treat dreams as oracles and augeries of meaning or as statements of the psyche that require analysis back into a personal context of history and relationships? Is the psyche fundamentally mythic and myth-producing, weaving a personal myth out of a warp and woof of archetypal elements with the intention of giving the individual life its meaning, or is the psyche fundamentally repetitious and pattern-restating and therefore in need of assistance when it gets stuck in its old ways? From this difference flows the archetypal school on one side and the developmentalist school on the other, the former treating the psyche as fundamentally unconnected to history and history itself as fundamentally of the imagination; the other considering imagination and emotional life as deeply controlled by history and its impasses. The classical Jungian school tries to straddle this fence by taking a both/and position: the dream is both a statement of historically created complexes *and* a symbolic statement of the psyche's drive for wholeness. The dream compensates one-sided ego-consciousness and thereby pushes for wholeness.

In the classic approach to analysis, the doctrine has been to practice reductive, historical analysis of complexes first (the "Freudian" phase) and the symbolic, synthetic method second (the Jungian phase); or (and this is an important conditional clause) as indicated by dreams themselves. The notion here is that dreams themselves indicate when they are to be taken historically and when teleologically and symbolically.

It is fair to say, I think, that an analyst trained in the developmentalist school will take dreams historically and reductively first and foremost; one trained in archetypalist ways will never take the dream historically but always in its own terms of image and internal structure; one trained classically will look to the dream itself to indicate how to take it—whether personalistically, historically, reductively or symbolically, teleologically, synthetically. This means, concretely, that these three analyses will be significantly different. The first will have great historical coherence, the second none, the third some but unsystematically (see Samuels 1985, for a full treatment of these three schools).

In what follows I will be assuming a modified classical position in that I will be taking cues about when to pursue the quest for the historical self from dreams themselves. My hope is that the therapeutic value of this quest will be clear.

Dreams of History

Some dreams simply cry out for historical reflection and demand it. In this group are recurrent dreams that bring up the past by reliving it. This dream classically replays a traumatic event, such as a battle scene, which recurs repeatedly in almost identical form and insists on the dreamer's once again going through the moment of terror. But there are other dreams, much less physically threatening and less dramatic, that fall into this same genre.

A number of men I have worked with in analysis have reported recurrent dreams of this sort that center on high school sports teams and events. In these dreams of football, basketball, or baseball, there is a particular setting, an important game, often a particular old coach, and a critical moment: "I am driving for the goal line and drop the ball"; "I tell the coach to put me in, but he won't"; "I am suiting up and can't find my shoes," etc.

Collecting the associations and the history represented in this recurring dream, one comes to the feeling that an essential psychic fact of this personality is being presented. This fact cannot be exposed and investigated without the historical setting, without the detail and exact associations. In one case, this psychic fact was expressed by the figure of the coach and by his conflicted relationship with the dreamer. The recurrent dream revolved on the centrality of this figure. Reflecting on this coach, who appeared in many dreams throughout this young man's analysis, we would eventually conclude that the central psychic fact depicted in these dreams again and again was a failed male initiation ritual and its aftermath (see Bernstein 1987, for a discussion of this problem in contemporary culture). Left in the wake of this arrested psychological development were distrust of male authority, tendencies toward a *puer aeternus* character structure, compulsive sexuality, and a search for adequate mentoring which invariably concluded in disappointment. While our analysis of this psychic fact was going on, the dreams began to change. The coach came down from his throne of power and authority and eventually appeared as a pathetic, down-and-out character in need of help and sympathy. Behind this coach, or buried in the image, was a father figure and a father problem that antedated the coach. This young man also reported many dreams of his father, more or less parallel in theme with the coach dreams but often less dramatic and less frozen in content. The father appeared to be a more realistic figure, the coach more set in a specific time period and therefore also more symbolic.

If we say, now, that the coach, or rather this particular coach, was an important dream symbol for this young man, we are using the term in a different way from the sense of "symbolic" as understood when it is contrasted with "historical." The coach clearly symbolizes an essential psychic fact in this man's personality, in that he represents a central complex in dream after dream. This image from dreams could be used, with effectiveness, in analyzing other relationships, including (to some extent) the transference. Had it not been for these recurrent dreams of the coach, it would never have occurred to this analysand to use his memories of the coach in such a central and psychologically illuminating fashion. The dreams presented the coach as a symbol, and as a symbol this figure had general applicability for interpreting other similar structures of relationship and life experience.

The complex represented by the coach figure also has an archetypal core, in which resides the Father. This complex was arranged in such a way that it impinged upon the ego as the Father archetype would: a male authority blocking or facilitating the way to work and libido commitments in the world. The dream figure here was symbolic in that it pointed beyond itself to greater psychic meanings, and yet it was also purely historical: this man had actually been the dreamer's coach some 20 years earlier.

The realization that a recurrent dream of this kind, containing a clearly marked and recalled historical figure or event, also carries symbolic significance is achieved when one gets a sense of its greater psychological meaning. It is more than a simple repetition of a memory or an attempt to work through an emotional trauma from the past. Perhaps a symbol could be defined as an event plus its meaning. If we say, for example, that a dream is a symbol, this means that we have captured this combination of the dream as an historical event and its meaning. Once rendered symbolic, the meaning of the event can also be transferred to other contexts.

Perhaps a general hypothesis for dream analysis could be suggested: when a person or figure or motif from an individual's history recurs to a noticeable extent in a long dream series, it contains symbolic import. Symbolic import means that the extent and range of possible meaningful reference to which this image can be applied is greatly increased.

In a long dream series, too, where one can witness a gradual change in the structures and figures of the dreams' dramas, one can also often glimpse how the psyche deals with history. The dreams rework a bit of history until it both becomes symbolic and transforms its shape. In this respect, we can affirm that psychological growth can be charted in dream sequences. The transformation of personal history into symbol makes it possible for past events that have inhibited or blocked psychological functioning, split the psyche, or limited the self in externalizing its functions in space and time to be gradually overcome.

A second kind of dream that calls insistently for historical reflection and reconstruction is one that hints symbolically at an historical event. Here a historical event is hidden by an image, barely alluded to, yet dreamed in a way that associations can lead to it quite directly and easily. Typically these hidden events are of a shaming, embarrassing, and painful nature, such as incest experiences which have been covered up and to some extent repressed.

A young woman came to see me because she felt overwhelmed by powerful dreams which she could not understand. The dreams were charged with emotion, they would often awaken her, and they were often innocuous in content. In our second or third session, she reported dreaming of her childhood home. She is exploring the back yard and comes upon a tree she has not seen before, a young fruit tree about to bear fruit for the first time. Her associations to the dream took us quickly and forcefully back into her early adolescence, when her family had moved into this house and her father had purchased the land next door for a garden. It was a garden rich with orchards and berry bushes. She had spent many hours roaming through it and playing there with girlfriends. At the place of the unknown tree in the dream, she recalled, she had had an early sexual encounter: another girl had shown her her pubescent breasts, and they had touched one another. This association led quickly to others, and particularly to painful memories of discovering that her divorced and lonely father would spy on her as she undressed in her room and would sometimes come into her room at night and sit on her bed. Suddenly her whole terrified adolescence sprang back into memory. From the innocence of a young fruit tree in the garden we came suddenly upon the serpent, upon an original sin, upon the fall from grace of her father in her eyes, and upon years and years of holding in a terrible secret. In this instance, an ingenuous dream, an Eden image, yields up a secret of personal shame, not on the mythic symbolic level but on the concretely historical level.

One interesting feature of this case is that it conforms to Jung's early formulation of the etiology of neurosis (Jung 1955, pars. 203–522). There was a task in the present that this young woman was avoiding: she was stuck in writing her dissertation. Libido would not flow to it. Furthermore, there was also a problem in her relationship with her husband: libido did not want to flow there either. The damming up of libido and the ensuing regression produced symptoms: overcharged dreams, nightmares, and anxiety. Following the dream mentioned above back into her personal history, the path lead to incest scenes with her father, and after these were uncovered and the traumas and feelings were brought into consciousness, libido was released for a new progression of libido. In fact, after some discussion of these memories that came flooding back, she was able to take up her dissertation and finish it. She also tackled her relationship with her husband.

What started out seeming like a dream symbol in this case, namely the garden, the tree, the fruit, turned into history and lost its symbolic meaning. This deconstruction of symbolic into historical meanings follows the old-fashioned notion of psychoanalysis as undoing repressions and working through incest issues. This dream presented a dream symbol in the Freudian sense of disguise rather than in the sense of event plus meaning.

And yet there was one detail in the dream, which did not seem particularly significant at the time because of all the material that flowed from the associations, that did have symbolic import as well. It was the new fruit of the tree. Unlike any of the trees in the actual orchard back home, this was a pear tree; the fruit was an incipient pear. Historically this referred to the period of adolescence when she became initiated into female sexuality, but it had a teleological reference as well. From a clinical viewpoint one could readily assess that she needed to further her feminine identity and maturity as a woman. As for the interpretive work, the deconstructive move in taking apart the symbol-as-disguise serves the prospective function of the dream, which is to advance the cause of personal psychological development.

History as Metaphor

When Freud abandoned the seduction theory and replaced it with the notion that childhood incest fantasies disguise themselves as historical memory, he was pointing to one of the ways in which the mind uses history metaphorically. Jung certainly supported this view of the psyche as creator of metaphor to express its essence and meanings. History can be used to this purpose.

In a metaphor, two things are compared in such a way that one can stand for the other and illuminate its significance. But it also may come to replace it. If I say, "My love is a red, red rose," this may engender some confusion about the object of my love. You could ask, "Does this mean that you love a red rose?" I would protest that I was speaking poetically. But when we speak or think in metaphors we are not far from a potential muddle. Straightening out this muddle and making the meaning come clear is one function of interpretation. A good interpretation will render the meaning of the metaphorical expression in a language that is considerate of poetic values; it will carefully suggest the meaning of the metaphor.

In a sense, every dream is a metaphor and needs to be so interpreted. Freud and Jung agreed on this. A dream interpretation says in prose what the dream says in poetry. Reading or hearing dreams, I often ask myself, "If I were to state this dream story as a thought, what would the thought be?" The mind dreaming is the mind thinking in images. (Equally, one could say that the mind thinking is the mind dreaming in thoughts.) This does not answer the question of where these thoughts come from or what they mean, but it does take us toward a theory of dream interpretation. To understand dream language requires us to translate it into the thoughts that it represents metaphorically. A dream can move us without this, of course, but it cannot be understood cognitively unless we make this translation.

There is a large group of dreams that begin something like this: "I was back home . . . ." The dream report opens with a statement of place, and that place is from the long ago: the childhood home, the school, the grandparents' place, the summer home, but in any case a place of origin where much important, formative experience took place. Then, after this typical opening, we are introduced to a cast of characters, often mixing the old and the new: some from the old home town, some from more recent days, some from the present. The dream then proceeds to develop into a drama that often has little or nothing to do with the past even though it is set there. While it has more to do with present matters, these are surprisingly stated in historical terms and images. It is as though one were to read about a current political campaign in terms of the Civil War or the Revolutionary period, of formative times.

A man in his late 50s was studying for a new profession, psychotherapy. He was in the midst of a practicum with a number of low-fee patients when he dreamed of being back in the town where he had been born and spent the first 50 years of his life. (This was the usual setting of nearly all of his dreams.) In this dream, he was playing the role of doorkeeper in a saloon. A sting operation was being conducted to capture drug dealers and users, and his job was to escort the potential customers to the back of the place, where they would be busted. Finally the operation was completed, and he was free to leave, which he did with trepidation, fearing an attack from the drug people. In associating to the dream, he identified this location as the snake pit of his hometown. Other associations led to his practicum, where he was dealing with a number of substance abusers. One of these had cancelled a session on the day of the dream, and he feared the patient was regressing to his old habit. Others of his patients were sociopathic court cases.

It is a cardinal tenet of analytical psychology that the unconscious assimilates experience by comparing it to the past. New experience is integrated by chewing it up with old teeth in an old mouth and digesting it in an old stomach with old gases and juices. As far as the psyche is concerned, new wine is always put into old casks. If this operation does not work, there is a breakdown and subsequent reorganization. This is the basis of transference: the patient assimilates the analyst, this new figure of importance, libidinal attachment, and authority, to former authority figures (usually parental, they being the earliest), along lines that were laid down long ago along an archetypal roadbed of truly ancient vintage. In a dream like the one quoted above, we see this process at work. The practicum was a new, and in many ways threatening, experience for the dreamer. He was not a novice to the world of work and to membership in the service industry, but this activity and role were new for him. He was an old dog learning a new trick, and in this dream we see his unconscious groping to grasp this new role on the basis of former life experience. The dream thought is something like this: "In your new job you are one part of a larger effort to change some antisocial behavior and to try to clean things up. This is a somewhat dangerous job, and you could be easily misunderstood and attacked by the people you are trying to help change. The kind of people you are dealing with are a lot like those characters who hung around on that corner back home where drugs were bought and sold. You are dealing with the shadowy side of life. Be careful and stay alert."

In this dream, the historical setting makes the statement that the present moment is something like it was back then. This assimilation of the present to past models is part of the adjustment and adaptation to a new situation that is challenging and somewhat frightening.

I am reminded of an observation that Miss Marples, the foxy old detective in some of Agatha Christy's novels, makes about how she is able to sleuth so well. She says that back in her small English village there were just enough characters to learn all she needed to know about human nature. What she does when she goes into a new situation is to get a sense of what the people are like by comparing them to the characters in the village. Her observation was that if you thoroughly know the people in one small village, you can understand any human situation.

What Miss Marples did was assimilate the new to the old through comparing them. This is the use of history as metaphor: for a moment the past stands in for the present so that one can understand the present more clearly.

"My love is a red, red rose" only works if one has earlier come to know roses and to love them; otherwise the metaphor is meaningless and could confuse the reader into thinking the poet is a gardener. Sometimes the would-be interpreter of a dream that contains a strong historical reference is like such a reader. If the historical reference is taken literally, as making a concrete reference to a past event or person, when this historical reference is actually meant to be taken metaphorically, the muddle becomes complete.

In the example given above, it would have been foolish to pursue the notion that the dreamer was in the process of uncovering some shadow activity that had actually happened back in his old home town. Not that this tack would be "wrong" necessarily; one could indeed look, perhaps even with some profit, at shadow issues from those past years. Similarly, one could also take the line, "My love is a red, red rose," and speculate that the poet's selection of precisely this metaphor had to do with a strong preference for red roses. Or was his mother's name Rose? But this would be missing the point of this poem, which is not really about roses but about his beloved. Similarly, in the instance of the dream, it would be missing the point to go woolgathering on that street from the old hometown.

The historical element in dreams where history is metaphor points to old and long-standing patterns of structure, identification, habit. The dream is saying: this is an old pattern that is now being applied to a new situation; this is a pattern that was laid down in that place because of the circumstances, identifications, persons involved there and your relationship to them. The unconscious is trying to assimilate the present by devouring it in the stomach of the past.

These dreams raise a further question, particularly if they are habitual and recurrent. Is this a good thing? Is assimilation of the present by the past the way of individuation, or is it a sign of defense? We come here upon the uses of memory. Memory can be a means of cognition, but it can also be an instrument of defense.

History as Oppression

"We are our complexes; they are our memory," writes Elie Humbert in an article in which he discusses how analysis attempts to dissolve the repetition compulsion through regression. His notion is that in order for change to take place, the complexes must be dissolved and re-formed through a therapeutic regression. This forms new structures. The implication is that memory alters as well. This brings us to the question, Do dreams indicate a process at work in the psyche that can alter the structure of complexes and change memory as well?

It is too facile an equation to say, simply, that our complexes are our memory. Memory is more than complexes. And yet there is certainly an important connection. Memory, in the sense depth psychologists understand it, goes beyond the conscious memory bank, short or long term. It extends to body memories and unconscious memories as well. The evidence that memory exceeds consciousness and its powers of recall is extensive and compelling. We dream of persons and places we would never retrieve through conscious effort. Too, we often realize that dreams contain memory images after a long and arduous process of association and interpretation; then we are surprised that this is the case. In recent years, body therapy has demonstrated that the very body tissues, when pressed and massaged in certain ways, can be made to give up the dead in the form of memory images of early childhood. Hypnosis has long been used to demonstrate the existence of memory far beyond the range of conscious recall, and it has even entered areas that may pertain to previous lives. Here we verge on the edge of a memory bank that extends through the ages. The collective unconscious is thought to contain memory traces of an ancestral origin.

As far as the contents of memory are concerned, therefore, we can say, with a fair degree of confidence, that they exceed consciousness and conscious control. We cannot control or retrieve what we remember at all levels. Freud's theory of repression deals with the human need to forget, while it simultaneously testifies that we do not forget the very things we want to: the memory of traumata and fantasies lives on. This is also true of Jung's theory of complexes. Complexes are made up of largely unconscious memories clustered around an archetypal core, and complexes are autonomous and free from ego control. Thus memory is controlled by the psyche, not by the ego.

When we consider how memory is structured we come upon a further set of considerations. Eli Humbert claims that memory is structured by complexes. This is to say that memory is structured largely by emotional dynamics, such as the operation of defenses. Moreover, the nature of complexes is to repeat their patterns, unchanged, until an intervention from outside alters them. The tendency of complexes to rigidify, to resist change, and to repeat was an early observation. Jung's differentiation between neurosis and schizophrenia rested on the relative malleability of complexes in the former and their utter imperviousness to change in the latter (1960, par. 141). In neurosis, the complexes will yield somewhat to treatment and to conscious intervention; in schizophrenia they are intractable. This is another way of saying, perhaps, that for normal neurotics memory can be changed and restructured somewhat; for the more seriously ill, it cannot. A sense of personal history, then, is structured by emotion (i.e., the complexes), at least to some degree, and the harder that emotion is frozen the less likely it is that memory will change.

As one observes dreams, it becomes evident that they both reconstitute memory and attempt to restructure and to change it. If memory changes in its contents, its repetitions, its structuring, then personal identity also changes, patterns of behavior and reaction and perception change, and personality undergoes a transformation. The change of memory, in content and structure, is an essential component of therapeutic transformation. More precisely, the change in affective charge, or valence, around certain areas of an individual's sense of personal history — mother, father, childhood, identity, etc. — is the critical factor in psychological transformation. An autobiography written after analysis is typically quite different from one written beforehand, both because of the additional detail and because of the rearrangement of the valued contents.

Dreams can be seen working on the emotional valences of past figures, presenting "positive figures" from the past in a negative light and "negative figures" with more positive cast and feature. Within dream dynamics there is an attempt to change the complexes, which are the emotional basis of memory and its structuring.

One class of dreams that shows this effort is the toilet dream. This dream has a more or less standard structure and two or three predictable outcomes. The dreamer typically realizes, suddenly, a need to go to the toilet, usually to defecate. Either this occurs successfully, or it runs into one of several problems. There are other people in the bathroom, and this interrupts the act; the toilets are stopped up and the place is a mess, and again this leads to difficulties in obeying nature's commands; the toilet is full and won't hold more content. In my experience, the people who have this dream recurrently are somewhat compulsive, rather unhappily entrenched in their habits and styles of living, and find themselves in a crisis that demands change. Their being stuck in the midst of a transformation process manifests itself in this dream: the toilet is stopped up, and the dreamer cannot get rid of a used-up past.

This dream indicates a need and a problem: the need is to get rid of some worthless material, the problem is doing it. An impasse results.

This dreamer is typically a person with high control needs, along with a strong fear of letting go of a secure position that in the past was of value but now no longer serves the needs of individuation. As a thought, the dream images would say: In the past this identity was of great value, but you've gotten what you can out of it. Now you must let it go. But you are not letting it go; something in your character (the plumbing) has created a blockage.

Both the requirement for change and the resistance to it belong to this same personality, of course, but they arise from different areas. The requirement derives from the self's need for something new, for new sources of nourishment. The resistance comes from the ego's defenses against the anxiety created by change. The complexes (i.e., emotionally structured memories) make up the material in the blockage, and they insist on repeating the past for emotional security. They constrict the personality and thereby create the blockage in the toilet. The complexes themselves are imaged as shit by the dream.

The message is unmistakable: it is time to remove this bit of outworn history and memory from the psychic body. What was once perhaps a nourishing repast is now chewed up, worked over by the digestive system, useless, and if retained will poison the whole body. The used-up past needs to be eliminated.

Toilet dreams can, of course, also give clues about transference issues that revolve around holding back and controlling emotion. Beneath this trait lie the intractable complexes and their repetitions. In a sense, memory will not let go. Our history will not be denied, and it insists on repeating tself. The complexes form a character structure. The separation anxiety constellated in losing a grip on personal history is enormous, and this anxiety provides the glue between ego-consciousness and its outworn past.

This may take the form of persona anxiety — "What will people say, or think, if I make such a change and release the past in this way?" Or the issue may revolve on security and display the notion of clinging to history for comfort and identity. This anxiety may also be an expression of a collective, clan, or family problem, reflecting the fact that many others, too, cannot make the necessary change and all are blocked; the whole interpersonal system may be stagnant and poisoned. The issue for analysis in all of these instances is separation anxiety, which presents itself with excruciating impact during periods of deep inner change. The analyst who is similarly blocked may contribute to the problem rather than help to relieve it.

At the conclusion of his paper "The Spirit Mercurius" (1948, pars. 299–303), Jung discusses two kinds of knowledge, following St. Augustine: *cognito vespertina* ("evening knowledge") and *cognito matutina* (morning knowledge"). The first is the kind of knowledge that becomes ego syntonic and eventually grows old and stale, losing its savor and value; the second remains eternally fresh. When insight and experience that was once inspired and fresh becomes integrated into ego-consciousness as personal history and identity, the need arises to renew oneself in a wellspring of fresh vision and awareness. The sense of a personal history runs this course. At first it is a feast and supplies the basic material for a personal identity. Personal history and identity rest, however, upon a set of complexes, which make up the emotional glue of memory and of its structuring. This emotional glue becomes hardened by anxiety, and history thus becomes fixated. It turns into a burden. The tyranny of a too fixed sense of personal history blocks life and new direction. So the husk of history must be shed, the complexes dissolved. The archetypal core of the personality, however, remains eternally fresh, filled with nourishment and value. The ego can renew itself in this level, in the Self. This "regression," according to Humbert, is the secret of therapeutic healing. We can add that it is also the key to all psychological renewal. From the Self flows the *cognito matutina*, a fountain of youth that also has the detergent power to flush the toilet clean.

The Child, Childhood, and Nostalgia

If one follows the lead of dreams and associations in analysis, one comes rapidly and inevitably upon images and memories of childhood. When these begin to crowd into consciousness, it is the dawning of *cognito matutina*. Dreams of childhood, of being a child again, of returning to important places of childhood, of caring for small children and infants, are indicators that analysis is reaching the soul. This re-entry into childhood is essential for the healing process that we anticipate and count on in analysis.

The constellation of this inner child is essential for healing the fundamental split in the modern adult psyche. This is the split between consciousness and the unconscious, between reality and imagination. The healthy child within is our capacity to dwell in a world of whole symbols, where the divisions between these elements are not yet existent. Whether this world is called "transitional space" (Winnicott 1971), "liminality" (Turner 1967), the operation of the transcendent function (Jung 1916), the "imaginal" (Hillman 1983), or the "secured symbolizing field" (Goodheart 1980), it is a kind of consciousness in which the literal and the imaginal are combined and allowed to mingle in such a way that the dichotomy between them, created by later ego developments, is suspended. This healing of the rift between inner and outer, real and imaginal, ego and unconscious is the function of the symbol, and the constellation of this healing symbol is the generally accepted ultimate goal of Jungian treatment. Jung spoke of the transcendent function as the means by which the opposites are reconciled and attitudes changed, and this function at work is represented by the child at play.

The return of childhood images in dreams in the course of analysis therefore indicates operation of the healing function. Dreams that speak of loss of the child, damage to the child, threats to the child, neglect of the child, etc., indicate potential hazards facing the working of this healing function. One recalls that Jung himself returned to childhood and to childhood games in his search for healing during midlife, and it was through these activities that imagination was released and the transcendent function discovered and allowed to release symbols of reconciliation (Jung 1961, p. 174).

At the heart of every analysand's history lies childhood. Dreams of childhood imply a particular story of childhood, a history, and remembering childhood has the psychological value of helping to constellate the transcendent function.

A woman in her mid-40s suffering from the turmoil created by a conflict between physical and emotional desire on the one hand and spiritual aspiration and commitment on the other, dreamed that she was playing a game with her younger brother, as they had often done in childhood. Suddenly she was no longer playing with him but with a favorite doll. This dream released a flood of memories from childhood, both of her brother and their relationship and of this favorite doll that she had kept with her into teenage years. This dream occurred at a point in her life when rational problem-solving methods for tackling her conflict had become useless, and she was simply ruminating over the same old ground. She was caught in her complexes. This dream suggested the activation of the transcendent function, first of all by drawing her back to scenes of childhood and, even more importantly, by providing her with recall of a transitional object. This magical object has the power to transform the ego's time- and space-bounded reality into transitional space, where play allows new combinations of old elements to form. From this dream she proceeded to try sandplay. In the sandtray she created a scene of conflict and resolution. This activity, in turn, coincided with a general lightening of the rending effects of the conflict, with a return of her sense of humor, and with the disappearance of some rather severe and embarrassing physical symptoms.

When a dream brings back childhood, the feeling tones evoked by it can smack strongly of nostalgia. One may awaken from such a dream with a sense of nostalgia so compelling that hours or even days may pass before mood and emotional tone return to normal. Typically these are dream reminiscences of times and places that emotionally contained and nurtured the dreamer in a particularly effective way. With such a dream, one is drawn into a set of feelings and images that smell of attachment and intimate familiarity and induce longing and sometimes short separation depressions. Separation from the mother is recapitulated, and there is a reminder that one cannot go back home again. A longing for paradise suffuses nostalgia, and the dreams tease us, seemingly, with a glimpse of what we once had and forever lost.

This type of dream represents a brief symbolic return to the mother. The significance of this return is not fully noted by pointing out that one cannot actually do that, that it is a romantic delusion and needs to be shunned. These dreams are not so much symptomatic of an unwillingness to accept present reality as they are an effort to return to a source of life and nourishment to gather energy for a new beginning. They speak of renewal. For nostalgia is both a sentimental attachment to the past and a hope for another chance at a future.

The Child and childhood itself are evocative of nostalgia. One can recall them as times of comfort, safety, and creativity, as existing beyond serious conflict and the experience of loss and limitation. But, as Jung points out, the child archetype fundamentally signifies futurity (1951, par. 278). The child faces into the future, not back to the past, and, paradoxically, the return of the child in analysis is a means of approaching the future via the past.

The reason this is possible and actually happens is that as the past recedes and becomes the distant past it becomes assimilated to the archetypes (Stein 1987, p. 68). Thus, my own personal childhood becomes Childhood itself; the home of my childhood becomes the Garden of Eden or that mythic and much sought after place called Home; my personal parents become Mother and Father. As memories recede, they sink further into the unconscious and come into contact with the archetypal substratum. Eventually they become assimilated to it. Another way to conceptualize this phenomenon is to see the archetype, which lies at the core of the complex, gradually absorbing the personal associations into itself; enriched by these, this memory trace more and more reveals itself as archetypal image in dreams and recollected associations. The emotional aura around memory changes with age. This is how personal history becomes personal myth.

Often this phenomenon is interpreted as defensive. In order to convert a painful and troubled childhood into something acceptable, or at least neutral, the ego defenses take off the edges, distort the memories through association with archetypal structures, and leave the individual with a defensively reconstructed memory of childhood. Traumas are repressed, injuries suffered at the hands of borderline or narcissistic parents are disguised, and a kind of sentimental haze conceals the realities of childhood in order to hide its gloomy and fearful truth. As these defenses are dismantled, the person who entered analysis with a glowing account of parents and childhood leaves with a Gahan Wilson vision of torture chambers and monsters. The ego has been strengthened to a point where it can now accept this harsh reality.

The advantage of following dreams rather than memories or free associations into childhood is that they do not lie. The ego and its defenses may well give a distorted account, in the form of a pasted together set of idealized or horrific memories, but the unconscious does not much cooperate in this. Dreams of childhood are both warm and exceedingly unpleasant. Witches, fires, floods, dismembered dolls, frightening animals such as vicious dogs and clawing cats, disemboweled and otherwise sick farmyard animals, scenes of violence and destruction are as common as teddy bears and Gardens of Eden. The painful dynamics of childhood do become manifest in dreams: separation and loss, oedipal rivalries, double binds that injure and maim. Dreams do not hide any of these in the course of a complete dream series in analysis.

But there is also a child at play, which feels like the soul's essence. This is the object of nostalgia; to return to this child is its goal. In order to preserve this sense of childhood, all the defenses of the self are mobilized. These are self defenses (Fordham 1985, pp. 152–160) rather than ego defenses, which merely guard against ego pain. Only when conditions of safety are in place can these defenses be dismantled and this child be allowed to come out of the closet or basement.

This child of play is a fusion of archetype and personal memory, mediating imagination and historical existence in a particular zone of time and space. And gathered around this child are the places and persons who are also symbols: Mother, Father, Home, Animals.

A woman in her late 30s who had been in analysis for about twelve months and had recently become bedridden with an anomalous illness, dreamed that she was in church. As she walked to the door, a gigantic butterfly flew past her and out into the fresh air. She steps out herself and is suddenly in a winter landscape. The place is Russia, and she is standing on a road that runs through a forest for hundreds of miles. As she looks down the road she sees a horse-drawn sleigh approaching and is surprised to see her mother and father coming her way. Associations to this dream only recalled that her father was a second-generation Russian American, that she had always been fascinated with stories told by her grandfather about Russia, and that she had read and reread the great Russian novels. But why the giant butterfly, why this landscape, why her own parents and not her grandparents or great-grandparents?

Quite evidently this is a symbolic, archetypal dream as indicated by the soul figure in the butterfly, the gesture of passing through a doorway, the land of ancestors. At the time of the dream, she was feverish and worried about the seriousness of her illness. A question of survival even occurred, although she was not hypochondriacal. Her parents called from time to time throughout the illness to encourage her. She has lived out a sort of counterdependent defensive relationship with them, in which they gladly colluded.

While this dream is clearly a return of sorts to childhood and to feelings of vulnerability, in short an image of regression during illness, it goes beyond that to represent transitional and archetypal space: the church as sacred temenos and place of souls; the butterfly as departing soul, flying off into another world; her own entry into that other world, the world of the ancestors; the experience of nostalgic reunion with parental imagoes. One could almost think this was anticipatory of death: the soul leaves the body and enters another world, where those who have loved one most deeply come to greet and lead one on into the other life. In this return to childhood, there is a penetration beyond it into Childhood, the childhood of her own genetic line and race, the point of origin, the source of life. In this respect, the dream implies birth, the renewal of life through a return to the point of origin, and entry into the realm of *cognito matutina*.

The timing of the illness and of this dream was meaningful as well. They occurred precisely during the period when a child would have been born to her had she not aborted it. The decision to have an abortion had been a sound one, practically speaking, but her psyche and her body had not given up the agenda of pregnancy and birth and followed through, after a manner. The dream, with its escaping butterfly and return to the world of the ancestors, charted the course of this unborn soul. It also brought the dreamer, the lost child's mother, to the place of her ancestral origins and roots.

The implication of a return to "deep childhood," to the point of ancestry even beyond one's own personal beginning, is futurity. Because the archetypes are engaged at this level, the psyche's progressive movement toward wholeness can be touched.

References

Bernstein, Jerome S. 1987. The decline of masculine rites of passage in our culture: the impact on masculine individuation. In *Betwixt and Between*, L. Mahdi, S. Foster and M. Little, eds. LaSalle, Ill.: Open Court.

Dieckmann, Hans. 1986. Opening address. In *Symbolic and Clinical Approaches in Theory and Practice*. Zürich: Daimon Verlag.

Fordham, Michael. 1985. *Explorations into the Self*. London: Academic Press.

Goodheart, William. 1980. Theory of analytic interaction. *The San Francisco Institute Library Journal* 1:2–39.

Hillman, James. 1983. *Archetypal Psychology: A Brief Account*. Dallas: Spring Publications.

Humbert, Elie. 1988. The wellsprings of memory. *Journal of Analytical Psychology* 33:3–20.

Jung, C. G. 1907. The psychology of dementia praecox. In *Collected Works* 3:1–151. Princeton, N.J.: Princeton University Press, 1960.

_____. 1916. The transcendent function. In *Collected Works* 8:67–91. Princeton, N.J.: Princeton University Press, 1969.

_____. 1944. *Psychology and Alchemy*. In *Collected Works*, vol. 12. Princeton, N.J.: Princeton University Press, 1968.

_____. 1948. *Symbolik des Geistes*. Translated as "The spirit Mercurius," *Alchemical Studies*. In *Collected Works*, vol. 13. Princeton, N.J.: Princeton University Press, 1967.

_____. 1951. The psychology of the child archetype. In *Collected Works* 9/1:151–181. Princeton, N.J.: Princeton University Press, 1969.

_____. 1952. *Symbols of Transformation*. In *Collected Works*, vol. 5. Princeton, N.J.: Princeton University Press, 1956.

_____. 1955. The theory of psychoanalysis. In *Collected Works* 4:83–226. Princeton, N. J.: Princeton University Press, 1961.

_____. 1961. *Memories, Dreams, Reflections*. New York: Random House.

Samuels, Andrew. 1985. *Jung and Post-Jungians*. London: Routledge and Kegan Paul.

Stein, Murray. 1985. *Jung's Treatment of Christianity*. Wilmette, Ill.: Chiron Publications.

_____. 1987. Looking backward: archetypes in reconstruction. In *Archetypal Processes in Psychotherapy*, Nathan Schwartz-Salant and Murray Stein, eds. Wilmette, Ill.: Chiron Publications, pp. 51–74.

Turner, Victor. 1967. *The Forest of Symbols*. Ithaca, N.Y.: Cornell University Press.

Winnicott, D. W. 1971. *Playing and Reality*. New York: Basic Books.

Dream Design: Some Operations Underlying Clinical Dream Appreciation[1]

Sylvia Brinton Perera

Pattern is born amid formlessness: that is biology's basic beauty and its basic mystery. Life sucks order from a sea of disorder. (Gleick, Chaos, p. 299)

Trying to unweave, unwind, unravel
And piece together the past and the future,
Between midnight and dawn, when the past is all deception,
The future futureless, before the morning watch
When time stops and time is never ending . . .
. . . To apprehend
The point of intersection of the timeless
With time, is an occupation for the saint —
No occupation either, but something given
And taken . . . (Eliot, Dry Salvages, pp. 22, 24)

Sylvia Brinton Perera is a member of the New York Association of Analytical Psychology, a teacher at the C. G. Jung Institute of New York, and a practicing analyst in New York and Connecticut. She is author of *Descent to the Goddess: A Way of Initiation for Women*, *The Scapegoat Complex: Toward a Mythology of Shadow and Guilt*, and co-author of *Dreams: A Portal to the Source*.

It is our occupation as psychotherapists to try to "apprehend" all the weavings and unweavings that pattern, "piece together," and point to the intersection of the timeless with time. Dreams "between midnight and dawn" are among the natural communications arising from that point.[2] They illuminate in images the interface where "time stops and time is never ending." Here the past is frozen and repeated in the patterns established by personal complexes (that shape and even "deceive" perception, action, emotion, relationships). Here also dream images provide access to the eternal archetypal energy patterns that underly the personal complexes. Through attending all communications from the interface, we seek as therapists to find the person before us (and ourselves) as he or she is and is "meant to be" and to celebrate that "point of intersection."

With those who come into our consulting rooms for the help and enrichment such communications can give, we seek "approach to the meaning [which] restores the experience / In a different form" (ibid., p. 24). Dreams offer primary assistance in this task. They provide a glimpse of the "different form" since their images reflect the dreamer's psychological, spiritual — and sometime external — reality as seen from the eye of the Self. Such perspective represents to the outer witness the situation of the inner world and thus helps to make conscious the dreamer's perceptual and emotional just-so facts and self-deceptions. It also points toward still unconscious potentials, which may sometimes provide avenues of transformation.

Over the years we continue to train ourselves, adding to the "given and taken" gift of apprehension new skills and practice in order to be able to attune more sensitively to the multiplicity of experience occurring simultaneously in and around the telling of each dream.

Dreams and Images

Poetry and the arts come from the same source and illuminate the same interface as do dreams. Both derive from the formative power of the archetypes which manifests to some extent in time/space and psyche in the form of images. And as Jung put it, "A great work of art is like a dream; for all its apparent obviousness it does not explain itself and is always ambiguous" (1966, par. 161).

In approaching our occupational task of dream appreciation then, a poet/teacher's statements about poetry are apt:

One does not take a poem [dream] apart for the love of dissection, but only in order to put it back together more meaningfully. (Ciardi 1959, p. 779)

The poem [dream] is not a statement but a performance of forces, not an essay on life but a reenactment . . . so the performance of a true poem is endless in being not a meaning but an act of existence. (Ibid., p. 674)

Dream experience, like poetry, "performs" in an altered state of consciousness. Dreaming consciousness or "mentation" (Glucksman, et al. 1987, p. 19) feels "otherworldly" for it reaches beyond rational categories of time and space to the timeless. It reaches, however, to dramatize and circumambulate the dreamer's current problematic (hence charged with energy) and/or individuation issues.

As Koffka, a Gestalt psychologist, put it, "where the center of our interest lies, there . . . a figure is likely to arise" (Deri 1984, p. 35). The "interest" in a dream is focused from the dreamer's Self and tends to interweave effectively potent and pertinent material from past, present, and future.[3] Since the dream manifests to "reenact" existence when conscious habits of perception are relatively passive (indeed dormant), it permits the emergence of new image and emotional structures from outside the dreamer's usual mind set. These structures combine relevant information that is familiar and unfamiliar. Such information may come from individual (subject level), communal (object level), and archetypal dimensions about which the awake dreamer is unconscious. By calling forth and integrating such new images and structures, dreams facilitate reorganization of the dreamer's psyche—probably on both unconscious and conscious levels (Gabel 1985, pp. 185–205; Deri 1984, p. 37). Thus dreams can be used for healing, for psychological insight and guidance, for problem solving, and for the nurturing of creativity.

To connect to here/now awareness in the witnessing dreamer, sleeping mentation presents itself in a language of sensory images— visual, auditory, proprioceptive, and/or kinesthetic. These may be metaphoric if their psychological-spiritual meanings can be more or less translated into rational concepts or shared and verbalizable analogies; they are symbolic if they point to "something suprahuman and only partly conceivable" (Jung 1942, par. 307).

When dealing with dreams in our occupation as Jungian analysts we sometimes use other images to amplify those of the dream to discover paths of meaning for our own orientation and ultimately for the waking dreamer.[4] This is the classical Jungian approach. Sometimes we encourage moving toward the world of images to participate in active imaginations (for summary, see Hall 1977, pp. 331-347) or to encourage the dreamer's consciousness to be infused with more "underworld" fantasy (Hillman 1979, Shelburne 1984, and Lambert 1984). Sometimes we use archetypal forms, such as that of the drama, to help us comprehend the underlying structure of dream communication (Jung 1948, pars. 509, 560-566; Whitmont 1978, p. 64). Sometimes a diagram is used to convey the relations of interlocking complexes revealed through the images of a dream (Mahoney 1966, p. 146, illustrating an example from Jolande Jacobi). In all these cases we use created/discovered image forms, which come from psychic processes similar or analogous to those of the dream itself, to help ease the dream's reception into fuller consciousness (Faber, et al. 1983, pp. 145, 158-159).

There are also other images which can help us understand the basic *operations* through which we come to appreciate and dialogue with the timeless depths of each dream performance and its verbalized text. These are images, originally of ritual processes, which have been used since our Stone Age ancestors first began scratching linear forms on the rock walls of sacred caves and mounds. These sacred designs depict energy in motion. They reveal the power of the line both to move our mind/body and to communicate as a metaphor of action (Klee 1953, p. 16). And they illuminate the dream in terms of its archetypal affect, or lines of force, by following the sensed intensities in any dream appreciation.[5] The line is like the energy of affect force pushing through the ground of chaos to create a surface pattern. Anthropology has found parallels between some of these basic design forms and ritual procession and dance (Levy 1948, pp. 247-249). In psychotherapy we also find certain analysands using such primitive visual notation to express an emotion-laden movement or a ritual interaction. I have seen the infinity sign repeated until it took the double-spiral shape of the Lorenz Attractor (Gleick 1987, p. 114) in the drawing by a woman to express and contain the power of her helpless rage. A series of mazes was drawn by another analysand to remind herself of the various ritual movements she wanted to enact with her analyst in order to discover and creatively manage her feelings about her envious mistrust and idealizing love.

The images provide access to the archetypal patterns underlying the contextual and emotional mental processes by which we work on nonlinear levels of cognition. They thus confirm the logos of a non-discursive, but clearly and effectively ordered method by which we can reach meaning. This logos is very different from the linear, hierarchical, and dichotomizing modes of cognition that underly Western, Judeo-Roman-based logic and grammar, for by it we work with the affect end of archetypal dynamics, tracking imaged emotion in its "cat's cradle" web of interlaced, simultaneous, paradoxical tangles toward perception of its meaning-filled, inner coherence.

In reflecting on design forms that express some of the operations involved in processing dreams, I have been guided in part by my current interest in Celtic mythology and art. I have plucked from that rich culture a few of the prominent design forms manifesting/channeling supernatural force and suggesting ritual dance plans. These are by no means confined to Celtic material, nor are they the only ones that could be so used. They may suggest, however, analogies to some clinical processes through which we appreciate and understand dreaming performance, the transpersonal energies revealed in dream images, and the interlacing of dream images with psychological and spiritual realities in the dreamer's daily and analytic/transferential life.

Both dreams and the ritual arts manifest and mediate transpersonal energies. Both are forms of enactment expressing the depths of existence and the energies flowing from the source through life. Both serve the function of the "feminine" form principle which envessels to transform cosmic libido for human participation. To use processes suggested by one to illuminate the other may permit us to relate to the dream in terms that do not lurch it from its matrix, yet facilitate and develop participant witnessing in the dreamer.

I am suggesting, then, that operations analogous to those underlying forms and processes of ritual art may be meaningful for clinical dream appreciation. For we can follow with them an energic process similar to the passionate, intuitive, aesthetic, spiritual energies underlying the dream text itself. They permit and train the witnessing mind to steer accurately by affect intensity, by embodied sense, and by trained intuition. Such modes are as important as those which operate according to image explanation and amplification, and indeed the interweaving of all these modalities and operations are part of the larger interlace process described below.

In writing about these processes my style is itself influenced by their curling weaving forms. It circles back, repeats, meanders much as do the designs themselves — and much as do our mental processes when confronted with an analysand's dream in our consulting rooms. The reader is urged temporarily to forego understanding in the heirarchical, straight-linear, rational, and deductive methods of Roman logic and grammar and to be guided by the weaving, circular patterns of Celtic mentation[6] and the ancient oral tradition — to go "a-mazing" (as Judith Hubback put it in her comments to this paper). This allows the interlacing order to take place or be discovered/created. Its pattern is unpredictable, unknown in advance. It is found only during and after the experiential process itself.

Celtic Design

The Celtic art style was based on the Celt's belief in "the aristocracy of the imagination," on the honored place of the druid/poet/ musician, and on the power of crafted forms. It conveyed the Celt's strong sense of the supernatural and of the constant interpenetration of the natural and supernatural worlds, much as we experience them in dreams.

It was a magic style, "as alienating to modern consciousness as *Finnegan's Wake*," one commentator puts it. "[It] repels and fascinates because its order, barely controlling an explosive anarchy, allows us to glimpse the chaos at the heart of the universe which our own Romanized culture is at pains to conceal" (De Paor 1981, p. 126). In recent decades we have come to know (via the mathematics of infinite sets) that chaos has an unpredictable order of repetition across scales—very similar to the kinds of symmetry and internal consistency across levels and perspectives that occur in dreams. The Celts seem to have known this order intuitively, for many of the image forms of the Celtic La Tene style are remarkably like those which derive from modern chaos theory (Gleick 1987, p. 114ff).

Like the forms generated by chaos theory and the dream itself, Celtic art concerns itself with translating energy into precise design. It uses forms expressing process, linear analogues of cosmic libido. Like the dream, which the Celtic druids sought as the predictor of kingship, much of Celtic art was created in altered states of consciousness, and meditative trance is induced by it even when a modern participant observer traces its coiled interlace forms. There is potential correspondence, I find, between the subject matter of Celtic art and the creative processes by which it was produced and the subject matter of dreams and the processes of their appreciation.

This can be felt by looking at some examples of Celtic La Tene and early medieval visual art. The style powerfully and congruently expresses its content. The extraordinary use of sinuous line channels the energy of life into coiling forms that are always sensuous and vibrant. But the supernatural energy (Figure 1) is so strong it twists natural forms into abstractions. Forms suggestive of nature are deprived of their specifics and revealed as impersonal designs by simplifying, condens-

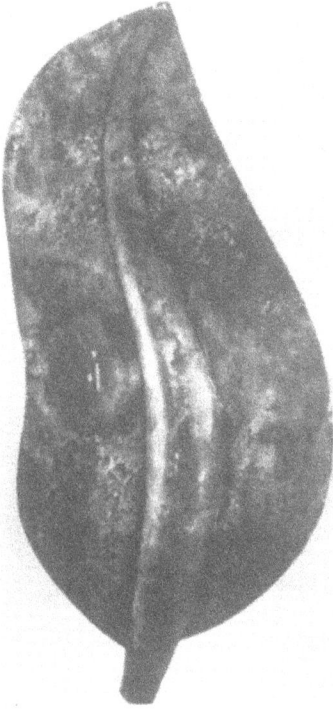

Figure 1.

ing, displacing, combining, and repeating forms in different scales (Figure 2). Such starkly simplifying abstractions are analogous to dream images—revelations of vast, not yet differentiated, psychological complexity conveyed in the simplest essential elements.

Beyond and through the stylized figures, the subject matter was, as I have said, libido in process—"The force that through the green fuse drives the flower [and] Drives my green age . . . " one modern Celtic poet put it (Thomas 1953, p. 10). Celtic art expresses this force in rhythmic, pulsing curves and knots and clusters (Figure 3). They are precise, elegant, magic forms that feel both driven and tightly ordered like the designs of the Mandelbrot Set (Gleick 1987). With careful, beautifully controlling line the artists focused, contained, and channeled intense libido by holding it in magic coils often set against a bare background. "As magic circles they bind and subdue the lawless powers belonging to the world of darkness, and depict or create an order that transforms the chaos into cosmos" (Jung, speaking of the mandala form, 1959b, par. 60). These nodes or clusters of intensity suggest the vitality of dream images against the ground of night's non-REM sleeping darkness.

The process by which the artist set his coils (and the reciprocating process by which the observer views them) creates a visual metaphor. It is analogous to one way the images "intended" by art, ritual, or dream can channel and mediate turbulent, archetypal affect. For the Celts such sacred power might also be danced with, propitiated, submitted to in meditations, possessions, and beserk seizures. Warrior camps and druid colleges trained men and women in the use of controlled, magical, mythical energies and consciousness. Thus they attuned to, perceived, and expressed cosmic energy in their creative and primarily magic-level processes of combat, art, ritual, and story. "[In] dream we have the ultimate transformation of emotion into design—ultimate

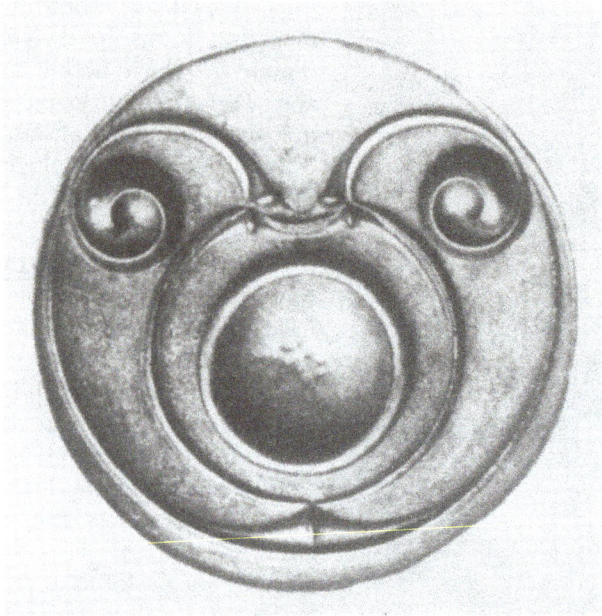

Figure 2.

because it happens completely in 'altered' consciousness, uncontrolled by ego, which can only receive and dialogue with the result" (David Massell, private communication).[7]

Celtic art orients along lines of force — much as we do when we follow the unfolding images of a dream. Basic patterns are the various spirals and the interlace — one restless, mobile line, coiling into knots and clusters based on magical analogies and correspondences (Markale 1976, pp. 76–77) and on sacred-emotional-aesthetic intensity (Figure 4). Such designs underly the cosmic motion of celestial lights, biologic growth as well as — I hope to show — the complexes of the human psyche and their emergence into dream images. Celtic consciousness provides orientation by showing us the process through which energic patterns manifest, interlacing through time, never-ending, leaping, crossing, always in change and motion, and always expressing, revealing, and channeling the energy of the sacred source as it shapeshifts into its many forms of manifestation.[8] For the Celts the process of following that energy — of seeing, letting the eye follow the lines, of telling and listening to the telling of a tale or dream — was as important

Figure 3.

and magical in holding the fearsome energies of existence as the precise and magical forms themselves.

The Spiral

The spiral path has been seen as a symbol of psyche's most basic developmental process:

Figure 4.

Mazes and spirals are symbols of the unfolding spiral of life; of the path from the cradle to the grave, of the path to the inner mysteries, of the finding of the body centers; a path now clear, now convolute, now back-tracking. It leads from beginnings in archetypal possibilities; through babyhood, childhood and adolescence, through marriage, parenthood and involution, and returns to the great mother in death. (Moore 1983, p. 120)

Erich Neumann has written also of the ritual journey by which the ego entering on the spiral path following "the unconscious intention of the way" receives and accepts "the spiritual direction of the uncon-scious," which leads both to "an ever new manifestation of the archetypal world, but also to an increasing development of consciousness" (Neumann 1976, p. 32). Jung points to the spiral as the movement of unconscious processes:

> We can hardly help feeling that the unconscious process moves spiralwise round a centre, gradually getting closer, while the characteristics of the centre grow more and more distinct. (1944, par. 325)

> The way to the goal seems chaotic and interminable at first, and only gradually do the signs increase that it is leading anywhere. The way is not straight but appears to go round in circles. More accurate knowledge has proved it to go in spirals; the dream motifs always return after certain intervals to definite forms whose characteristic it is to define a centre . . . . As manifestations of unconscious processes the dreams rotate or circumambulate around the centre, drawing closer to it as the amplifications increase in distinctness and scope. (Ibid., par. 34)

Such a rotation around the central ordering Self in analysis and in a dream series has a "symmetry across scale" to the process of discovering the ordering form pattern underlying any dream image. The journey on a macroscale is that of individuation. On a microscale, it is the journey into and out of the essential core determining the Self-generated complexities of each dream image.

Relearning to perceive the spiral process — to discover the clustered facets around an energy core or theme — trains us to work patiently and imaginatively with dreams and their associations and amplifications, with the pulsing levels of affect that run through the analytic session and life itself. It trains us to be able to companion the deepest and farthest reaches of imaginal, creative consciousness. We learn thus to find the central points we need for orientation.

The spiral form expresses a path circumambulating a center of power — a going easily into and from that center (see below, p. 60 for an example of this operation in a dream). It suggests the winding process through which participants in a ritual dance into the secret core of the mystery (Robertson 1963, pp. 111-135) — where transpersonal energy is found and made available to human participation. As its line is followed, the spiral process creates/discovers a plane, the ground or underlying matrix of the journey — analogous to the psychic field depicted in dream images, which is structured and empowered from its archetypal center.

Every dream is a natural pattern,[9] like the snowflakes Gleick describes, representing:

a delicate balance between forces of stability and forces of instability; a powerful interplay of forces in [micro and macro] scales [that] . . . records the history of all the changing . . . conditions [the dreamer] has experienced and the combinations may as well be infinite. (1987, pp. 309, 311)

The dream thus expresses and represents the powerful interplay between "basins of attraction" (ibid., p. 299), and thus it records the conditions the dreamer is experiencing — the relational/psychological/spiritual situation as it is — in terms of present energy configurations.

The text of a dream may be similar to that of any poem, painting, or narrative: "a system of internal energies and tensions, compulsions, resistances and desires" (Brooks 1984, p. xiv), depicting personified psychological qualities and objectified psychological events and relationships circling around a central theme or patterned in dramatic sequence. But it may also be a single image — visual, auditory, and/or kinesthetic — to be enriched in the web of associations, explanations, and cultural/mythological amplifications (Jung 1944, par. 403) that inevitably radiate out from the node of psychic energy that the image expresses in sensate form for (partial) revelation.

When we have found the relevant psychological/spiritual dynammic manifesting through the image, the dreamer's emotional, embodied assent affirms that the core is found (Whitmont 1978, p. 68). Then we can circle out, retracing the ground from the perspective of the core energy pattern into the whole field of its ramifications in the dreamer's current, transferential and historical psycho/spiritual dynamics.

Each dream image, then, can be seen as manifesting and taking its focus from such a gravitational, energic center. Sometimes it is relatively easy to proceed from the shared present moment of the analytic encounter with its verbal or painted depiction of the dream to the essential core of psychic reality that each dream image manifests. Together dreamer and analyst can sometimes sense its energic pull and let consciousness spiral in, aided by the dreamer's personal associations and emotions which are aroused by its presence. We can also tune in meditatively to the unknowable essence of the symbolic image and let those qualities reverberate to pull us toward the core of the spiral. Inevitably there is an interlace between all these circumambulations as they manifest the central core in their various and differentiating modes. Being able to discover the methods of this interlacing trains us in the logic of symbolic thought. For the design is not random, but rigorously determined.

Image Logic

The magic level modalities operative in Celtic literature and art as in dream mentation involve shapeshifting and associations by analogy, similarity, contiguity, and accretion through a time cycle. These same factors underly the organizing principles that enable/create perception of a coherent gestalt (Deri 1984, p. 36). In such dream and poetic or symbolic modes, a part may stand for the whole, forms may transform, or one stand for another that has a similarity of core essentials. Nonetheless there is a logic in these modalities. This logic ensures the integrity of the images that limits their misuse and calls attention to any crossing of the boundaries of their own coherence. We learn, thus, that when image forms are mixed or twisted or occur with fantastic juxtapositions, there are inevitably deeper and pertinent psychological points to be discovered.

Dreaming of "a loaf of bread made of loosely packed grain" focuses attention on an image of basic human nourishment. Grain is a pertinent part of the image, but its description as loosely packed (and uncooked) suggests that the transformation process to permit normal creation of a loaf of bread — and hence ensure assimilation of basic life and therapeutic food — was too quick and incomplete, lacking psychological grinding, moisture, and leavening. In working through such a dream image, we would need to delve into the dreamer's personal associations and explanations of grinding, moisture, and leavening as well as into their collective, metaphoric, and symbolic and mythological significances. We could then apply the image as a metaphor of the dreamer's problems, and perhaps also of problems in the analysis — since the image may refer to the transforming and feeding functions of the analytic process (Whitmont and Perera 1989, chap. 12).

When the dream image is, instead, "the loaf is made of feathers," we know there is a radical distortion in the coherence and meaning of the images. Bread and feathers have no structural correspondence between them, nor to reality as we commonly share it. The dream witness feels their juxtaposition to be disturbing and cannot find closure of the image. Yet the image is just so, a fact of the dream. We can assume it is isomorphic with some actuality in the dreamer's psyche, but its resistance to closure alerts us to disturbed psychological dynamics.

Here the dreamer's initial association to feathers was "lightweight and spiritual." Thus we are shown that the basic nourishment of life is being made of inedible, "lightweight and spiritual" stuff. The intersection of this personal association with the dreamer's rote amplification, that birds are "creatures of spirit," already tells us something about the incoherent and impersonal process by which psychological and spiritual nourishment occurs in the dreamer (and perhaps in the dreamer's analysis). Further questioning about feathers, however, led the spiral further in to memories of a childhood pillow, through which feathers unexpectedly protruded, and to the dreamer's secret fear that he would be pierced or suffocated in his sleep. From the intersecting perspective of each part of the disturbed image, a deeper meaning became clear. The quick, lightweight verbalizations, by which a seemingly possible nourishment was rendered impossible, could then be appreciated as a defense against the dreamer's fears to trust any holding environment. Bread of feathers aptly imaged his ensuing, unsatisfactory attempts at self-feeding.

The Maze

Sometimes, as in the second example above, it is relatively hard to discover what complex of psychological reality underlies the image. Then we must proceed as if traversing a maze. Its form creates a linear procession protecting the sacred place from those who do not know its secret, admitting only those willing to follow its devious route. For even when the maze path seems to be going in the wrong direction, it is still leading to the center. We find an opening and proceed with stops, retracings, turns. We get lost, ask the dreamer's psyche and our own access modes to the depths, which gave the image, for help to follow it. Slowly over time we may discover the direction to the sacred maze center where the mating/meeting (Levy 1948, pp. 247–248) with the Other can take place.[10] In dream work the core is the particular archetypal field that underlies both the dream and the process of its work. We are guided by the pull from the center, and frustrated also, in order to be made to cover the psychological ground that the complex itself covers.

An example of such a maze came with a depressed woman's very simple dream:

Dream: *In the dream there is my blue trunk. I wonder what to do about it.*

The blue trunk had no remembered setting. "There" it was — an issue without known context or particularized relation to the dream-ego. It only becomes in and through the dream an object of the dream-ego's wondering. Thus its image beckons for reflection. I thought I had a head start into the dream knowing the dominant, metaphorical connotations or explanations of the image of trunk and knowing also some mythological amplifications suggesting the basic analogy of trunk to vessel, treasure box, coffin, womb, etc. — all of which imply valuable, potentially transformative, contents to be closed away and protected in a manner analogous to maternal holding. But I was also aware that without knowing the dreamer's personal reactions and context, the dream image can only generate hypotheses in the analyst's mind. Mine were not communicated to the dreamer, for I expected they would detract from the emotional experience of the ritual process between dreamer, analyst, and dream material as well as arouse the dreamer's idealization or envy. Rather the path opened in a search for affect-filled personal association. I have adapted the following dialogue and reflections from my verbatim notes:

Upon reflection the dreamer could remember no blue trunk. The process of searching through the path of personal associations immediately hit a wall. As often happens, the stop caused the path to bifurcate into its parts: trunks and blueness:

—What about trunks? The dreamer "never used a trunk only suitcases." Why? "Trunks are" (and here she switched from the path of personal association to that of explanation) "for people who have a lot to carry, who go on long trips, or who store things in the attic."

(Again the path divided. The container is for journeys and storage. There is no emotional charge to any of the verbalizations, however. This tells us the path is still far from the archetypal, energic center.)

Further rumination was equally limp. I decided to explore some implications of the explanation of the image, a path opened by the dreamer already. Consensually, trunk implies contents held during journeys or in storage. The dreamer's explanation was in agreement with collective meaning; there was no aberrant divergence. But there was no attention yet to the contents.

—What might be inside? "I have no idea."

—Can you imagine? "I don't think so. No."

I heard the note of aggression and wondering if it was protectiveness, decided to comment.

—Perhaps she didn't want to let me in on what had been stored away.

In response the dreamer veered away and said she thought "the trunk was open in the dream." (She was brushing away my comment. Like the maze path itself, an opening seemed to be found. It suggested psychological availability, but turned out to be a tease, another dead end.)

—Open? "I think it's empty."

—Can you imagine going back into the dream to look? "No, it's empty."

(Instead of closed away, the potential matter seemed now denied or affirmed as void. There was a dead end.)

I wondered silently if emptiness was part of the psychological contents. She said the protective vessel is open to see emptiness. Am I to focus on the emptiness, or the sense of seemingly open, but teasingly palpable resistance? Given the choice I felt my ignorance and chose to wait. I could not see enough about the emptiness and such veiled, prickly aggression was usual for this dreamer and often served as a rote cover for more personal reactions.

During a long silence I felt the dreamer's distance from me and herself. I wondered if it was an expression of emptiness or of the trunk closed again. I realized I was doing the wondering of the dream, and wondered how to convey a sense of it to the dreamer. A possibility might lie in refocusing on the image. There was a path opened by the color we had not tried. As I was considering what to say, the dreamer began associating, confirming to me that we were together in the dream field: "blue sky," "blue trunk," "blue sneakers," "blue is spirit, isn't it?" "blue eyes or brown eyes."

(Here was a spurt of intellectual reverie and less blank passivity, but everything mentioned seemed like an association test—content without present affect—and had the quality of defensive holding away of emotion. The protective resistance was itself, however, part of the quality of the trunk image, and hearing the transferential message, I finally got the hint from "blue eyes or brown" that an element of competition had entered the work. My blue eyes were questioning, perhaps intrusive, perhaps experienced as threatening to steal.)

I commented that the dreamer wanted to find out with her own brown eyes, and that the dream puts it that it is her own trunk. I felt that my initial sense of having entered the maze before her was dead-ended. Now she had taken the lead and I was to wait.

(Both her emotional emptiness and the aggression seemed to shift.)

After a long silence the dreamer said, "Hmm, maybe my high school notebook." (There was another silence, but it had a felt charge in it. Much later, reviewing the session, I realized that the image of school had been present from the beginning unconsciously. I had responded by "knowing" and questioning as a teacher might, and this had exacerbated her rebellion and impoverished emptiness defense.)

I cautiously maintained her own "wondering" momentum with a mirroring—Hmm? "Not that notebook, but that was the one I took to school."

(This did not feel like another wall, but a pause to choose which route led to the now palpable emotion. Guided by the intensity and intuition, I repeated her last two words.) The dreamer blurted, "That was the first year of high school." She was physically tense.

—Yes? "Oh, I don't know?"

—Umhmm, sometimes it is hard to know. (I was speaking from my own experience in this maze.)

The dreamer made a sound of despair. "That's when I wrote a lot." (I wondered if the despair was at the unknowing or at her own opening memory. The emotional core of the image felt very close.)

Further silence led to painful remembrance of a story written for her idolized English teacher when she was twelve years old. The story was about lovers who were separated by death. This memory opened further into her feelings for and felt-rejection by that teacher as a surrogate mother/beloved.

The core and contents of the "blue trunk" image were reached. From this center the rest of the associations and explanations, indeed the whole process of the dream appreciation itself, were seen to be meaningful and related together, although they were not discussed with the dreamer. As in a Rorshalk, a Celtic design, or a natural object, nothing in the dream field is random. But the meaning in the seemingly chaotic maze cannot be seen until the center of the psychic reality is sensed and all that has been traversed can be seen from its perspective. As information theorists put it more superficially, "You don't see something until you have the right metaphor to let you perceive it" (Gleick 1987, p. 262). The details are made meaningful by the order of the underlying image energy which structures the whole field. Such synchronicity or "self-symmetry" shows the power of the energic process underlying seemingly disparate and previously unpredictable events (ibid., pp. 109, 306, 309). Indeed it is often found in clinical work that a session expresses or discovers the intent of a dream not told by the dreamer until the end of the hour.

Here, the details of the process confirmed the central order, once the core was known. The energy imaged in the trunk was indeed "a lot to carry" on the dreamer's "long trip" of life (she was 42 at the time of the dream) and "to store." Its color tinged her relation to the transpersonal ("sky" above), to the shabby, athletic footwear with which she sought to cover her own unentitled standpoint. It related also to newly undertaken learning; she was in the first year of her analysis. And the idolized teacher suggested issues of idealization, competitive performance goals, and fear of dependency in the transference which help to explain the various pain-reducing and aggressive defenses that were already part of the dream operation. The ground of the maze had an integrity structured from the core image.

Returning from the maze center in the dream process involved the analyst and dreamer's "wondering" about the beloved and spurning teacher and of the hold of that surrogate-mother complex in the dreamer's life. The teacher was contrasted with the dreamer's own mother, and transferential implications were "wondered" about. Returning out of the maze, then, led to considering the psychological issues raised by the dream in the dreamer's history and current reality. This "wondering" became part of the ensuing analytic process as her connection to symbolic thinking deepened.

Presymbolic Dreamers

With dreamers who are unable to work with dream images, the analyst is accustomed to taking the analysand's dreams as offering guidance about the transference/countertransference, the dreamer's psychological dynamics, and/or the therapy process. Then hypotheses about dream messages may be generated and spoken. But these are often accepted or rejected by the dreamer without his or her having adequate access to an interior center of affirmation or authority. The dreamer may even feel the dream is a deflection from attention to his or her own person and resent the dream source and the therapist who appreciates and understands the images.

Often identified with the complex inside the core of the maze walls, such severely damaged dreamers give the impression that they wait to be found yet feel equally distrustful and may even repudiate the analyst's work. The dreams help the therapist in that search. But the dreamer's envy, leading to noncooperation, may feel subjectively to the analyst as if all his or her good interpretations are blocked or destroyed. Often there is a sense in the analyst of being scrutinized by the dreamer's hidden ego, which may feel somewhat relieved to be sought and hopeful that there is someone (the analyst on whom the Self and the caring parent is projected) worthy to receive trust. Yet the dreamer may also expect or feel the dreams to be spoiled by working with them and despair. This occurs when the therapist carries a transference of the negative caretaker—and is "such a clutz" as one dreamer put it with unusual (for him) humor in his bitterness.

There are many individual variations on this theme. In all, however, the therapist, who has never walked the particular dream maze before, hits dead ends, "bruises heart and head" (as one colleague put it), gets frustrated, but also knows that the dreamer is afraid, unable, and even unwilling to help with the work. Tiny, bodily felt attunements of energy, like muffled sounds, may orient the therapist seeking through the dream imagery, but these often turn out to be on the other side of a suddenly appearing blind wall and the therapist has to leave the seemingly valid approach to dream and dreamer, circling back to find another opening. The hope, frustration, rage, and despair in the transference/countertransference serve to reconstitute the mismatch of dreamer-child to the analyst-parent and may bring out the dreamer's aggression against the dream itself as well as against the analyst who respects it as a message from a source still unknown and fearful to the dreamer. This is all part of the field on which dream appreciation may play.

Rather than entering the labyrinth together as can be done with dreamers with more firmly established egos, some dreamers may initially rely passively on the analyst to bring an image piece of the dream from the maze and take care of both it and the dreamer. The analyst provides a feeling focus that bridges the image to the dreamer and holds both person and dream product with respect and willingness to mirror the dreamer's need. Then the presymbolic dreamer may be able to begin to explore the image and its effects in the relative safety of the analytic container. Sometimes the dreamer can be invited to play with an image piece of a dream, picking it up, turning it over in nascent reflective consciousness, beginning to associate and define, refusing to accept the analyst's interpretation, enjoying the rejection. Such shared play with the dream products of the dreamer's own psyche initiates a creative process even as it helps to build a witnessing consciousness and sense of the ever-creative Self matrix in the dreamer.

Interlacing

The disciplined art of interlacing is another important operation of dream appreciation — and indeed of all analytic work. It is a pattern so common in later Celtic art that interlace design and Celtic are popularly held to be synonymous (Figure 5).

The interlace is made up of one or more continuous lines that cover a surface to create an intricate and orderly network. From a more distant perspective, it forms a texture that defines a shape; from a closer one, it forms a weaving processional path that leads the eye in subtle undulations around and in and out. The eye can start at any point to follow the paths traversing the whole. Sometimes the sinuous lines coil back on themselves in convolutions. Sometimes, in Celtic art, they seem to extrude human or monster parts. Always they seem to manifest the processes of life energy on the ground of being, like sacred ivy coiling up the great druid oaks, or human-knit fibers twisted into cloth.[11]

As a typically Celtic expression of intense, intentional, interactive energy currents, the interwoven net was used as magic ornamentation. It may have originally been a design plan for dances (Robertson 1963, p. 125). It has been so used by modern analysands (Patricia Finley has kindly shown me an example) suggesting the patterned process unfolding through time and movement. It may have been a form of meditation: the perceiver's eye drawn into "contemplating the knots of eternity" (Sharkey 1975, p. 92). It was also used to convey exchange—of energy, of form. In one of many similar margin illustrations in the Book of Kells (Figure 6), an interlace between two beard-pullers suggests a ritual verse or energy exchange between two bards or a communication between ego and Self. Other interlaces demonstrate the mystery by which line and energy shapeshift to generate the forms of plant and animal life.

The interlace is a visual correlate to a mode of processing reality that is intuitive and symbolically logical. Intuition picks up the cogent facts; symbolically trained perception and its rationality tells us where the facts fit meaningfully together.

This is not the consciousness that arises by "discrimination of opposites . . . the paternal principle, the Logos"

Figure 5.

(Jung 1959a, par. 178), for this consciousness recognizes that the separate-seeming strands must cross and recross to find resonance on the deeper ground of being. Nor is this like the spiral/maze operations whereby we reach the affect core of the single image. Rather this consciousness seeks the nodal crossing points where discrepancies interlace and conjoin and separate to convey significant affect-image meanings. It decides what elements belong together because they hold basic, isomorphic similarities or provide differentiating contrasts. It discovers, also, and can discriminate the multiple, simultaneous, nonhierarchical strands compressed into one image.

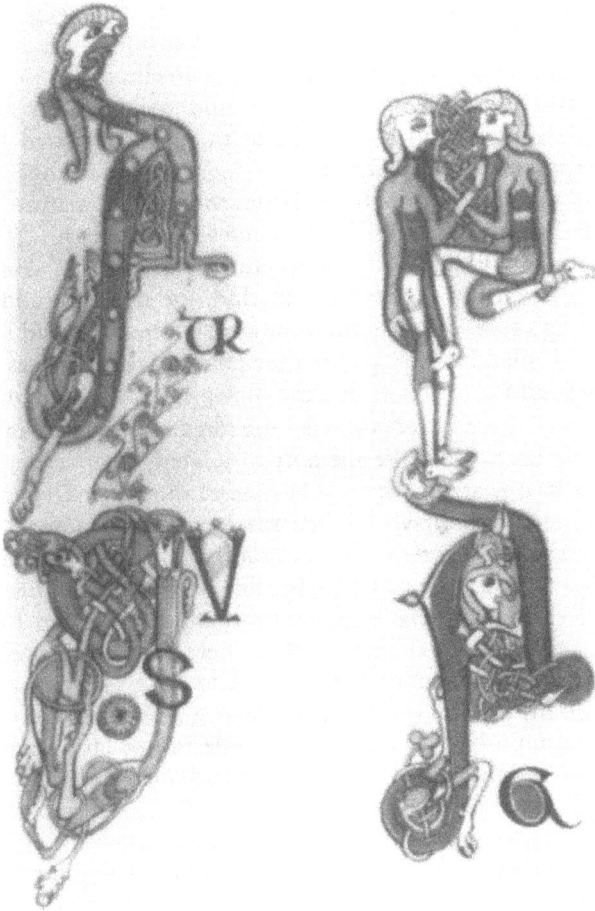

Figure 6.

It is an archetypal mode of working which includes time, ismorphisms, and clustering, as well as seeming leaps, loops, and discrepancies; and overall meaningfully interlaced context, as well as the ego's inevitable ignorance—all as parts of its ordered pattern. Knowing such a method is archetypal and based in ritual design, the analyst may find it less difficult to sit with the unmediated turbulence, instability, and chaos that is so fearful to the infant part of the dreamer until pattern emerges.

In dream work, the simplest interlace operation finds the psychologically meaningful crossing point between associations, explanations, and amplifications. An example of this was provided by a depressed man of 48, whose initial dream image was of "an elm tree." His association was to an elm from which he and a childhood friend had built a rope swing during vacation—a poignant memory of shared, playful activity. By explanation, he said that "elm logs are hard to chop because the wood is particularly tough, and they burn with many so many flying sparks" that he thought them "somewhat dangerous." Furthermore, elm trees have "died off due to Dutch elm disease." Amplifications of the tree of life, the trees of paradise, the shamanic and family trees, and Jung's essay on the symbolism of the tree came readily to the analyst's mind, silently alerting me to the power of the image as symbol of life growth and connection to basic biological/spiritual dynamics.

Interlacing these three strands, the dream provided an image expressing life energy and the memory of related, creative play which gives zest. It is contrary to the present state of the dreamer, yet also an image of a lone, "elmlike," organic wholeness pattern that seemed congruent with the dreamer's tall, dour presence in my office. Contrary to the dreamer's assumption, its vitality had not died off in his psyche. But because of the fact that elms had actually disappeared from our landscape, I silently hypothesized that there may have been some "unreal" or unrelated manner in which he had had to keep its symbolic value alive in his psychological environment. (This turned out later to have been accomplished through a secret collection of erotic paintings.) He was to be reconnected to the meaning and energy of this "elm" in the shared dialogue of analysis, much as he had built an instrument of free rhythmic swinging with his friend. But there was warning that the task was presently conceived of as chopping and burning tough wood. The difficulty of the work and the dreamer's fear of the danger of flying sparks—all were expressed through this simple operation of interlace.

Perhaps the primary interlace design is that between the deeper archetypal *gestalt* and the perceptions and events that compose ordinary life—suggested visually by the simple looped interlace between the double spiral "eyes." We know that the patterns of perceptions themselves are structured by underlying archetypal dynamics. We know from experiments in Gestalt psychology that "vision imposes a conceptual order on the material it records" (Arnheim 1971, p. 22, cf. 13). "Perception is purposive and selective" (ibid., p. 19). The mind perceives in patterns, finds or creates simpler, relatively closed, meaning-filled structures in the chaotic panoply of perceptions, emotions, and events. Thus there is an interlace by which ordinary life depends on the deeper patterns. Equally, by perceiving the patterns in the ordinary, we discover depth.

Symbolization and analogy are cognitive tools based on interlace. They find correspondences between images, events, and dynamics and pair these on the basis of isomorphic similarity (Deri 1984, p. 103, quoting Kohler). The symbolic mode finds the correspondence by attuning to the underlying and ultimately unrepresentable archetypal pattern *behind* images and events. The analogic mode attunes to simi- lar structures and themes *between* them.[12] In this paper, for example, I am using my experience of Celtic material and interlacing it with my experience as a therapist to find analogies that might bring illumina- tion in both realms.[13] The common symbolic theme behind the mate- rial for both Celts and Jungians is concern for the processes whereby this world and the other world interpenetrate. Hence dream appreciation is a fitting subject to illuminate the points of intersection. Dream menta- tion, like Celtic magic/mythological-level design, and ritual move- ment, is an area where conscious and unconscious meet to exchange and interact on the ground of being, the only partially knowable "unus mundus."

We learn and can ever again assume such intersections are opera- tive within the dream itself and also within the psychological/spiritual field constellated with a dream—no matter at what point we start. Thus we seek the meaning-filled points where dream images cross with affects, currently active complexes, daily events, memories, transferen- tial and countertransferential patterns—each strand converging and separating to illuminate the whole field. Our endless tracing of the interlacing designs leads to experience of inner coherence "embedded [with]in a continuum."[14]

Dream: *I am lying down. Mr. A comes up and starts to hit me with the propeller of his boat.*

This stark dream, from the dreamer who brought the blue trunk image, tells us from its drama that a cruel animus is attacking her passivity. As analyst, I could not help but wonder about the transference/ countertransference implications of the scene. But the potential preci- sion of the dream first required more careful work.

The dreamer's associations spiraled easily into the core meaning and emotion of the image: Mr. A is "very helpful, picks up subtle cues; he's a good father to his children, very supportive."

What has this to do with the dream action by which the figure of Mr. A is brutalizing the dream-ego? We need to find how the image of the "good" paternal authority, which operates with sensitivity to sustain the new life, is interlaced with sadistic threat. We could try weaving together "helpful, supportive, good father," attentive to other's "cues," and brutalizing. Is she being warned on an object level of qualities she did not suspect in Mr. A? How does helpful, sensitive support brutalize her as an attitude to her own life? How does brutalizing operate through her? These questions remained held in my mind as more was explored.

In the dream, the dream-ego is lying down. What associates to that? The dreamer reported, "I am so tired, but I never lie down in the day." (There may be a maze deadend here.) I asked: why not if she is tired. "Because there's always a lot to do." What? "Oh, anything." (Impasse; thus, try another route to the emotional meaning.) I restated her words: you don't feel you can rest. "No," said the dreamer, "it's not very safe." (The affect core begins to reveal itself.) Not safe? I repeated. "I never do enough. It's like when I was younger and my father would come in from work in a rage and order us to get supper, clean things up. He was always angry." The core of this image spiral, then, is fear defended against by activity. It, too, needs to be held until a meaningful interlace pattern can come into focus.

What is the setting in which she is lying down? "In the teacher's room, there's a cot where you can rest during free periods." The place makes it legitimate to rest, but I felt a tonal change as the dreamer said the word "period" and questioned the word, intuiting that it had something to do with menstruation. The dreamer confirmed that she was about to get her period and felt her female cycle's pull to introvert. Interlacing this association/explanation with the teacher's room and dreamer's memory of her father, the psychological setting of the dream becomes clear. The dreamer is in the place of legitimate, feminine introversion and self-nurture. There is an archetypal feminine pattern to be honored. But it is disturbed by fear of paternal animus attack. The attack is both personally constellated and, as an aspect of the Western Puritan performance ethic, it is an archetypal opposition, which will have to be worked out, nonetheless, in personal terms in the dreamer's life.

The attack comes in the dream not from a raging perfectionist like the dreamer's remembered father, but from a "good father" who is supportive and helpful. He uses a propeller. There were no associations to the image, but the explanation of that propelling instrument suggests that it is what makes a ship go; hence, it is an aspect of impersonal motivation. I recalled the spinning mandala machines common in schizophrenic imagery and examined the amplification silently to see if it fit the dreamer. The image suggests a mechanical-compulsive motivational system used by the animus to drive the validly introverted, feminine dream-ego.

Here there is an interlace between the helpful and good parent who extrovertedly attunes to other people's cues and the propeller by which the dreamer is driven away from her needed introversion and the reflective processes of her periodic weekly sessions of analysis. The various strands suddenly wove together to permit an appreciation of the dream's picture of beleaguered femininity at the mercy of having to be supportive and nice to others.

Working further with the images helped us to begin to see the complicated interweavings of this fear-driven compulsion in the dreamer's daily life and in her analysis. The dreamer was drawn to reflect on the unconscious propulsion that had ensnared her life in childhood and kept her focused on the need to stay extrovertedly active away from her own depths and needs. Transferentially we both needed to see that she experienced the brutal propeller in the "helpful" and "supportive" parental therapist, and her fear kept her scrambling to placate projected performance demands. The propulsion complex kept her conscious will and perception "lying down" on the surface of life and held within its magnetic currents in a repetitive thematic design.

Dream and Countertransference Interlaces

In this dream there is a suggestion of possible countertransference. As the dreamer's therapist, I felt the confused entanglement that intimates the path beyond syntonic to illusory countertransference (Fordham 1960, pp. 240–250). I needed to open the intermeshed field to the outside to find perspective on my part in the knot. A colleague could readily help point me toward the countertransference piece with an objectivity I lacked. The knot could then be untangled and its strands interlaced appropriately back into the dream message, for the image pointed accurately to the propeller-wielding, "kind father" aspect of my own psychology. This intersected with the dreamer's complex and its inductive force in the countertransference to collude in an unnecessary and ambitious hope about the dreamer's analytic process.

As in this dream and the psychological field which it represents, it is rare that any interlace pattern is truly closed. The lines can slip under or over any frame we build because they are expressions of the life flow. Some Celtic interlace designs exist within arbitrarily closed circles (Figure 7) to represent the complexity in the cosmos. In analysis we try to draw delimiting forms around our therapeutic vessels to contain, concentrate, focus, and clarify our work. But the interlace operation shows us repeatedly how the energy slips into the countertransference and beyond to supervision and life. Like artists we are forced to endure an ever-again open gestalt, even while we struggle to find containing forms and to return into the relatively closed vessel whatever spills out so we may come to an enhanced perception of its patterns.

Figure 7.

Interlacing Method

The interlacing operation relies on a capacity to hold the weaving strands and to feel/recognize relations between different kinds of material within the "total structure . . . in simultaneous, integral presentation" (Langer 1951, p. 97). Its meaning is "non-discursive" and based upon a sense of the deeper or "total structure" of the strands, which often seem to coalesce suddenly in the perception of the witness. "A good reader must be prepared to respond at all levels simultaneously" (Ciardi 1959, p. 866).

Listening in a session through the analysand's verbal description of a dream, we tune into our emerging sense of the currents flowing — as spontaneous emotions, sensations, thoughts, and images arising in our bodies and minds and/or the analysand's communications. We seek the design of correspondences and divergences between the varied elements. We begin to find and expect repetitions of the underlying issues and structures.[15] This provides us with a sense of basic themes and variations in an hour, a dream, a dream series.

The unfolding verbal and nonverbal communications occurring in the context or field of the dream—about daily events, the patient's history and complexes, the workings of the transference and countertransference—in turn, resonate with the pattern of symbolic images and mythic themes emerging through the dream material. We learn to attune to the undertones through which these deeper crossings create correspondences across all the simultaneous modalities of life expression. Holding all of these perceptions, conceptions, and emotions on the ground of attentive consciousness to see where the energies cross to make valid or meaningful metaphoric and/or symbolic patterns is working with interlace.

The operation works, then, both from the surface and from the depth. On the surface, we use it with two or more seemingly divergent experiences to seek how they balance or fit relative to one another and how they may converge at an assumed/intuited, psychologically meaningful convergence point. This becomes the relevant intersection, because it is also a manifestation of the deeper and unrepresentable energic form, which elicited and brought the elements together synchronistically (Jung 1952, pars. 840, 849, 859). In the dream discussed above, the image of the dream-ego lying down intersects with memories, present emotional and physical reality, body dynamics, and transference to point to the deeper issue of threatened feminine identity. Thus, to the trained participant-witness, the surface elements coexist with perception within the archetypal energy field as partial manifestations of that field; and each element or strand will be found to resonate with the others in a relatively unified, interlacing balance.

The pattern may readily reveal this coherence to the witness, or it may seem incoherent and still inaccessible. Like any image, it will nonetheless have its own internal consistency or truth and its own intentionality even if these must be sought through patient work.

Valid and Invalid Interlace

A sense of aesthetics and an appreciation of emotional subtleties and the careful taking of associations can steer toward valid and meaningful connections and avoid rigid, simplistic, or frivolous crossings. Such meaningless interlaces hold experience arbitrarily against a theoretical pattern or reduce it to explanations and contexts too cramped for the vitality of living psyche. An approach to dreams, for example, that interlaces all images with preoedipal or transferential dynamics or a drive pattern (sex or rage) distorts as much as an approach that reduces the images to signs or collective metaphors without personal associations and/or mythological variants when these are relevant. The therapist's crossings also can be indiscriminate, implausible, too hasty — even wrong. This will lead to the dreamer's entanglement in confusions and make it hard to find any personal and appropriate focus to separate from an entrapping web of interconnections that can drown consciousness.

There is inevitably an interlace to be found between the dreamer's conscious perspective and the dream. The dream material may conflict, may complement and enlarge, compensate, support or parallel (when the conscious position is split or weak). It may mirror unseen spoiling complexes, warn the therapist of transferential and countertransferential problems. It may point to future events, but it is always divergent from the dreamer's current consciously held position, and often the therapist's as well, opening an objective perspective into a hitherto unknown area on the subject and/or subject level (Whitmont and Perera 1989, p. 86).

After realizing the separate strands and interlacing them by grounding the dream images in psychological reality, the insights gained from the dream need also to be interlaced responsibly into attitudes and actions in daily life.

Space for Reflection

As stated above, every dream appears at the intersection of a number of energy currents and dimensions; its images are the expression of currently vital interconnections. Usually the interstice, where two strands cross, is a place of power. In the dream above, for example, when the dreamer could see the intersection of the dream image of "lying down" with its association to the female body mystery of menstruation, she became motivated to protect her introversion.

Not only is this the point where the thematic intersection becomes visible and potent, it is also where one part of the linear pattern is raised to let another through. Thus, it is the place where psychological space and the capacity for reflection begin, beyond the two-dimensional magic-level mystery which captures and compels the psyche toward action (as in the more primitive spirals of all peoples and children). Here in the beginnings of a third dimension, consciousness can begin to see the crossing of two patterns and to learn to perceive itself—against the background of and directed from psychological/ spiritual depths. Then the ground is no longer mere surface on which energy plays and drags the unwitting subject. It becomes a multileveled matrix with depth, space, tensions, and overlappings. As the analysand can see the interrelation of two disparate but analogous themes, she or he can begin to reflect and find some sense of disidentification from the unconscious events that pull on him or her. In the dream above, the crossing of "propeller" and helpfulness allowed the dreamer to begin to disidentify from a masochistic pattern of which she was previously unconscious. Thus she gained some nascent sense of control as her observing ego found space to function, separated from the underlying and blinding compulsion.

The moments when this occurs in the arts of the world and in the individual psyche are numinous. They readily occur when, working on a dream, the dreamer can feel, "Ah, yes, that's it; that's the connection that makes sense." Meaning and freedom result, thus, from such points of interlace. Like yantras—meditation patterns—they steer and discipline our mind's working toward wonder as we witness and can separate somewhat from the intricate archetypal basis which weaves our personal life.

Learning to trust their dream images over time, analysands may find a web of created/discovered meanings—"like a new bridge," as one man's dream put it, "to stand on above the abyss." We come to learn that even the most chaotic panoply of images has a pattern and meaning if we can but find and bear it.

The Double Spiral Interlace

Combining several spirals into one design is another very ancient and widespread motif. One of the earliest Celtic examples we have (Figure 8) is the pair of bronze shoulder ornaments belonging to an older woman of the fourth century B.C., buried near the salt mine entrance at Hallstatt, Austria. Each is a typical double spiral interlace, seeming to uncurl from two centers that circumambulate nine times outwards like two dark pupils, reminding us of the Stone Age Eye Goddess forms. In the center between the spirals, the bronze is looped twice, and behind this "infinity sign" the horizontal clasping pin runs. It is all one wire, shaping what seems an endless line of simple intricacy. On closer inspection, however, what seems visually to be two spirals opening from the center is more complex. One side emerges from the center; the other spirals in and its line ends behind the other center.

Figure 8.

One unfolds, one returns. The two motions are linked by the infinity sign that itself makes two small loops which echo the dark circles of the "eye" centers.

Magic meaning can be inferred or projected here, for the viewer's mind is gripped and moved by the forms, as it would be meditating on a dream image. The double spiral suggests the union of opposites in movement, the unity of life and death, of creation and destruction. I thought of the wearer, an older woman, one of the few women buried with the unarmed miners and other men in graves surrounded by the graves of guarding warriors. Was she their priestess, wearing the emblems of unfolding and returning life to signify the transpersonal matrix that the Celts from their beginnings served and celebrated? Did she wear the sign of the double spiral to mark her as one holding initiated vision?

The double, emerging/returning "eye" centers of this spiral suggest the binocular perception that sees both the ordinary and the other-worldly, natural and supernatural. It sees both life on earth and the sacred, unrepresentable energy forming and playing through incarnated existence. It is not unlike the operations of interlacing and the transcendent function whereby we maintain conscious relationship between personal and transpersonal, between emerging ego life and its transcendent matrix, which we can see only symbolically, through a glass darkly. Such vision is necessary in dream appreciation for the dream occurs at just the point of interface — where deeper energic structures manifest as image patterns of the energy itself to create a formed and coherent design out of nearly unrepresentable forces.

Not all dreams may have such depth. Many come from the personal unconscious with metaphoric images of psychological dynamics, and these are vital in any analytic process for "grounding" archetypal dynamics in personal life. But others plumb the profundities of the dreamer's existence and require knowledge of collective unconscious dimensions gained from familiarity with the mythological storehouse of humankind. Then the analyst must know not only the mythological motifs themselves as they have been expressed in art, literature, and ritual, but must know them well enough to be able to recognize their forms in the "modern dress" usually worn when they emerge into dreams. We must be able to help the dreamer to experience the archetypal patterns as they are manifesting in personal, psychological dynamics. This may, however, not include discussing the mythological images per se (see Whitmont and Perera 1989, chap. 8).

The double spiral conveys the operations whereby "archetypal image and personal complex and adaptation need to be seen and worked on together as mutually interwoven aspects of the individual dreamer's life situation" (Whitmont and Perera 1989, p. 180). The interplay of archetypal and personal material in a dream or a pair of coinciding dreams (one archetypal and one more personal) depict both the symbolic overview of the dreamer's present situation and the particular, concrete actions and attitudes that ground and manifest the archetypal drama in ordinary ego life. Frequently there will be structural similarities between the pair of dreams. Other times the dimensions will be interlaced, and archetypal and personal elements will need to be separated out and then interrelated for their more conscious perception.

A rather detailed example of this operation of the double spiral in dream appreciation was brought by a young woman (ibid., pp. 92–96):

Dream: *While I am walking on the street, I am attacked by a hoodlum, who snatches the purse I carry. I run after him, now over fields and hill and dale; but, even though the man walks exceedingly slowly, the faster I run, the less I can catch up with him.*

The motif of not being able to move effectively, either to catch up or to flee in spite of one's extreme effort, occurs quite frequently in nightmares. It images a sense of frightening ineffectiveness or helplessness.

The language of the dream, by staging the action with the phrase "over the hill and dale," immediately brings out a fairy tale mood. But even without this detail, the magical quality of the discrepancy in the inability to catch a slow walker, even while running faster than he, points to a symbolic motif. It is one well known in several mythologies. A story precisely corresponding to, and thus amplifying, the dream lies in the Celtic-Welsh story of Pwyll, Prince of Dyved, and the Mare Goddess. There, the prince beholds an unknown lady pass by on a pure white horse, "a garment of shining gold around her." He sends others and then himself to pursue her, but "the greater his speed the further was she from him." Only when, after repeated failures to catch her, he speaks to her and asks her to stay for him, does she respond: "I will stay gladly, and it were better for thy horse, hadst thou asked it long since" (*The Mabinogion*: 11).

The silent assumption that the robber might be a potentially helpful and transpersonal figure was the result of the therapist's silent amplification. I had read *The Mabinogion*. The dreamer had not. This fact, as such, does not preclude the validity of the amplification, for dreams operate out of a dimension transcending space/time and individual awareness, and routinely use facts and motifs beyond and outside of the dreamer's (and sometimes the therapist's) present awareness. However, the therapist's assumptions, associations, and even the selected amplifications, can also apply only to the therapist's psychology. Their appropriate fit to the dreamer can only be confirmed as the dream is worked through.

In this dream a suprapersonal power is indicated, one which will not be "caught" or forced by willful ego effort but, according to the amplification, demands to be addressed and related to respectfully. This may be said to be the general meaning of the mythological motif in the dream. But what are we to make of the fact that the "divinity" or transpersonal power happens to be imaged as a purse-snatching hoodlum? And how may this all be relevant to the dreamer's psychology?

Association, explanation, and further amplification were needed to provide answers to these crucial questions. The dreamer described the purse as her wallet. By explanation, a wallet is a container for essential personal belongings — in this particular dreamer's case (which always needs to be ascertained), for personal identification, money, and credit cards. Translated into psychological language, we may regard this wallet as a metaphor for the container of her sense of personal identity, available energy or libido (money), and psychological potential value and/or credibility in the world (credit cards). Nothing less than her sense of personal selfhood and identity, her trust in herself and her capacities, is depicted as being stolen from her in the dream.

What is it in her psychology that is the thief? To find out, the figure and its action need to be "grounded" — that is, understood and felt in personal, psychological terms. The figure was unknown to the dreamer.

The dreamer now immediately wanted to enact the scene as she had learned to do in her gestalt training group. I considered her insistent and hurried style — a repetition of behavior in previous sessions — to be relevant to the dream's message, but I held my interpretations of it to be used later to bring this aspect of the dream's message to the dreamer's awareness. On the other hand, since I also respect the potential value of enactment and fantasy to ascertain whether or not the amplifications and even interpretations were relevant and valid, I sometimes find such imaginal methods helpful. In this instance, too, the dream is relatively unfinished. There is no lysis. But waking imagination can be used to continue otherwise unfinished dreams.

I suggested, however, that the dreamer try to address the running robber verbally instead of pursuing him. As she called out, "Stop, stop!" and "Hey you. Stop!" she felt nothing happened. Frustrated, as she had been in the dream, she became impatient and increasingly loud. Then she fell silent and looked to me for an intervention. In discussing the impasse, which merely repeated the dream action, I pointed out both her imperious and impatient tone and the easy abandonment of her position. The dreamer had some difficulty finding an alternative. She finally managed, "Would you stop. I really need that purse. It's not yours, so let me have it back. Please." At that the thief, in her active imagination, turned around. He now looked to her like a professor from her college days, and she imagined in her enactment that he said, "Just take it easy; you need to learn a lot." When she asked if he would give back her purse, he only said cryptically, "Walk with me, and you will get what you have to have."

To circle closer to the essential core of the image, personal associations were needed. The college professor of literature (revealed when she addressed the hoodlum) had been, the dreamer said, "truly inspiring." This transformation into a positive figure fits the mythological amplification, but the description is too general. What was inspiring about him? The dreamer remembered his poetic imagination and sense of slow strength and quietly assertive self-confidence. He seemed to know what he wanted and how to get the best out of his students; thus, she assumed, out of life, too. He was strong; yet the strength was paired with a quiet, unassuming, highly sensitive and responsive adaptation to people and situations. There was a palpable sense of emotional validation from the dreamer.

It is not important that the dreamer's view of the man may have been highly idealized or even unrealistic. As her association to the figure, it depicts her projection onto the professor of an unconscious potential — a cluster of energized qualities. As she actively and desperately "pursues" him, the figure is a hoodlum who withholds her selfhood and self-potentials from her. As she changes her approach, this figure turns out to be a teacher. The dream's message urges the dreamer to revalue her own approach and to learn from the teacher's sensitive, strong, reflective style. Rather than feeling robbed of her accustomed identity with its defensive and willful rush to control, she will get back her wallet and all that it symbolizes — potentially transformed.

For added clarification, it is important to do what should routinely be done at the very beginning of working with a dream, namely to consider the dream setting. The dreamer described the place where the beginning of the dream occurred as the street to her present employment — metaphorically her approach to her life work. Her associations spiraled in to focus on her driven, ambitious attitude and on her sense that she needed to use willpower, pressure, and political ploys to further her chronically insecure positions in her job and in her relationships. This anxious and manic style was the core issue addressed by the dream. It could be now interlaced with its childhood antecedents and its effects on the dreamer's current behavior in relation to the analyst and the therapy.

Throughout the working on the dream, I had silently reflected on the transferential implications of the image. Had there been an experienced sense of theft in the last session? Was something actually happening and/or projected onto the therapist or the therapeutic process that was stealing away the dreamer's habitual sense of identity and energy resources? Even if the amplification implied that this might be positive and a potential encounter with a transpersonal or Self figure, issues of idealization and envy of the therapist (as carrier of the projection) as well as frustration with the process might need to be met and made conscious. I remembered that in the previous session the analysand had talked urgently about her current relationship, seeking advice for immediate implementation. When this was met with a reflective interpretation about her style of compelled and anxious rushing to solve the problem on a practical level, the analysand had lapsed into somewhat depressed, angry silence. The dream followed this interaction as a comment from the Self on the transpersonal life process, imaged in the figure of Mare Goddess of the Mabinogion story, as this process is manifest also in the therapy. The dream thus encouraged further exploration of the feelings of the dreamer after the previous session's encounter, imaging them in a mythic context—as a life problem far larger than the transference relationship, but also manifest within it.

Since the setting of the dream places the problem in her approach to work, the reference is primarily to her style of work and her obsession with willful active work as her style of life. This needs to be explored first. The problem could subsequently be interlaced with the transference issue. Had the setting been a metaphor describing the therapeutic process, it would need to be explored in the reverse order. For it is, inevitably, most helpful to approach the problem where the dream locates it. In this dreamer's case her obsessive defenses against relationship made initial transference interpretations less acceptable, even though they came readily to the therapist's mind.

Woven together, the many strands revealed the pattern of the dream's intent. It suggested that the dreamer's driven attitude to life and work and therapy results in the theft of her true identity and self-potentials and life energy by a figure embodying that very insecurity and driven willfulness. Thus, her assertive capacities turn against her and she cannot avail herself of what is hers. But instead of rushing and pushing, she is enabled to establish—through the mutual play with the dream itself—a conscious relationship of "talking to" what is in her. When she relates humanly to the "thief," she discovers that he is a teacher with qualities of the professor who impressed her. Such sensitivity, receptivity, poetic inspiration, and different strength can indeed teach her by opening her to those potentials in herself, if she will trust herself to walk and experiment with the new style.

The therapist had silently held initial musings about the dream: that it may have indicated that the dreamer needed to confront unconscious feelings about the robbery of her defensive personal identity in the previous session; that it may also have indicated the dreamer's feelings that now she wanted to reconnect to the therapist/thief, but her idealizing and envy seem to make connection impossible. Or perhaps there is a helpless despair similar to that which made her wish to destroy herself because her mother left her in childhood. Holding these questions I let myself be guided by the dream images and the sense that playing with them together would create meaning and would serve to build new inner, reflective processes and structures. These might then serve to hold the frantic, envious parts of the dreamer. The correction of the transference could thereby be built from the archetypal level — depicted as the Mare Goddess/admired teacher in the dream — as this was mediated by the attentive dream appreciation process between dreamer and therapist. The musings and amplification were not discussed with the dreamer, but their effects structured the therapeutic field.

This single dream revealed a life pattern that exceeded in significance the present job issue, to which the dreamer associated. It structured her relationship to her partner (the subject of the previous session) and to the analytic process (revealed in her behavior around and during the enactment and in her negative reaction to the analyst's reflective style). Further, the archetypal elements in the dream pointed to the healing pattern of relationship between ego and Self, between personal and transpersonal, against which the misconstellated elements in the dreamer's complexes needed to be seen. The myth behind the dream revealed a whole, prediseased or preconditioned structure, which could provide the underpinnings and the lysis of the dreamer's life drama.

Seen through the operation of the double spiral, both transpersonal and personal elements can be revealed and interlaced. The infinity sign loop is analogous to the endless weaving together between personal and archetypal levels that take place in the dream appreciation work, in the transference and countertransference, in art and in life. It is that process whereby we "unweave, unwind, unravel and piece together" to find the "intersection of the timeless with time."

Conclusion

In the dreams I thought I had chosen at random for discussion I see with afterthought two common themes. Not only do several refer at least indirectly to teaching (analogous, perhaps, to my task of the presentation of material), but most show aspects of the problem of psychological movement from outer action to inner reflection and back to outer action. This is not the only function of dream appreciation, but it is the one called forth, I now think in retrospect, by my focus on Celtic art derived from ritual movement.

Using process-oriented operations akin to the Celtic art that moves dance action to drawn images, I find by hindsight that several of the dreams which came to mind for attention do indeed show congruent movement. It is a vital one especially for clients held back on the border of their own interior capacity for symbolic consciousness. But it speaks also to the function of dreams for all of us who struggle to live the symbolic life, transmuting compulsion and complex-based action to image and image back to responsible, lived action. And the mode of consciousness of dream logic described here applies, I think, to all dreams.

Because the ritual dream operations are actions in tune with psychic energy and its revelation in dream images, they have the potential of creative play and healing ritual (cf. Winnicott 1971, Davis and Wallbridge 1981, Perera 1986). Such operations can, therefore, be adapted for clinical use with any dreamer, including borderline and undeveloped personalities hitherto unable to use imagery except in neutral, uncomplicated, areas of their lives. For these clients clinically interpretive work on dreams has often been seen—especially by non-Jungians—as counterproductive (Grolnick 1978, pp. 213–226) except for the therapist's own orientation. Sometimes the dreams of such clients are considered such intensely private fantasy (Khan 1972, pp. 307–311) that dialogue seems impossible. In such cases, however, variations on the ritual operations mentioned in this paper may be found to begin to integrate dreams in the shared space of therapy.

Rather than using only verbal descriptions of my understanding of the major operations underlying dream appreciation, I have tried to interweave my descriptions with examination of Celtic designs as well as of relevant material from literary, perceptual, and mathematical theories.

The ritual design forms of the spiral, maze, and interlace provide useful analogies in thinking about processes crucial to modern clinical dream appreciation. For the designs—very archaic and seemingly simple—are patterns drawn with lines which represent and evoke universal elements of motion, growth, and transformation. They come from the same magic—mythological levels of consciousness which produce dreaming mentation. Thus they reach through the same dimensionalities to the interface of psychic depths and current clinical dynamics.

Whether one calls these processes the foundation of a "logos of the feminine" (as John Beebe dubbed it, Ghost Ranch Conference, 1988) or those underlying a nondiscursive, "integral consciousness" (Gebser 1953, p. 97), they weave together preverbal with cognitive, verbal modes. They are the ways many analysts work. Reflecting consciously on these processes can train our minds, then, to work better with the complexities of the affect-image language of dreams.

Such an approach to dreams does not separate them from the rest of therapy or life, for the ritual operations of dream appreciation are not alien to any ongoing and overall process. Rather they both express the whole and can be woven together with work on transferential and countertransferential issues and the dreamer's basic psychological dynamics. Like the interlace line which moves under and over, disappears or comes forward over another strand to exhibit itself, so the various processes of therapy itself interlace to create the web that makes new bridges of consciousness and relationship across and expressing the transpersonal depths.

Notes

1. I want to express my thanks to the participants of the Ghost Ranch Conference for their questions, comments, and amplifications in response to the presentation of this paper, in particular, my respondent, Judith Hubback. I am also grateful to members of The Women's Gathering, an annual women's retreat preceding the Ghost Ranch Conference, for their support and encouragement. Finally I am indebted to my New York colleagues, Patricia Finley, Gertrude Ujhely, and E. Christopher Whitmont, for their comments at various stages of the writing.

2. We see these shapings in dreams, transference/countertransference dynamics, gesture and bodily armoring, verbal communications, and artistic expressions.

3. The "objectivity" of the dream perspective Jung has compared to nature itself. Our reading, however, must take into account the common finding that the dream-ego is most often the dreamer as the Self views it and seems to "want" identity to be perceived by the dreamer for current purposes of individuation. Thus representations in dreams may mirror the dreamer's actual attitudes and qualities, fragments of split identity, ego ideals, or even the supraordinating personality, the Self.

4. Amplification is a method of interpretation reached by "recalling similar images . . . for comparison, a method which may not allow us to define the psychic meaning by means of an abstract concept, but will enable us to describe it in a way which at least throws light upon the underlying energic processes" (von Franz 1980, p. 3).

5. This mode is the other side of the coin of an approach to the dream via its form. Both sides are necessary: there can be no drama without affect, nor affect without the potential for dramatic form. Yet we have our own particular and natural modes of approach to the goal, which is appreciation of the dream in the dreamer's life field. Much has been written about the dramatic, amplificatory, formal methods. There is less material available about the process-oriented methods by which we discover and explore the emotionally based patterns created by the turbulence of therapy and life in the dream.

6. The word itself in Celtic languages is different from that in Latin-based systems. A Celt would say, "Love is at me to him," relativizing the subject to its place within an encompassing energy field. Such relativization of the ego is appropriate to the world of dream (Neumann 1988, p. 17).

7. I am not dealing with the phenomenon of lucid dreams here.

8. Neumann puts this as "the paradoxical multiplicity of [the archetype's] eternal presence, which makes possible an infinite variety of forms of expression" (1959, p. 82).

9. "Nature forms patterns. Some are orderly in space but disorderly in time, others are orderly in time but disorderly in space. Some patterns are fractal, exhibiting structures self-similar in scale. Others give rise to steady states or to oscillating ones" (Gleick 1987, p. 308).

10. J. Hubback reported at Ghost Ranch that she knows of a garden maze constructed in 1986 in memory of the deceased owner of a house. This form of the persistence of the custom seems to corroborate the theory that many British turf mazes "were, in origin, prehistoric sites where ritual dances, representing the triumph of spring over winter or life over death, were performed" (Whitlock 1979, p. 116.).

11. Knitting was started by men in ancient Arabia. The weaving of cloth in ancient Egypt was associated with knowledge (June Kunin, communication at the Ghost Ranch Conference, 1988). Mme. La Farge in Dicken's novel of the French Revolution provides a modern variant of the ancient cultural theme (Norns, Fates) that the knitter's or spinner's thread holds fated information.

12. The psychoanalytic tradition tends to see the primary interlace as that between dream images and the day residue and uses this kind of "linking interpretation" to teach a patient to be curious rather than fearful about psychological processes (Giovacchini 1969, pp. 179–186). This is certainly a valid approach, but it illustrates only one aspect of interlacing.

13. Some understanding of gestalt perceptual and mathematical chaos theories is useful in both areas.

14. E. Neumann (1988, pp. 17–18) puts this: "The ego experiences the occurrences of the inner and outer world as parts of a whole . . . and begins to experience the continuity of the soul."

15. If we are finding what seems to be a known pattern, we can be alert to unexpected divergences.

Bibliography

Arnheim, Rudolf. 1971. *Visual Thinking*. Berkeley, Calif.: University of California Press.

Brooks, Peter. 1984. *Reading for the Plot: Design and Intention in Narrative*. New York: Knopf.

Ciardi, John. 1959. *How Does a Poem Mean?* Boston: Houghton Mifflin Co.

Davis, Madeleine and Wallbridge, David. 1981. *Boundary and Space: An Introduction to the Work of D. W. Winnicott*. New York: Brunner/Mazel.

De Paor, Liam. 1981. The art of the Celtic peoples. *The Celtic Consciousness*, ed. Robert O'Driscoll. New York: George Braziller, 121–142.

Deri, Susan K. 1984. *Symbolism and Creativity*. New York: International Universities Press.

Eliot, T. S. 1943. *Four Quartets*. New York: Harcourt Brace and Co.

Faber, P. A., G. S. Saaymann, and R. K. Papadopoulos. 1983. Induced waking fantasy, its effects upon the archetypal content of nocturnal dreams. *Journal of Analytical Psychology* 28, 2:141–164.

Fordham, Michael. 1960. Countertransference. *Technique in Jungian Analysis*. London: Heinemann Ltd., 1974, 240–250.

Gebser, Jean. 1953. *The Ever-Present Origin*. Translation by Noel Barstad with Algis Mickunas. Athens, Ohio: Ohio University Press, 1984.

Gleick, James. 1987. *Chaos: Making a New Science*. New York: Viking.

Grolnick, Simon A. 1978. Dreams and dreaming as transitional phenomena. *Between Reality and Fantasy: Transitional Objects and Phenomena*, ed. Simon A. Grolnick, Leonard Barkin, with Werner Muensterberger. New York: Jason Aronson, 211–231.

Gabel, S. 1985. Sleep research and clinically reported dreams. *Journal of Analytical Psychology* 30, 3:185–205.

Giovacchini, P. 1969. The influence of interpretation upon schizophrenic patients. *International Journal of Psychoanalysis* 50:179–186.

Glucksman, Myron L. and Warner, Silas L., eds. 1987. *Dreams in New Perspective: The Royal Road Revisited*. New York: Human Sciences Press.

Hall, James A. 1977. *Clinical Uses of Dreams: Jungian Interpretations and Enactments*. New York: Grune and Stratton.

Hillman, James. 1979. *The Dream and Underworld*. New York: Harper and Row.

Hubback, Judith. 1988. *People Who Do Things to Each Other*. Wilmette, Ill.: Chiron Publications.

Jung, C. G. 1921. *Psychological Types. Collected Works*, vol. 6. Princeton, N.J.: Princeton University Press, 1971.

———. 1942. A psychological approach to the dogma of the Trinity. In *CW* 11:109–200. Princeton, N.J.: Princeton University Press, 1958.

———. 1944. *Psychology and Alchemy. CW*, vol.12. Princeton, N.J.: Princeton University Press, 1968.

———. 1948. On the nature of dreams. In *CW* 8:281–297. Princeton, N.J.: Princeton University Press, 1969.

———. 1952. Synchronicity: an acausal connecting principle. In *CW* 8: 417–531. Princeton, N.J.: Princeton University Press, 1969.

———. 1959a. Psychological aspects of the Mother archetype. In *CW* 9/1:75–110. Princeton, N.J.: Princeton University Press, 1969.

———. 1959b. *Aion. CW*, vol. 9/2. Princeton, N.J.: Princeton University Press, 1959.

———. 1966. *The Spirit in Man, Art and Literature. CW*, vol. 15. Princeton, N.J.: Princeton University Press, 1966.

Khan, M. Masud R. 1972. The use and abuse of dream in psychic experience. In *The Privacy of the Self: Papers on Psychoanalytic Theory and Technique*. New York: International Universities Press, 1974, 306–315.

Klee, Paul. 1953. *Paul Klee: A Pedagogical Sketchbook*. Introduction and translation by Sibyl Moholy-Nagy. New York: Praeger.

Lambert, K. 1984. Reflections on a critique of Hillman's approach to the dream by W. A. Shelburne. *Journal of Analytical Psychology* 29, 1:57–65.

Langer, Susanne K. 1951. *Philosophy in a New Key*. Cambridge, Mass.: Harvard University Press.

Levy, Rachel. 1948. *The Gate of Horn*. London: Faber and Faber.

The Mabinogion. 1906. Translated and with an introduction by Gwyn and Thomas Jones, London: Everyman's Library.

Mahoney, Maria F. 1966. *The Meaning in Dreams and Dreaming: The Jungian Viewpoint*. New York: The Citadel Press.

Markale, Jean. 1976. *Celtic Civilization*. London: Gordon and Cremonesi.

Moore, Norah. 1983. The archetype of the way. *Journal of Analytical Psychology* 28, 2–3:119–140.

Neumann, Erich, 1959. *Art and the Creative Unconscious: Four Essays*. Ralph Manheim, trans. New York: Harper and Row.

———. 1976. On the psychological meaning of ritual. *Quadrant* 9,2:5–34.

———. 1988. Stages of religious experience and the path of depth psychology. *Quadrant* 21,1:11–32.

Perera, S. B. 1986. Ceremonies of the emerging ego in psychotherapy. In *The Body In Analysis*, Nathan Schwartz-Salant and Murray Stein, eds. Wilmette, Ill.: Chiron Publications.

Robertson, Seonaid M. 1963. *Rosegarden and Labyrinth: A Study in Art Education*. London: Routledge and Kegan Paul.

Samuels, Andrew. 1985. *Jung and the Post-Jungians*. London: Routledge and Kegan Paul.

Sharkey, John. 1975. *Celtic Mysteries: The Ancient Religion*. London: Thames and Hudson.

Shelburne, W. A. 1984. A critique of James Hillman's approach to the dream. *Journal of Analytical Psychology* 29,1:35–56.

Thomas, Dylan. 1953. *The Collected Poems of Dylan Thomas, 1934–1952.* New York: New Directions.

von Franz, M. L. 1980. *The Passion of Perpetua.* Dallas: Spring Publications.

Whitlock, R. 1979. *In Search of Lost Gods: A Guide to British Folklore.* Oxford: Phaidon.

Whitmont, Edward C. 1978. Jungian approach. In *Dream Interpretation: A Comparative Study*, ed. James L. Fosshage and Clemens A. Loew. New York: Spectrum Publications, 53–77.

_____. 1987. Archetypal and personal interaction in the clinical process. In *Archetypal Processes in Psychotherapy*, Nathan Schwartz-Salant and Murray Stein, eds. Wilmette, Ill.: Chiron Publications, 1–25.

Whitmont, E. C. and Perera, S. B. 1989. *Dreams, A Portal to the Source: A Clinical Guide for Therapidst.* New York: Routledge.

Winnicott, D. W. 1971. *Playing and Reality.* New York: Basic Books.

Zinkin, Louis, 1985. Paradoxes of the Self. *Journal of Analytical Psychology* 30,1:1–17.

A Pedestrian Approach to Dreams

Thomas B. Kirsch

As a manifestation of the unconscious, the dream has been the cornerstone of Jung's analytical psychology from its earliest formulations. It is not necessary here to review the development of Jung's theory of dreams from the beginning to the present. Jung himself has most eloquently described the nature of dreams and their function in "General Aspects of Dream Psychology" (1948) and "The Practical Use of Dream Analysis" (1934), and countless others, including myself, have painstakingly rehashed what Jung has already said. (See for example Mahoney, *The Meaning in Dreams and Dreaming* (1966).) For the most part, these rephrasings of theory have not been terribly enlightening. One can only speak in general terms for so long; after awhile one has many questions of a more specific nature. The one new area in dreams has been the development of the neurophysiology of dreams and its relationship to a psychology of dreams. The discovery of the REM state has been an important breakthrough with which, as clinicians, we have to reckon. I can refer you to papers by Meier (1969), Rossi (1986), Hall (1977), and Kirsch (1968), which have dealt with the phenomenon of REM in relationship to Jung's psychology. The discov-

Thomas B. Kirsch, M.D., is an analyst in private practice in Palo Alto, Calif. He is president of the International Association for Analytical Psychology and clinical research associate professor of psychiatry at Stanford Medical School.

ery of the REM state has helped us to demystify the nature of dreams and helped us to study dreams in a more objective fashion.

What is fascinating is that although the phenomenon of REM was discovered in the early 1950s, no one has been able to decipher its function. It is present in all mammals and has been noted in the youngest *in utero* fetuses. It can be interrupted in various ways, but it always returns whenever allowed naturally. Hence, it seems to play an extremely significant role in the human. But authorities vary in their understanding of that role. As an example of a current notion, Nobel–prize scientist Sir Francis Crick (1983) has suggested that dreaming is a kind of mental waste disposal. As we dream, the waste products of the previous day's thinking are eliminated from our minds. Remembering and holding onto one's dreams, to his mind, can therefore be destructive, rather like saving one's garbage, and just as potentially harmful to one's health. Other investigators have postulated a problem-solving function which makes trying to understand one's dreams more sensible. Dreams may be symbolic answers to an individual's difficulties. One thing most theorists seem to agree upon is that it is much more likely that REM sleep is initiated in order to make dreaming possible than the other way around.

It is good to realize that in the wealth of scientific opinion Jung's hypothesis and research as to the nature of dreams has held up remarkably well so far. Traditional psychoanalytic dream theory has been difficult to validate by the study of dreams in the lab. Freud's (1899) original idea that individual dreams occur to express, in disguised form, specific repressed wishes is very difficult to support using laboratory data on the regularity and periodicity of dreaming. Why would these wishes come at such regular intervals? The dream process follows its own conflict-free course, quite independent of the contents of individual dreams. The adaptational point of view of later psychoanalytic thinkers, such as Bonime (1962), French (1969), and Fromm (1957), that dream interpretation is the search for missing connections among the content of the dreams, the associations to the dream, and the dreamer's life experience, makes it possible to take the dreams as they come and to recognize the dream process as a continuous source of fuel for insight. The theory that dreaming is part of the process of becoming better adapted is close to the Jungian view, although it still leaves out the faith in the autonomy, meaningfulness, and inner richness of the symbol which is explicit in our approach.

Thus, the new physiology of dreaming has not essentially altered our approach to working with dreams. Despite Crick (1983), I remain reasonably assured that dreams have meaning and that they are not just an epiphenomenon to a physiological process. Certainly any of us who have had meaningful dreams can attest to their emotional significance and to their utility in furthering self-understanding. If the new physiology of sleep has not changed how we view dreams, has anything else changed in how we use dreams in analysis? The answer is a good Jungian one, both yes and no.

Let me begin by sharing with you my attitude toward dreams 25 years ago within the Jungian culture of that time. They were the be-all and end-all of Jungian analysis. Although one came in with one's personal problems and predicaments, the main way to gain insight into the situation was through dreams. They were even the final agenda-setters for the focus of the analysis. Many analysts wanted their analysands to bring in the dreams typewritten with a duplicate copy for the analyst. This "assignment" was very much like homework, and analysts and analysands would laughingly refer to it as such. If one did not have a dream to present, there was the definite feeling that one was not being a good patient. (As a patient, this was perhaps stronger in me than in others, for I certainly felt it.) I must honestly say that this attitude was not promoted by my analyst; he was accepting of whatever I brought into the sessions. It came from within me, and it was collectively supported by other analysands whom I knew as part of a small subculture who chose this seemingly strange pastime of being in Jungian analysis. I was then also in psychiatric training.[1]

It is interesting to ask myself how my current attitude toward the dream has changed from that of 25 years ago. Certainly much is the same in my *approach*, and my analysands do not act as if they think there is anything new in dream interpretation. Let us begin by examining the ritual of how a dream is presented in analysis. Do we begin the hour with a patient presenting a dream to the analyst? In my practice, I prefer to begin by hearing about conscious events in the patient's life. Then I like to hear a dream. I listen carefully, and it triggers my associations. I then ask my analysand for associations, which I allow to mesh with my own. Amplifications by either of us are then added into the mixture. Included in the amplifications are associations of a contemporary cultural or social nature, such as our perceptions of current political and media figures, and so on. A dialectic between us is maintained over the dream and its associated material. Throughout this process I am pondering, first to myself, the transference implications of the dream. Often these, too, are interpreted to the analysand, though not always. Eventually there is a sense that the dream has been understood. This sense of understanding between patient and analyst is not necessarily a verbal one, but it is felt in the room. We have somehow exhausted the possibilities of the moment, and it is time to go on in the therapy to another dream or to something else. If the dream is *not* understood, we try for further associations and amplifications, and the hour may end with an unresolved feeling to it. If at the end we still feel unresolved about the dream, I make sure we say we do not understand the dream, often with the stated hope that a future dream will help us to understand the whole process better. Then we can go on to another dream or other issue. This ritual, much as I became initiated to it 25 years ago, seems deceptively simple, and I feel we have essentially dealt with the dream in the same manner as did the early Jungians. Everything seems the same.

However, there are subtle differences in my attitude toward this ritual from 25 years ago. I do not feel the same compulsion to be talking about dreams in order to be a good Jungian analyst. The dream is one way for me to get a kind of data other than the conscious one, and its objectivity is extremely helpful. But when I do not hear dreams, then I use other ways to listen for, hopefully, the same kind of material in the kinds of projections made onto issues in the outer world. I do not any longer require analysands to bring their dreams in typed or photocopied for me. I want the analysands to bring in their dreams in any way that feels comfortable for them. That means there is a great deal of latitude about how dream material enters the session. In terms of quantity, the range now goes all the way from no reporting of dreams to the main part of the sessions being on dreams. It depends more upon the individual than before, as a sort of Jungian superego about dreams has become relaxed.

Does this mean that I think that dreams have become less important to the analytic process? No, but it does mean that there have been some shifts in how I approach the patient who does the dreaming. First and foremost in any analytic session, I seek out where the affects or emotions are located in the patient's psyche. This can be in some recent outer event, in a transference reaction to me, in a childhood memory which has come to the surface, in an inner event such as a dream or vision, or in a current mood. When I have located the affect, I ask for any dream which might have a bearing on that particular affective experience. My rationale for this is my belief that by seeking out the emotion in the analysand, I am tapping into the archetypal level. One of the basic attributes of archetypal experience is that it is laden with affect. If we can tap into that level of the patient's psyche through emotion, the dream that is then related is likely to touch that level, too, and to be taken seriously.

Let me give you a recent example from my practice. My patient, a man, is a middle-aged, highly successful professional with a good home life and marriage. He has always made the right moves to get to the next rung on his professional ladder. He is extremely "nice" — quiet, controlled, a little "wimpy," and he never seems to get angry. He reported the following dream while in the middle of deciding whether he should accept the next step on the professional ladder:

Dream: *He is in an African jungle on a safari. He sees two dogs fighting each other. Then a cougar comes out and eats the dogs. Next, a rhinoceros comes out and eats the cougar. He tells all this to a woman therapist. She says that he is in touch with his aggression and that he has changed. He is uncomfortable with her, does not like what she says, and awakens, with a bit of anxiety.*

My patient is a man who travels a lot for his work, but he certainly does not go to the jungle or anywhere typically primitive. In his dream, the animals are becoming bigger and also more primitive. To this highly rational, scientific professional, this scenario is quite surprising and at the same time very uncomfortable. There is a lot of primitive energy which is manifested in this dream. Also, in the dream his therapist is a woman. He is much more trusting of women, and he endows them with a great deal of authority. I see some of myself in this woman therapist. I have been a strong maternal figure in the transference, experienced by him as being supportive, nurturing and forbearing, as for instance not charging him when he has had to miss appointments because of work obligations. The maternal nature of the transference–countertransference situation was also upsetting to him, however, and he felt threatened by the disquieting feelings that were coming from inside him. In his work, he was being asked to take on more and more administrative tasks which were prestigious, but which were taking him away not only from therapy but from his true love, research in the lab. On the basis of dreams like this one and others, he was able to recognize that he did not want the increased power and prestige of the administration job, which all of his friends and colleagues were urging him to take. Instead, he was able to return to his lab. This dream and its interpretation became a turning point in his therapy. Very shortly thereafter he started feeling much more comfortable with himself.

We have just discussed a dream in which the patient experienced anxiety as a result of the dream, not an infrequent occurrence. At the other end is the analyst who is listening to the dream. This is not an easy process for the analyst, and I have a similarly disquieting experience whenever a patient begins to relate a dream. There is an anxiety in the pit of my stomach. This comes because I wonder what is coming now. And indeed, as the unconscious really is unconscious, one never knows what may come up in the process of relating the dream. I would have thought that over the years of doing this work, this feeling would have abated and, in some ways, I am more comfortable listening to unconscious material. But I have thought at times that anxiety might be a result of needing to know what the dream means, to be the expert, to not appear dumb. Certainly the fact that as the son of analysts I heard a lot of discussion about the importance of dreams in my childhood may have placed an extra burden on me to *know*. But despite my efforts to analyze it, this anxiety has remained relatively constant over the years. I have come to believe that it goes with the territory of exploring the unknown. There is an instant of both terror and fascination as one listens to a dream. Or it may produce boredom and falling asleep; one gets lost in the detail and one's mind wanders.

So, what does the therapist do with this anxiety? As I was writing this paper, *Practical Jung* by Harry Wilmer (1987) came out which in part addresses this problem, among others. The subtitle of the book, *Nuts and Bolts of Jungian Psychotherapy*, tells us that he is dealing with some of the same issues that I am discussing in this paper. He states:

> In confronting the dream world, don't take yourself too seriously, but take the dream seriously. Honor the dream and at the same time learn to play. (p. 212)

The key word for me in this paragraph is "play." In a book about play, the Dutch philosopher John Huizinga (1950) points out that the human is *homo ludens*, "playing man." Playing helps the therapist enter the imaginary world. Jung (1934) tells us that we should look at each dream anew without preconceptions, theories, etc., and then try to understand the dream from what the manifest dream images say. We need as well to play with the images and the affects that a dream arouses, without feeling that we have to know what the dream means. Wilmer (1987) has various rules of thumb for the Jungian therapist and the one he invokes for dream work is, "Not taking yourself too seriously."

Wilmer has classified dreams into various kinds. Many of the classifications are well known to all of us, but with new twists. One classification that particularly appealed to me was the one called "The On-and-On Dream." This kind of dream goes on and on and never seems to get to the point. The parts seem unconnected. It is very difficult to find a thread. I often find myself forgetting whole segments of the dream sequence and berating myself for not being able to remember better. I think, what's wrong with me? Sometimes I *can* make a connection between the various parts, but it requires mental gymnastics to do so. When I engage in these interpretive gymnastics, I feel awfully clever at the moment, but they do not seem very helpful to the patient. He or she will say, "That sounds very interesting and, mmm, maybe that's true. I'll have to think about that some more when I am alone with my thoughts." Of course, I know that I am being told that the patient is not going to think about it for one second more and would be relieved if we could have changed the subject ten minutes before. (As always in therapy, being right is not enough: what is unrelated or too complicated is finally not worth very much. I blush to recall what I used to do: repeat myself in a pedantic, insistent fashion in order to have my brilliant intuitive insights accepted by the patient. Of course, this did not increase the level of understanding. In fact, it would often only increase the resistance to the interpretation. Now I find that I get the best results if I can keep my statements simple.)

The issue here is that the patient is expressing resistance through the presentation of the long and complicated dream that does not seem to have a thread. It is a subtle resistance: the patient has been so "good" in presenting all this wonderful dream material, and the analyst feels so helpless, left out, not knowing what to do. In my experience, the best thing to do in this situation is to focus on one image or sequence that appeals to you, as the therapist, and leave the rest alone. Wait for another opportunity when the dream or pattern of behavior appears in a less convoluted form, and then it can be discussed more readily.

Resistance can take a much more direct expression in dreams. There is a type of dream which almost every patient who has a deep analysis brings in at one time or another; sometimes it is brought to many sessions in a row. The dream is a variation of the "intruder" theme, involving someone or something that is keeping the analysand from talking with the analyst. Typical motifs are that the patient arrives at the analyst's office, and the analyst is nowhere to be found; or that there is a group of strangers in the office with the analyst; or that the analyst is on the phone, and the patient cannot speak to the analyst, etc. Basically, there is a disruption in communication between the patient and analyst. One also often finds that in the dream the patient is far away and will never make it to the appointment, or that the patient arrives on the wrong day. If the image of the analyst is taken as some aspect of the patient's own relationship to the Self, then it speaks to a disruption in the ego–Self axis. Obviously, one needs to acertain whether any of the criticisms of the analyst by the patient's dream have some basis in fact. For instance, does the analyst take phone messages during the session, thereby breaking the analytic temenos? Only after the dream has been looked at from the objective perspective of interpretation should the subjective inner layer be analyzed. Yet, when we turn to this level, a deep disturbance in the ego–Self relationship is the rule.

Let me present a dream of a 35-year-old woman, recently married for the second time, which demonstrates this kind of resistance. She has had an on-again–off-again relationship with another man for the past ten years which became more intense as her analysis began to take hold. After one-and-a-half years of twice-a-week analysis, she had the following dream:

Dream: *I went to my hour with Tom at his house. We were outside in a garden with bricks and lots of shady trees. There were lots of young children running around playing and making lots of noise. I was trying to talk to Tom about all the dreams I had all week, but the children kept distracting us. Our hour kept ticking away, and I was getting more and more frustrated because we could not talk. Tom asked me if I would like to go downstairs to his house. We walked downstairs into his kitchen. I was looking at the cabinets noticing that they were just like the ones in the house I lived in as a child. But they were restored to their original beauty. His wife and daughters were there. They showed me the living room which I thought had the original carpeting of my old house. I sensed the house was similar to my parents' old house but down at the other end of the block. The living room was strangely partitioned off, and I commented to Tom's wife that it must make entertaining rather interesting. We went to their bedroom which was just like my parents' old bedroom but there was no furniture in it. Instead there was a slide projector which was projecting a painting of a woman's face on the wall. It would disappear and you could paint over it and change it. I was fascinated by it and wanted to try it. We left before I could. Tom left the house and I stayed with his family. I suddenly wanted to tell him that I had dreamt about that image on the wall in a previous dream. I had to wait until he got back so we could have another hour together. His daughters and I went down to an even lower level to the patio and sat out by the pool. I was sitting in a lawn chair and I looked up to a second-story window and saw C. R., my old boss from work. I asked her if she remembered me, and she said yes, D. M. I was surprised she knew my last name as M., not McC. I was reading about Tom in a magazine while lying by the pool. He had been having an affair with a very famous celebrity who looked up to him as her mentor. But his marriage survived. I felt very happy and contented sitting out by the pool with Tom's family when I awoke.*

Let me show you how I work with such a dream. I place a great deal of significance on the initial setting of the dream. It takes place at my house, a place she has never actually visited. So I have the feeling that I and my family represent her psychological family and, as such, are both a part of and separate from her original family. She has the desire and curiosity to have another kind of family experience than her own, and she experiences the potential for this in the analysis. She is trying to relate her dreams to me, but is unable to do so because the children kept distracting us. Here we have the "intruder" which keeps us from doing the analytic work. The intrusion comes from these small children playing and making noise. If one thinks about how difficult it is in real life to have an adult conversation with children running around, one can imagine a similar difficulty in one's inner world and ask what might cause it. These children personify the undeveloped, unintegrated complexes that are keeping us from relating to each other in a more mature fashion. Whether these complexes belong to her or me is hard to say for sure, because we do not know to whom these children belong. In any case, they are an interference to our communicating on an ego-to-ego level. The setting in the garden is too uncontained for us to do proper analytic work. She has had a number of other dreams where we have been in exposed places where everyone could hear what we were talking about. Then, I lead her into the kitchen, and now my wife and children are there. The kitchen represents the maternal side in its domestic surroundings. We quickly leave that and go into the bedroom, but it is bare. Instead there is a picture of a woman on the wall which changes. There is no real intimate communication in the bedroom; it is all in projection on the wall and otherwise empty. The patient is fascinated by the image of the woman on the wall. This attraction toward a woman is new for her. I think it represents a new potential feminine development which has never existed before. She wants to linger on at that place because she senses some new value there. Instead she stays with the feminine part of my family while I am away. She wants to experience more of what it is to be a woman in a family context. As the dream continues there is further validation of herself as a woman by her former boss, who even knows her by her married name. I come back into the dream as a powerful and famous authority figure who is having an affair but whose marriage survives. It occurs to me that it may be symbolic of her own situation where she has the fear that her own marriage will not survive her affair. My having this authority is a good thing because it allows the transference to contain the conflict between the affair and her marriage. This means that on one hand the actual transference relationship contains the warring opposites, whereas on the other hand the figure of me as the analyst represents an inner healer containing the conflict within. She is an extremely attractive woman who has been addicted to having a long series of affairs and acting out the typical anima woman for a whole host of men. There is and has been an extremely strong erotic transference toward me, which has manifested itself through both dreams and consciousness alike. When she is with the "other" man, she often fantasized that it is me she is with. She has tried to pull me into her sexual orbit, but I have been validating her feelings toward me without being seductive toward her. I sense her insecurity as a woman as well as her underlying feelings of inferiority. As a result, in my countertransference reactions I am able to keep a reasonable distance, although I find her to be a physically attractive woman. I experience her need to have affairs as a somewhat desperate attempt to validate herself as a woman.

Having gone through the whole dream, I am ready to build an interpretation, part of which I will tell the patient. The earlier part of the dream where the children as intruders interrupt our session represents the resistance. I experience this resistance by her silence, her bringing up socially acceptable topics, talking about tangential matters, etc. My usual way of responding to the resistance is to suddenly feel sleepy and lose my sense of concentration. I have not labeled her behavior directly as resistance, but have said that she seems to not be talking about important things. She usually realizes it, begins to tear up a bit, and sometimes begins to talk about something of more significance, or to complain that she seems out of sorts.

The latter part of the dream reveals imagery which is prospective in nature and exists as potential development for her. As her therapist, I derive a sense of optimism for the overall therapeutic outcome: she will work through her transference neurosis and make a better connection to me as a psychologically minded animus figure. This dream demonstrates, I think, a point which Jung made very early in his writings and which has been repeated by Mattoon (1978):

> A prospective dream can be likened to a preliminary exercise, sketch, or plan which is roughed out in advance. It may outline the solution of an unusually difficult conflict or it may prepare the dreamer for a future attitude that may not be recognized as needed until weeks or even months after the dream.

There are two more extended connections to this dream which are of significance to me. One is the relation of subsequent free associations to the dream that has been related, and the other is its place in highlighting the developmental aspect of the patient's psychology. Free association is very important in my work. I think it highly important to consider the *very first thing* that a patient says about a dream. Often, after the patient has thought about it, he or she may want to retract this first spontaneous thought, but I find that initial authentic association to be significant. In the interpretation of this dream, I have amalgamated the patient's associations with my own amplifications to come up with the present interpretation.

From the developmental point of view one gets a glimpse of the family dynamics. From the anamnesis, it is clear that the father is the love object in her childhood fantasy. The mother's domestic and living-room world is one to be gotten away from as soon as possible. The living room is partitioned off in a strange way which suggests that the relationship to the mother is divided, to say the least. The bare furniture in the bedroom suggests the lack of intimate communication between the parents. In what I said to the patient I chose not to use this particular dream to emphasize the childhood dynamics. There are many other dreams and childhood memories which have given us a better entree into this material. What I said to the patient was to stay close to the actual images of the dream.

Now, how do we know that this way of looking at the dream has any validity, or is it just some mental gymnastics to make the analyst feel better? Intuitively we often know from the patient's response that the interpretation feels correct. Here we are back to this sense that a dream and its interpretation just *is*. Mattoon (1978) has formalized this into a paradigm for correct dream interpretation. Mattoon observes that an affirmative answer to any one or more of the following questions verifies the interpretation:

1. Does the interpretation "click" with the dreamer?
2. Does the interpretation "act" for the dreamer?
3. Is the dream confirmed (or disconfirmed) by subsequent dreams?
4. Do the events anticipated by the interpretation occur in the dreamer's waking life?

The first question cannot be objectively tested since it is purely subjective, but when an interpretation "clicks," there is always the feeling that one has struck "pay dirt." It is a patently affective reaction experienced affirmatively. Occasionally this is a clicking into entrenched ego-attitudes rather than deep self-understanding, but usually I find one "click" reliable, a sign that the point of view of the Self has been tapped. However, some affective affirmations of an interpretation may meet subsequent resistance and be repressed, so their verification may be in doubt. To say it more simply, a patient may agree to an interpretation at one time and then when the therapist refers back to that interpretation, the patient may deny the interpretation or claim to have never heard it that way. In the case above, the patient felt that the interpretation "clicked," was "right on." The patient had just finished school and was really floundering, but shortly after this dream and others, she was able to begin to mobilize herself to act in a less diffuse manner.

The second question provides a more reliable test. Mattoon notes that dream interpretation can be verified by "setting the dreamer's life in motion again" (Jung, quoted in Mattoon 1978, p. 177), whether or not it is accepted cognitively by the dreamer. The new vitality may become apparent in the stimulation given to the therapeutic process and the flow of positive feelings between therapist and patient. The obverse occurs also, Jung found: errors in dream interpretation are reflected in "bleakness, sterility, and pointlessness" of the sessions (ibid., p. 178).

The third question is the most important one from a clinical point of view. Is the dream confirmed or disconfirmed by subsequent dreams? Mattoon reports that when a dream has been interpreted incompletely or incorrectly, the dreamer sometimes brings in a subsequent dream in which the major motif of the first dream is repeated more clearly or given a negative twist through "ironic paraphrase," or the interpretation of the first dream is opposed (ibid., pp. 179–180).

If there is a positive transference, subsequent dreams of the patient can comment, often with humor, about the wrong interpretation of the previous dream. When the resistance in the analysis is uppermost, the corrective dream may be repressed, leading to an even deeper resistance. The patient described above had a positive transference, and other dreams, both before and after, confirm the interpretation. She has continued to have dreams where there is a disturbance in our relationship, either because it is too public or because there are intruders of some kind in the consulting room with us.

The fourth question is answered very clearly by Mattoon as follows: Jung's fourth test for verification of dream interpretations consists of facts from the dreamer's waking life: events that are anticipated by dreams, including the occurrence or avoidance of difficulties; the persistence or disappearance of symptoms; and other physical events, such as accidents, organic illness or death. A dream interpretation providing a differential diagnosis between organic and hysterical symptoms may be verified by the subsequent course of the illness (ibid.).

Not enough time has elapsed to say whether the dream and its interpretation have had a lasting effect on her life. Here is a dream which she had seven months after the last one:

Dream: *I went to my hour with Tom. I sat in his office and started to talk about my week and the dreams I had. Everything was fine until I got to the part about a woman friend of Tom's. I felt uncomfortable about having to talk about her since I knew they were friends. It was at this point that I started noticing the difference in Tom's office. He had just painted his office, he had completely remodeled everything. The ceiling had opened up and there was a loft above me with a receptionist sitting at a desk. There was an orange-colored carpet and a blue tile-pattern wallpaper. It was very garish. He had lots of patients coming in off the street. His door opened and his daughter was standing there. I saw a woman walk by looking for a box of Kleenex because she was crying. Tom got distracted and started walking in and out of the office. He walked me outside. I told him I liked his new carpet and wallpaper (which I really didn't), but I didn't like the receptionist sitting above us listening in. We stood outside facing the side of the house. It was gray stucco. He was talking to me about something, and I kept thinking we had only 20 minutes left in our hour. He kept moving closer to me and his arm touched my arm. I put my left hand on the wall, and he tried to touch it. I moved it away but finally let him touch me. He then reached over and gave me a long romantic kiss. It felt very real and I liked it very much. I* *couldn't believe it was happening after all this time. I thought maybe he had waited until I had finished my affair with P. I wondered if I might end up like a woman friend who had married her therapist. I kept wanting to finish our hour but time was passing and he walked me to my car. It was parked in a large parking lot. We couldn't find it. We searched and searched. We went back to his office to find his kids to help. They were seven years old, a boy and a girl. I offered $20 to them if they could find my car. Tom said I should multiply that amount by six. We all searched but still could not find it. I started feeling funny. Mentally and physically exhausted. I really wanted to talk to Tom, but we were too busy looking for the car. I told Tom that I had spent all day with my analyst and I felt like I needed to see an analyst. We went back to the house. His wife was there. We were sneaking through the rooms so she would not notice us. I ducked into a small laundry room and saw a child's drawing of Tom's family with the father, mother, son and daughter standing in a row. I ran into another room, and Tom's wife saw me. Somehow I knew that she had stolen my car, and I said in the dream that I knew she never really did like me.*

This dream is an extremely complex one. She had recently been to a social gathering where other therapists were in attendance. One had married a former patient and another therapist's wife was a long-time friend of mine. Although she did not discuss her analysis and none of the above knew that she was in analysis with me, this event clearly stirred her up psychologically. I think this accounted for the beginning of the dream. She has great difficulties in confronting potentially disturbing topics. It also made her feel less safe and contained in my office. The office opened up and the temenos became porous. Patients have walked in off the street, and the secretary has listened in. It all has become too public. One could also see this dream as a criticism of how I have been working with her. I have been amiss in containing her anxiety. Then she remarks on many changes in my office. She is now more able to stand up for her own opinions even when they go against me. She can be openly critical of me, for instance, she does not like the wallpaper or the receptionist, etc. Next the erotic aspect of the transference is expressed. I touch her left hand and then kiss her "romantically." I am reminded here of the second and third pictures in Jung's *Psychology of the Transference* (1946), where the king and queen begin by touching left hands to indicate that the connection is an unconscious one. The linking of left hands is followed by the sexual union in the bath. She has the fantasy that we might end up married like the friend of hers, but this fantasy does not last long. Instead, she wants to finish out the analytical hour. The dream moves on to her looking for her car. Her car probably represents the autonomy of her ego. Without it she falls into a dependent lassitude which she cannot seem to get away from. The car is in the hands of my feminine aspect. At least she has a beginning awareness of where her female autonomy is, even though at present it appears hostile toward her.

This dream shows the motifs in the earlier dream: the sense of exposure of the analytical relationship; not being able to really talk with me; the erotic transference; loss of her ego, as expressed by the loss of her car; criticism from the feminine (my wife not liking her); childhood complexes (the children running around). As one can see from this dream, the work goes slowly, and any deep resolution of these issues is painstakingly slow.

The analysis continues and it has managed to weather the crisis precipitated by this social gathering. She continues to dream, and the interpretation of her unconscious material has continued to elucidate her deep negative mother complex and corresponding incestuous father tie. In spite of the leaks in the container, we can conclude that the analysis has been therapeutic.

As I was searching for a summary statement on dreams, I came across this eloquent comment by Henderson:

> Regardless of whether the dream is personal, cultural, or archetypal, or whether it is referred to past, present, or future, and in spite of its few exceptions, the unconscious core of the dream is compensatory to the life situation and normally provides a therapeutic correction to any one-sidedness it may show. (1980, pp. 369–384)

Let us now return to the title of this paper. We see that we have been dealing with the all too human realities of everyday life. Human relationships in and out of analysis form an important basis for much of our unconscious life. Much has been made of the spiritual dimensions found in archetypal symbolism of dreams. There is an equally prosaic and pedestrian aspect to dreams which is no less important and which deals with the all too human problems of everyday archetypal realities. This paper in part has been an attempt to show how these dream images are expressed in an ongoing analysis.

Notes

1. As an aside, I can remember that when I told my superiors in training that I was in Jungian analysis, it was thought of as so far out that my clinical competence was suspect on that basis alone! Indeed when other residents who had talked to me about the possibility of going into Jungian analysis mentioned their interest to these same supervisors, they were told that by going into Jungian analysis, they would be throwing away their careers in psychiatry. The attitudes against Jungian thinking were strong then, and it took a great deal of fortitude to go against the collective pressure of the times. It was somewhat easier for me because I had the strong support of my family, and because I had known so many of the early analysts. How times have changed! Jungian analysis today is almost too respectable, and its culture has been altered by its assimilation into the wider psychotherapeutic spectrum.

References

Bonime, Walter. 1962. *Clinical Use of Dreams*. New York: Basic Books.

Crick, Francis. 1983. The dream machine (REM sleep acts as reverse learning to raise memory): Theory of F. Crick and M. Mitcheson. T. Melnechunk, interviewer. *Psychology Today* 17:22–24.

French, T. and Whitman, Roy. 1969. A focal conflict view. In *Dream Psychology and the New Biology of Dreaming*. Milton Kramer, ed. Springfield, Ill.: Charles Thomas, pp. 64–77.

Freud, Sigmund. 1899. *The Interpretation of Dreams*. New York: Science Editions, 1961.

Fromm, E. 1957. *The Forgotten Language*. New York: Crown Press.

Hall, James Albert. 1977. *Clinical Uses of Dreams: Jungian Interpretations and Enactments*. New York: Grune and Stratton.

Henderson, Joseph L. 1980. The dream in Jungian analysis. In *The Dream in Clinical Practice*. Joseph E. Natterson, ed. New York: Jason Aronson Press, pp. 369–384.

Huizinga, Johan. 1950. *Homo Ludens: A Study of the Play Element in Culture*. Boston: Beacon Press.

Jung, C. G. 1934. The practical use of dream analysis. In *Collected Works* 16:139–162. Princeton, N.J.: Princeton University Press, 1966.

———. 1946. The psychology of the transference. In *CW* 16:167–323. Princeton, N.J.: Princeton University Press, 1966.

———. 1948. General aspects of dream psychology. In *CW* 8:235–297. Princeton, N.J.: Princeton University Press, 1969.

Kirsch, T. B. 1968. The relationship of REM to analytical psychology. *American Journal of Psychiatry* 124, 10:1459–1463.

Mahoney, Maria F. 1966. *The Meaning in Dreams and Dreaming*. New York: Citadel Press.

Mattoon, Mary Ann. 1978. *Applied Dream Analysis: A Jungian Approach*. New York: John Wiley and Sons.

Meier, C. A. 1969. A Jungian view. In *Dream Psychology and the New Biology of Dreaming*. Milton Kramer, ed. Springfield, Ill.: Charles Thomas, pp. 101–115.

Rossi, Ernest Lawrence. 1986. *The Psycho-Biology of Mind-Body Healing: New Concepts of Therapeutic Hypnosis*. New York: W. W. Norton.

Wilmer, Harry. 1987. *Practical Jung*. Wilmette, Ill.: Chiron Publications.

Some Comments on Knowing: Discussion of "A Pedestrian Approach to Dreams" by Thomas B. Kirsch

Caroline Stevens

Let me say first that I am delighted with Tom Kirsch's title, "A Pedestrian Approach to Dreams," with the image and the attitude it evokes. I imagine how it is to be walking around the dream, round and round, and then perhaps gently and carefully a spiral in, into the dream's countryside or cityscape or house or shopping complex, walking in dream space, attentive, respectful, observant of the happenings there. We may see so much more at this slow pace — and after all, what's the hurry?

I imagine some of the other possibilities that have tempted me: the interpreter as, say, Joan of Arc, guided by her voices, mounted and ready for the battle against evil; or the Priestess of the Tarot, enthroned in her power and dispensing wisdom; or, perhaps, the Mother, even the Great Mother (but only her positive side), possessed of and prepared to provide whatever the dreamer may need. When I imagine these, I see that they may all have their place and time in the consulting room. But

Caroline T. Stevens, Ph.D., is a training analyst at the C. G. Jung Institute of Chicago and conducts a private practice in Chicago. She is a contributor to the forthcoming *Psyche's Stories*, M. Stein and L. Corbett, eds.

the pedestrian, the walker-about in dream time and space, is a human-sized image, befitting an analyst very well, and guarding against too easy flights of intuitive fancy, warning against too quick a conviction of understanding.

I also value Kirsch's mention of the social and cultural factors that affect both the plot and the *dramatis personae* of the dream drama. Again, the image of the pedestrian appeals to me. The gods may indeed manifest on any street corner of any neighborhood, but the form of their manifestation, as Jung observed, absolutely depends upon the time and place, the cultural neighborhood, inhabited by the dreamer. If we walk through the neighborhood of the dream, through the personal and cultural neighborhood inhabited by the dreamer, we are less likely to fly too quickly into a fantasy of the eternal archetype, or to assume too easily the relevance of a given mythologem. A constant reference in the mind of the analyst to archetypal images from a given past—the Greeks, for instance—can block a recognition of more ancient sources and meanings, or of imaginal possibilities newly emerging, new myths in the making.

It has been said often that it is the analysand's agreement that guarantees the correctness of a dream interpretation. Of course, the analysand is the ultimate authority in these matters. Quite pragmatically this is so, as all of us know, for regardless of the brilliance or even the simple accuracy of an analyst's interpretation, if the analysand does not accept it, or cannot take it in for reasons of his or her own psychological readiness, then the interpretation is wrong and perhaps should not have been offered. It is wrong because it will not "work"; it will have no effect or ill effect. But the converse, I think, is not true. An analysand's agreement is not a guarantee of correct interpretation. It may simply be the issue of a *folie a deux*, a collusion between complexes. A good feeling in the room is not enough here.

Heaven knows, it would be nice to have this, at least, to rely on: the sense of rightness, of released tension, that can come when analyst and analysand share a vision, an understanding of the dream. But though there may, indeed, be an objective truth to be grasped by the mutual efforts of the two dream workers, our chance to approximate that truth is largest where the analyst's self-awareness is large. And our self-awareness is always, always incomplete.

We must try to know, as well as we can, not only the neighborhood of the dream and the dreamer, but our own neighborhood as well. We must continually be looking down *its* alleys and into *its* basements to find out the cultural, personal-biographical, and the theoretical-philosophical assumptions from which we operate. I do not believe in the possibility of dream work unencumbered or unclouded by such assumptions.

We must hear and respect the patient's perspective, and we might exercise artistic judgment, as Christopher Whitmont suggested, in choosing to focus on certain dream particulars. We may often rely on that felt, bodily sense that Sylvia Perera has mentioned: "Here it is, here is the place to look deeper." And we may ask ourselves the questions Kirsch quotes from Mattoon; an affirmative answer to any one of the four is supposed to provide "verification." All of the questions are useful, but again, who asks and who answers? The analyst has only a particular vision or bodily sensing capacity, and these are unavoidably conditioned by the factors I have mentioned. We each of us have a particular stance, relying on particular givens from our personal and cultural past, and it is just those givens that we must continually seek to discover and to question.

Let me here elaborate just a bit on two of the areas I have mentioned, the philosophical and the cultural. I suppose it is not common for many of us to ponder very deeply the philosophical assumptions which underly our work as analysts. Indeed, it is not altogether common for practitioners of any of the arts or sciences to give much explicit thought to these matters, or to try to develop their own statements of belief regarding the nature of reality and of human nature, the means to adequate knowledge, or the values they hope to serve in their work. To try to do so opens the door to uncertainty and perhaps to challenge by others. Surely we have enough of challenge and uncertainty hour by hour, day by day, in the consulting room. And yet there is something to gain if we hear and attempt to answer questions which may arise in us.

Do I imagine my patient's struggle to be totally determined by his developmental history, current complexes, or by the archetypes which live through him or her? By some combination of these? Then what is the role of the will of the patient? Does he or she, perhaps, have some real choice to make, however conditioned, in the matters at hand, or in the more fundamental questions of health or sickness, life or death?

How "objective" can my knowledge ever be? How certain? How do I achieve it? Do I think dream figures speak for the Self, that their advice should thus be taken? Is it true that the Self always acts for the good of the dreamer, and does it speak, if only in the long run, unequivocally? Is the dream ego always "wrong"?

What is "the good" of the dreamer? Am I committed to the flowering and fruiting of life, or of this life? But what is the meaning of death, of sickness, of limitation? And what of the unexceptional, simple falling short? (No tragedy, no transformation here; mere failure, and no apparent meaning to it.) Am I too in love with meaning?

What have I learned from my culture, of feminine moons and masculine suns, feminine matter and masculine spirit? Do we "progress" from bondage in the one to eternal freedom in the other? What of the obligations of gender performance and the "happy ending" or mystical significance of the heterosexual bond? Must we always be thinking in twos? What are the structures of relationship and value? Are they hierarchal, triangular (masculine?) or multivariant, circular (feminine?)? Or is each such structure significant and "good" in different settings?

These are only some of the questions that have occurred to me, and I have answered them differently, more or less consciously, as the years of my life have gone by. Of course, we cannot be mulling and wondering constantly; there's work to be done. But in the analytic hour I will act or fail to act on the basis of my beliefs. Should I not, then, know somewhat clearly what I think and why? The more that I do, it seems to me, the more responsibly and effectively I work.

I have been broadening the question: How do we know what the dream says? And I am suggesting that a pair of the many tensions, the seeming opposites, we must hold in our work are just these: the inevitable not knowing, and the obligation, nevertheless, to try to know more rightly.

I feel it can be dangerous simply to embrace our ignorance, celebrate mystery, and rely on the Self. We don't get off that easily. But it is also dangerous to imagine that we ever can be sure that we know, no matter our techniques and our tests of truth, however we may honestly strive to understand. Yet always, always we have to be open to learning more, specifically about ourselves.

One of the ways that we learn of ourselves is in listening to one another, and it is the difficult task of someone reporting analytic work to tell us what he or she knows of himself or herself in those interactions. Omissions are falsifications. They can be misleading as to what is really going on in the hour reported, and, worse, as to what the reporter believes it is important to know about ourselves in our work.

I am speaking, of course, of the countertransference and of the third set of factors which condition it—the personal-biographical. Kirsch warns us, quoting Harry Wilmer, that in working with dreams the analyst should not take himself or herself too seriously. But I don't think Kirsch has taken himself quite seriously enough as a participant in his patients' processes. The affects and emotions in the patient's psyche may lead ultimately to the archetypal core of his or her current struggle, as Kirsch suggests, but not without the interweaving effect of the analyst's own affects and emotions, and only then, I think, by way of the complexes of both analyst and analysand. There is agape aplenty in Kirsch's report, but I seem to look in vain for an adequate recognition of eros — of his own, of the analysand's, and above all of the palpable (to me) and potentially creative eros between himself and his analysands, both male and female.

So, from my perspective, the man who returns to his true love, his first love, is stuck, still, in the Mother. And the woman seeks in vain for an acknowledgment of her erotic child self through Kirsch's conscious and acknowledged response to it; she is let down, once again, by the Father.

But then I return to my beginning, deciding to be true to the pedestrian image I like so much. Two of us walking the same dream space must differ in discerning the points of interest, and might, therefore, comparing notes, enrich the journey for both of us. But this is not the place to treat the dreams more fully. It requires time for discernment and time for dialogue between oneself and the dreamer, or here, between myself and the reporter of the dreams of others.

Meantime, I am glad to remember again Whitmont's observation that the dream moves the dreamer toward completion. I think that we are weaving a pattern of theory and of practice, a shifting complexity of oppositions and complementarities whose final form, as always, we cannot yet discern.

Dream Experience

Elie G. Humbert
Translated by Ronald Jalbert

Common language speaks of the dream as though it were an object. In French, one says that one "made" (*faire*) a dream, in German and in English, one "has" a dream, while in the Greek of antiquity, one "saw a dream." The dream would then be a sort of film that one views during sleep and that one more or less remembers upon awakening. The *Dictionnaire Larousse de la Langue Française* (1961) describes dream phenomena as "a series of thoughts or images that parade through the mind during sleep." This common point of view is quite well summarized in this observation made by a psychologist: "We perceive dreams just as we do the exterior world . . . dreams are a succession of frequently detached images that unfold in one's mental being and that thrust themselves upon it."

This film-object that we remember the following day holds our attention both because of its composition, which apparently bears no resemblance to anything else, and because of its spontaneous emergence during the night. Short of rejecting the dream as impenetrable,

---

Elie Humbert, one of the few remaining who knew and worked with Jung, is France's foremost Jungian. Co-founder of the French Society of Analytical Psychology, past president of the French Jung Society, and editor-in-chief of *Cahiers Jungiens de Psychoanalyse*, he lives and practices in Paris and is an internationally known lecturer, author of *C. G. Jung: Theory and Practice* and numerous articles.

one must, if one is to deal with it at all, seek out its relationship with the day world. "An uninterpreted dream is an unopened letter" (*Talmud*, Berakhot 55b). It is striking to see that this quotation from the Talmud appears throughout the ages, in the writings of authors of many orientations. It seems, in fact, that in examining the nature of the dream, one necessarily ends up dealing with it as though it were an object of information.

I would have held onto this same point of view had experience not taught me otherwise. The dream is not psychic material that is only to be perceived and remembered. To dream is not merely to perceive a dream.

One notes, upon waking, that certain dreams are very much the memory of a scenario within which one is more or less involved. Other dreams are merely perceptions that the morning interrupts: a scene was being played out before our very eyes. In these two cases, the analogy of the dream to a film that is perceived and recalled is valid.

But there is another experience of the dream. This is one within which the dreamer hesitates, seeks, decides. The dreamer may be frightened or experience pleasure. He or she hears sentences or phrases that stir or that perplex. The dreamer participates in events involving him or her and reflects upon these events or reacts to them. In a word, the dreamer is situated within the dream. Circumstances provoke the dreamer and he or she responds. All around the dreamer, dream-figures initiate activities. The dreamer also initiates activities of his or her own. This is not to say that the dreamer observes himself or herself make decisions, such as happens in certain situations. The experience to which we are referring has all the intensity and the suspense of the events of the day world. It is a lived experience.

Dream: *We are in the country, my mother and I. We have to return to Paris. My mother settles into the driver's seat of the car. I do not like that and seek to get into the driver's seat myself but I find no way to express my objections. My mother starts the car and we leave. Obviously, she suits herself by taking charge of the trip and we stop by a large restaurant for lunch. I have no desire to have a formal meal and wonder how I might get out of it. I look around, but there are no other restaurants in sight and there is no way I can convince her to eat elsewhere. We settle into our places in the dining area. The service is endless. My mother relishes every moment, while I am irritated by her. I can say nothing and I fume inside.*

This is a mundane example of a story every moment of which the female dreamer experienced within the dream. The dream is first of all a lived experience. To dream is to live an adventure that is so real that the following day or the next weeks or even months will be marked by what was pulled apart or brought together in the dream.

Yet, not all dreams convey this kind of experience. Some dreams are more like films. For instance, one can clearly differentiate between characters in the dream who give the impression of belonging to personal history and those who have a reality all their own as partners within the dream. How are we to understand that the dream can at times be an adventure that one lives out as if awake and that at other times it appears like a cartoon strip that one observes even at the risk of seeing oneself in it, while, at other times still, the dream is simply the memory of a past story?

These modalities of being present or absent to an experience are not surprising to one who observes to what extent they also affect daily life. Days unfold without us. Activities pass us by like ghosts. Entire years escape our attention. These things come and go without any awareness of them on our part except in hindsight, through memory. One experiences the dream as one does the day world, by being absent most of the time.

In the day world, there is the illusion of the permanence of sensations. Since the body is located in a particular place, we believe that that is where we are. The dream, on the other hand, objectifies differences, insists that we take them into account. There is already the perceptible split between the scene that is lived out and the scene that is recalled, however vivid it might be. Above all else, the dream stages the coefficient of presence. It allows us to sketch out a stylistics of presence.

1. The events that we see without being present, episodes that unfold upon a stage and that turn into a film, sites that we visit as if we were tourists. Actions that involve us as spectator or that give us a secondary role within a play. In one event, we are passive while, in another, we are ultimately called upon to be protagonists.

2. Chromatics. This is not in reference to the color of a particular character or of the clothing worn, but to color in general. Dreams can appear in black and white even while the action within the dream is supposed to take place in daytime; sombre greys; monochromatic ochre upon faces and walls; greenness

and redness; clearly diverse polychromatics. These shades of color express the modalities of participation in life.

Disconnected almost entirely from external stimulations, one lives at night the pure states of the different ways of being or of not being in the world.

Dream experience is characterized by the structure of what is lived experience. This structure is the original state of the dream experience, from which we can have an adequate point of view on dream phenomena. Why have dream studies not taken this simple observation into consideration?

In fact, we have confused the dream with the form it receives at the moment we wake up, at the moment the dream appears to consciousness. By being placed in memory, the dream becomes a sequence that is perceived. Because of this, we assume that the recalled dream had always been a sequence unfolding within consciousness. The emotion in the dream would then have been that of a spectator so caught by the object that he or she was moved by it. This confusion is due to the point of view of the interpreter for whom the dream is the retelling of memories. Dream books and psychoanalysis, both the works of interpreters, have reduced dream phenomena to a linkage of signs. By abstracting dream experience, the interpreter takes hold only of an "object-for-the-interpreter," that is to say, the interpreter ends up with an imaginary entity. This is what has happened to dream studies in Western civilization since post-shamanic Greece. But all of the psychology of the unconscious is subject to the same danger: the point of view of the interpreter that ignores everything of the psyche that is not reflected at the level of logos. Thus the dream, which has become confused with the status it acquires in consciousness once the dreamer wakes up, paradoxically becomes a representation from the day world; furthermore — and this is a second blind spot — psychoanalysis retains of the dream only what fits into the schemas used to reflect upon it.

To avoid this trap and to take into consideration what we have observed, this study on dreams must differentiate and interweave three levels. There is, first of all, the moment the dream happens, which moment may be that of a lived experience. Then comes the dream sequence, the story that appears in the form of memories. Finally, there is the dream text, the narrative that one tells oneself and that one sometimes shares with another person.

By coming back to dream experience, that is, to the fact that dreams are lived events, one becomes aware that certain conclusions can be drawn.

Formerly, one used to ask: Why do you not dream? Since the advent of laboratory research on sleep, one asks: Why do you not recall your dreams? These questions clarified the psychology of the dreamer, particularly his resistances. To these questions, one must add another: Why do you not live your dreams? What we have here is a criterion of the general relationship between consciousness and the unconscious. Whoever habitually lives his dreams has less rigid or, at least, less impenetrable defense mechanisms. When applied to a particular dream, this third question allows us to know the distance the dreamer has taken from the elements that appear in the dream.

Valery once quipped, "The dream is a hypothesis because we know nothing of it except through memory." A similar theme can be heard currently among psychologists. "The dream as immediate experience can never be the object of psychology. The psychology of the dream can only bear upon the dream that is remembered" (*Le Rêve*, 1987, p. 128). We know, in fact, that this is not the case. Psychology begins with experience and not with the sequencing of images. This point is obscured by the imperialistic point of view of the interpreter. One way to come back to what is essential is to return to the problematic nature of what is involved in being present to lived experience. The problem of presence is one that psychologists have up to this day relegated to Eastern spirituality, even to Marxist philosophies. In the area of the dream, this leads to the integration of the body within the dream itself. One can no longer be content to study REM (rapid eye movement) as a condition that gives rise to this or that phenomenon.

Let us pursue our discussion further. It was once intellectually fashionable to think that cerebral functioning taking place almost completely during REM sleep served to restore somewhat freely the flow of representations. How are we to understand that REM sleep is the locus of a lived experience that consists not only of images that are of sufficient intensity to give the impression of a lived event, but of images that are real events and activities? I am not a physiologist and can only formulate a general idea on the subject of the physiology of dreams. What must the brain be to act as the locus of such an activity? Dream experience deals a final blow to inadequate comparisons of the brain to electronic circuitry, for example. It is also clear that we can no longer rest easy with the schema of the reflex arc, a schema implicit in many theories. When we again come back to psychology, the question becomes: What does the fact that there is experience in the night world mean to waking life? If, in the isolation of the dream, we are in the grips of a field of exteriority comparable to that of the outer world, one that is equally provocative and equally replete with the opportunity for initiative, what then is the concrete world?

For most ancient civilizations, the dream meant the entrance into another world. Dream experience, which we have reintroduced at the beginning of this study, did not pose a problem. These ancient peoples acknowledged dream experience the very way they lived it, that is, they gave it full reality. It was natural for them to interpret dream experience the way one interprets the concerns of the day world, as an encounter with beings who are real even though, in the case of the dream, they are not embodied.

In his study on the practice of dream fasting among the Ojibwa, Hallowell describes a people whose life structure involves a sharing between human beings and nonhuman forces. This relationship becomes effective when the young man retreats into the forest to prepare himself by fasting for a dream visit by one or several spirits who decide to protect him and who will henceforth define his social role by conferring particular powers on him.

> W. B. dreamed that he was out hunting and met one of the *memengweci* [a spirit endowed with therapeutic powers]. He asked W. B. to visit his home. "On the northwest side of the lake there was a very steep rock. He headed directly for this rock. With one stroke of the paddle, we were across the lake. The fellow threw his paddle as we landed on flat shelf of rock about level with the water. Behind this the rest of the rock rose steeply before us. But when his paddle touched the rock this part opened up. He pulled the canoe in and we entered a room inside the rock." In this dream, the geographical details are very precise. W. B. said that some time later, when awake and out hunting, he recognized the exact spot he had visited in his dream. He could go back any time in the future and obtain the special kind of medicine for which the *memengweciwak* are famous. (Hallowell 1966, pp. 285–286)

Don Talayesva, a Hopi Indian, found himself dying in the infirmary of an urban college where he had been learning the trade of the white man. In his sleep, an ancestral spirit comes to get him, drags him to a faraway ravine from which the human race is said to have emerged, shows him the traditional places in which Don Talayesva no longer believed, helps him through many dangerous trials that bring him face to face with spiritual forces, and finally takes him back to the infirmary (Talayesva 1958). Healed, the dreamer returned to his native village where he contributed to the restoration of cultural kinship and where he was still living at a very old age when he recounted his story to an American ethnographer.

"The angel of the Lord came upon him while he was sleeping." It is with words like these that many accounts of religious vocations are expressed. The dream was for Mohammed at the origins of his personal adventures, of the rallying of the Arab people, of the founding of the Islamic religion.

In these examples, the dream is an event and it is taken as such. It carries forth its own meaning. It meshes in with everyday life. The only issue is that of submission to it.

Such an attitude toward the dream world is not particular to ancient peoples. Many contemporaries, who in all appearances are rationalists, admit that such and such a dream affected the orientation of their life.

In these experiences, two traits come together: the dream opens the way to another world; the dream provides a forum for the superior part of the psyche to act. For Pindar, the soul, which is divine and which sleeps while we are awake, reveals in dreams correct judgments while we sleep. Xenophon states that it is "in sleep that the soul best shows its divine nature; during sleep it enjoys a certain intuitive foreknowledge." Plato declares that a dream can reveal the supreme truth. Philo tells us that the dream is a phenomenon whose pneuma is the protagonist (Dodds 1965, p. 135).

Seen from this perspective, the ancient practice of incubation is most significant (Meier 1949). While sleeping in a renowned temple, the sick receive a visit from the god who heals.

This same practice of incubation illustrates the passage to another sort of relationship with the dream: a relationship that consists of taking a certain distance from the dream world. The day world consolidates itself and closes up upon itself. The dream becomes a message. The god or goddess no longer acts directly. Whether he or she appears or sends a delegate, it is in view of prescribing a course of treatment that is to be followed if it is to heal. The dream is transitive, a scene that is seen and recounted.

We have moved to the plane of divination, which brings along a submission to consciousness. Thus the question of origins is now posed and it is up to consciousness to understand. Is the dream an *a deo missus* or a trap, the work of treacherous spirits, a deceitful message? In order to be deciphered, these complicated or strange images are naturally submitted to conscious reflection, that is, they are analyzed for their semantic value; they are catalogued. Dream experience is transformed into themes. We end up saying, "I dreamed that I was killing the king" and no longer "I killed the king in the dream."

The process of translation puts the dream through the network of the social and cultural structures of the day world. The dream does not have the same meaning if it comes from a pauper than if it comes from a prince. One raises a question about dreams that is typical of consciousness: Is the dream "good" or is it "bad"? This question is answered according to cultural norms. In these matters, medieval theology provided a principle: a dream was good and of divine origin if it conformed to matters of faith and morals — otherwise it was the work of Satan.

At the moment when so-called Western civilization began to emerge, an evolution took place in the way dreams were considered. At the end of the fifth century B.C., Heraclitus observed that each of us, as he or she falls asleep, retreats into a world all his or her own. The dream world is no longer elsewhere, but it is, rather, in the most intimate regions of the dreamer: the dream is an expression in phantasy form of this region. Hippocrates seeks in dreams a correlation to the physical state of the dreamer and even devised a table showing the correspondences between images and organs. In this way the dream became a subjective fact, either a sign or a symptom.

The dream is so evidently a lived experience that we first interpret it realistically, then see it as a message, and finally take it for a symptom. The historical evolution as to how the dream is seen is certainly not simply linear. The importance of this evolution is foremost typological. It demonstrates how in each structure the attitude that one takes toward the dream depends upon a differentiation of consciousness. Everything happens as if the human spirit struggled to extricate itself from something. The history of humankind's relationship to dreams is, from way back in time, that of resistance. This is so perhaps because human beings have always been fascinated by dreams. We are reminded of what Hallowell wrote:

> The culturally defined attitude toward dreams which we find among different peoples is often a direct clue to the basic premises of their world view. Among other things, it provides insight into how what we are accustomed to designate as "objective" and "subjective" phenomena are sharply differentiated, fused or blurred. (Hallowell 1966, p. 272)

Christianity pushes the process of differentiation to the point of exclusion. The verb "to dream" does not appear even once in the New Testament. In the Gospels, three dreams are reported, and all three belong to legendary tradition and represent popular elaborations. In the *Acts of the Apostles*, a few spoken words and callings emanate from the night world, which one obeys as one had usually done in the Old Testament. These are the only references to dreams in the New Testament. The New Testament represents the effort to remain awake and aware. It is addressed to the moral side of human nature, the side that is part of the day world, in order to invite it to a spiritual experience that outshines all other experiences. Psychologically, everything aims at strengthening the conscious ego, but at the price of rejecting the dream.

Freud managed to continue this effort toward greater consciousness while still taking the dream into consideration. He sees within dreams a complete psychic activity, but by introducing the principle of the egocentric character of dreams, he dissipates everything that has anything to do with the dream world as dream world, as another world. For Freud, the dream-image has a relationship to a meaning found elsewhere, but this "elsewhere" is intrapsychic, relates to sexual etiology, and has nothing in common with the immaterial and concrete world known to mythology. Thus Freud allows for the possibility that dreams can be taken seriously while acknowledging that they are composed of images. On the other hand, by asserting that there is no dream discourse, he dismisses any attempt to seek a message within the dream. His understanding of the unconscious allows him to reclaim the psyche without, for that matter, returning to spirits. He re-opened the way to the dream.

However, Freud refuses to enter the dream. He interprets the dream world by resorting to what is already known, and, in order to uphold his hypothesis, he imagines a "dream work" (*Traumarbeit*), which is an unverifiable mechanism theorized a posteriori.

By situating the dream on the continuum of neurotic and psychotic phenomena, Freud sees it as a symptom, which reintroduces a duality, for example, between the manifest content and the latent content, between the unconscious image and desire. Lacan's theory seeks to tone down this duality by shifting away from the symptom and toward the signifier: the latter does not become meaningful because of something hidden but because of another signifier.[1] In this way we arrive at a radical semiotization of dreams.

This process has the advantage of freeing the study of dreams from all metapsychologies. However, a semiotization that sees dreams through the lenses of an abusive reduction is unacceptable. The observation of what happens when we dream leads us to turn our attention to dream experience, this time within the framework of psychology. It is this same experience that the ancients integrated within their metaphysics and within their religion. In this way, the study of dreams is given a fresh start.

If one remains semivigilant at the moment of falling asleep, one can see in flashes the emergence of objects and persons that are transformed one into another. Their contour is generally crisp, their presence intense. There is one, there are two, three of them, and then they seem to meld into a flimsy weave of beings and gestures that are barely perceptible and, finally, one falls asleep.

This phase, referred to as hypnagogic, is characterized by a peculiar EEG pattern. One can recognize the typical EEG pattern present in those who come to an unknown place, for instance, as tourists in a vacation spot, or as invited guests where others remain unknown. There are a few vividly focused impressions, then everything blends into a jumbled haze.

There are times when this continuum seems to come to a focus. A street corner whose mood stays with us, someone speaks to us and we respond. In the insignificant thread of people and things, an action begins to coalesce. Each element asserts its autonomy, encounters other elements but in its own terms. In daily life, it is a moment; in the course of this psychic activity that does not ever seem to stop completely during sleep, it is "a" dream. Whether he or she intervenes or not, the dreamer is caught in the movement that arises, unfolds, and comes to a close as in a small drama.

Physiologists have noticed that cerebral activity registered during periods of REM sleep is comparable to that of waking life; it even appears to be more important than cerebral activity associated with waking life. The observations to which we have just pointed suggest a parallel between the conscious structure of waking life and that of the night world.

Must we not speak of consciousness when referring to the dream? At any rate, if we are not content to see the dream as a phantasm formed only upon awakening, and even if we limit ourselves to seeing it as a series of representations that unfold during certain phases of sleep, this psychic activity must be conscious enough to be remembered. There is, therefore, at the very least, a dream consciousness that consists of a field of perception. Dreams appear in this field of perception with an intensity that parallels the reality of the day world, but since we discover, after waking up, that these perceptions were merely images from the inner world, we tend to liken them to hallucinations.

This first conclusion adequately accounts for dreams that are perceived as though they were films; it does not apply to other dreams. In this latter case, if we attend not to the story that unfolds but to the way in which we are engaged in the dream, we can make several observations. First of all, the dream is a field within which willed activities are undertaken. An owner-fisherman invites me to the bar of a port, the waitress sits by us. I will know later that these were images and, when I recall the dream, this event will become a scene. For the moment, while I am in the dream, these people are persons in an "external" world who speak to me, affect me, require me to react. When the owner-fisherman invites me to join him, this seems to be simple enough. A sort of natural impulse impels me to follow him to the bistro. We cross the port together. The dream is a field of action. But when the owner-fisherman proposes to hire me, I am perplexed. How much is he going to pay me? How many days of shore leave will I have? Will I refuse to get on board in Paris? I hesitate, and finally, I refuse. Reflection, deliberation, decision. One must conclude that the dream is a field where there is voluntary activity.

In his *Memories, Dreams, Reflections*, Jung tells us a dream where the decision he took marked the turning point of his existence.

> I was with an unknown, brown-skinned man, a savage, in a lonely, rocky mountain landscape. It was before dawn; the eastern sky was already bright, and the stars were fading. Then I heard Siegfried's horn sounding over the mountains and I knew that we had to kill him. We were armed with rifles and lay in wait for him on a narrow path over the rocks.
>
> Then Siegfried appeared high up on the crest of the mountain, in the first ray of the rising sun. On a chariot made of the bones of the dead, he drove at furious speed down the precipitous slope. When he turned a corner, we shot at him, and he plunged down, struck dead.
>
> Filled with disgust and remorse for having destroyed something so great and beautiful, I turned to flee, impelled by the fear that the murder might be discovered. But a tremendous downfall of rain began, and I knew it would wipe out all traces of the dead. I had escaped the dangers of discovery; life could go on, but an unbearable feeling of guilt remained. (1965, p. 180)

At the opposite end of the spectrum, here is a dream where the dreamer decided to do nothing.

Dream: *There is before me an altar made of huge stones. An unsheathed sword lies upon the altar. The sword had been broken and welded back together; the weld line appears like the trace of dripping blood. To the left, a woman in black, Theresa of Avila, invites me to pick up the sword. I am scared, afraid. I hesitate. I get a sense of all I will be called upon to suffer and to struggle with if I pick up this sword. I do not pick it up.*

This choice weighed upon the dreamer's life for two years.

To assume that nothing else is involved in a dream save the staging of a scene does not account for the facts. A feeling of freedom, similar to that experienced during waking states, ensues with decisions made in some dreams. On the other hand, experience shows that the choice made in the dream has an unimpeded continuity with that of the day world. It happens that one does in a dream what one is unable to do in the day or, inversely, that certain attitudes are rejected in the dream that one was unable to reject in day life. The nature of the freedom involved in the dream arises from and relates to the problematic nature of freedom in general. It seems to me, in return, that freedom experienced in the dream makes an important contribution to the understanding of the overall problem of freedom.

The dream is a perceptual field, a field of initiatives, of voluntary activity. We must conclude that there is consciousness in the night world.

What is most disquieting is the exercise of the will in the dream. One might be tempted to reserve the will as the perogative of consciousness in the day world, to make of the will the sign and the privilege of the ego. What are these choices that I make while I am asleep, choices that are made outside my control? Speaking of the unconscious life becomes a weighty issue when one thinks of all these choices made at night, choices made with emotion, but reflection of which one has not the slightest recollection upon awakening. Who am I then in this sort of double life?

If one considers the dreamer's actions in his or her dream, one notes from the start that the dreamer is frequently engaged in astounding behavior, highlighted with traits and with costumes that he or she does not wear in daily life. Thus the dreamer finds himself or herself as a Roman general, the god Pan, or endowed with the genitals of the opposite sex. The attempt has been made to explain these phenomena by referring to unconscious desire or to compensation.

These events are not impervious to analysis. The dreamer might well have met a general, seen the sexual organs that he or she is supposed to lust for, or participated in a Pan-like bucolic rite of spring. The fact that, in the dream, the dreamer is actually a general or is lustful presents a different situation. By analyzing the lived experience of the day world, I have most often discovered the characters that the dreamer played out in the night world. Dreams of this kind do not stage repressed or isolated contents, but rather a dominant of consciousness, that is, a content of consciousness that comes into play periodically at the command of the personality. The dreamer unequivocally acts this or that part of his or her plural self.

In certain dreams, the dreamer is never who he or she is in the day. A passive woman found herself swimming against the current. A conventional employee found himself robbing a bank. I thought that, in these situations, where the motivating force of the dream is essentially compensation or an unconscious desire, the dreamer was the whole of his or her personality, putting into play unsuspected potentialities of the psyche. It should be noted that the compensatory activity of the dream comes into play only if there is reason for it to do so, that is, if the individual's psyche contains a possibility that consciousness can activate. This is what happens in these dreams.

Aside from those cases where the possibility for activating a certain aspect of the psyche does not exist and where compensation does not play a part, there are countless cases where the discarded psychic content comes out in dreams but at distance from the dreamer. A thirty-year-old woman, who had been diagnosed schizophrenic, dreams that a little man comes to sleep next to her so as to comfort her. This happens regularly. Each time he has to leave at dawn, otherwise he will be murdered by a large man who waits outside. She would definitely like to keep the little man's coat since it would suit her well and make her feel more feminine. But then the little man would have to risk great dangers. She has to let him go with his coat. In this dream, the woman is her ego-complex that is severed from everything this little man represents: the spirit of nature, the phallus, and a zest for life. She can only find this little man at night and lives her daily life as a dissociated personality. This dream shows that she is not really schizophrenic. That such a diagnosis could have been made at all underlines the fact, however, that the dissociation in question affects even the ego, which confirms our interpretation.

The dreamer who acts in the dream can then be three different realities: the ego-complex, the conscious personality dominated by this or that psychic content, the whole personality.

What we have mentioned above represents a first set of answers to earlier questions. We must go further. When I am dreaming, I am not only the one who intervenes in a story, but I am also the one who is in the process of dreaming. Where am I when the dream unfolds outside of me like a cartoon strip? This question is even more relevant when my dream is a sentence. We have already dealt with this question. To return to it now should allow us to see to what extent consciousness that belongs to the night world demystifies consciousness that is found in the day world and to what extent the first form of consciousness reveals the internal structures of the second. Because the body is there in the space of the day world, we believe that we are present. Because the body is at the juncture of perceptions and reactions, we believe ourselves to be the center of our own actions, whereas the center of our own actions is so often found in another person. We inhabit another place, another scenario, another idea. Psychoanalysis has strongly emphasized the absence of the other as other. Someone is missing, it is claimed. In fact, it is oneself who is missing.

However banal the expression "to dream that one is dreaming" may be, it nevertheless points to lived experience turning in upon itself by means of reflection: "to see oneself act," a division by means of mirroring; "to be in the process of doing something and to know that one is doing something completely different elsewhere," a splitting into duality. A patient frequently dreamed that he observed his dreams and tried to intervene in them. He lived everything once removed, just as much when he cultivated a false persona, spoke in the past tense, remained passive in love affairs, as when he remained in second place relative to his different bosses. There were once two autistic persons, one who in moments of exuberance could not fall asleep because the flow of his dreams continued the mental life of the day world, the other who intervened in his dreams in order to make them up.

This second series of observations, taken at the level of the structure of the dream, shows that we are more explicitly ourselves in the lived experience of the dream than in the lived experience of the day world. Tell me what your dreams are and I will tell you who you are. This raises the question about the responsibility of actions performed in the dream. The ancients devised a harsh system of casuistry to deal with the violation of taboos in dreams. We find this, for example, among converted Papoo, who go to confession for sins committed in dreams (Caillois 1967, pp. 28–29). Even though Saint Augustine was steeped in the tradition of Graeco-Roman rationalism, he is nonetheless sensitive to the reality of the dream.

> But there still exist in my memory—of which I have spoke so much—the images of such things as my habits had fixed there; and these rush into my thoughts, though strengthless, when I am awake; but in sleep they do so not

only so as to give pleasure, but even to obtain consent, and what very nearly resembles reality. And to such an extent prevails the illusion of the image, both in my soul and in my flesh, that the false persuade me, when sleeping, to that which the true are not able when waking. Am I not myself at that time, O Lord, my God? And there is yet so much difference between myself and myself, in that instant when I pass from waking to sleeping, or return from sleeping to waking! Where, then, is the reason which when waking resists such suggestions? And if the things themselves be forced on it, I remain unmoved. Is it shut up with the eyes? Or is it put to sleep with the bodily senses? But whence, then, comes to pass, that even in slumber we often resist, and, bearing our purpose in mind, and continuing most chastely in it, yield no assent to such allurements? And there is yet so much difference that, when it happens otherwise, upon awakening we return to peace of conscience; and by this same diversity do we discover that it was not we that did it, while we still feel sorry that in some way it was done in us. (Marjasch 1966, p. 72)

In me and yet not from me. Dreams highlight the plurality that we are. If we look at it from the point of view of guilt, this plurality leads to an impass. Who committed the crime? Rarely I, almost always a drive that possessed me. The rational basis for the penal code is founded on the need to protect society and not on an archaic conception of reflective will. On the other hand, each person is responsible for the totality of self. It is even from this perspective of plurality that responsibility makes sense. Having to answer to everything one has done raises the question of the conscious unity of the individual. It is not a question of guilt, but of total responsibility for one's own dreams.

Who then is seen as responsible? The conscious individual of the day world. The day world knows the dream, interprets it, takes it up. The reverse is not true. The dreamer is totally in function of the action taking place in the dream. Consciousness belonging to the night world has, for instance, very little of a memory structure. What comes from the past is staged immediately. The dreamer hardly remembers anything: sometimes the impression of déjà vu, occasionally the recalling of an experience, and always an incarnation into a decision. I have not seen any dream where the dreamer was engaged in remembering the events of the day and in trying to understand himself or herself. In the eyes of the person who is awake, dreams are often a reworking of the past, attempts to coordinate the psyche but, in the unfolding action of the dream, this structure of reworking and coordination barely exists. It seems that one has to compare consciousness in the night world to a consciousness that is strictly extraverted. The consciousness that the dreamer has of self in the dream is minimal. It rarely goes beyond anxiety or narcissistic gratification and one notes then that it is repetitive, that is, that it is not constituted in the dream but takes up one's many relationships to oneself such as they are lived out in the day world.

Here is a third dimension with which to address the question of dream experience: Who am I in this sort of double life? In the dream, I can be present, active, willful. It can happen that I intervene in the structure of the dream. But I am not aware within it of any passage of time as it relates to me, I do not have to take up the totality of myself. Integration belongs to the day world. Only consciousness in the day world can allow for self-consciousness.

This conclusion can appear a truism. It has considerable importance for interpretation, however. It articulates in a radical way the difference between the dream and the representations of the day world. The latter take shape in a field dominated by self-consciousness, which they come to represent. The dream is in itself the totality of a field of consciousness that is structured differently. What happens in the dream is affected by the nature of consciousness in the night world and appears in the form of memory to the human world once it is awake. When it appears in dreams, the psyche is not filtered through self-consciousness. This is why Jung wrote: "To me dreams are part of nature, which harbors no intention to deceive, but expresses something as best it can, just as a plant grows or an animal seeks its food as best it can" (1965, p. 161).

The dream is not an "elsewhere," nor is it a stock of supplementary signs. Human life unfolds in two different fields of consciousness: one appears in the area where an explicit drama is staged, the other in the area where integration takes place. In the first instance, psychic elements appear in their autonomy and with their own dynamisms, whereas in the second an awareness of self is constellated in the confrontation between the concrete world and the psyche. Attending to one's dream is a task that belongs to the day world, which attempts to bring together different life forces.

Notes

1. "The symptom is a return to truth. It is interpreted solely in the order of the signifier which has meaning only in relation to another signifier." J. Lacan, "Du Sujet enfin en Question," in *Ecrits* (Paris: Seuil, 1966, p. 234).

References

Caillois, R. 1967. Prestiges et Problèmes du Rêve. In *Le Rêve et les Sociétés Humaines*. Paris: Gallimard.

Dodds, E. R. 1965. *Les Grecs et l'Irrationnel.* Paris: Aubier.

Hallowell, A. I. 1966. The role of dreams in Ojibwa culture. In *The Dream and Human Societies*, G. E. Von Grunebaum and R. Caillois, eds. University of California Press.

Jung, C. G. 1965. *Memories, Dreams, Reflections.* New York: Random House.

Marjasch, S. 1960. The 'I' in the Dream. In *Spring.* New York: Jung Foundation.

Meier, C. A. 1949. *Antike Inkubation und Moderne Psychotherapie.* Zurich: Rascher.

Talayesva, Don. 1958. *Soleil Hopi.* Paris: Plon.

Forward into the Past: Re-emergence of the Archetypal Feminine

Betty De Shong Meador

I

The north Texas town where I was born was situated just across the Red River from former Indian territory in Oklahoma. The town sat on another frontier, between the rich farmlands of east Texas where the culture is more akin to the deep south and the vast plains, ranchlands, and oil strikes of west Texas whose culture boasts a wild and hearty freedom.

My parents were upward striving. My mother had been a schoolteacher in Tennessee and married late for those days, when she was nearly 30. My father was born in the French settlement of Paris, Texas, and although he had little formal education, he became a successful businessman. I was the second of three children. When I was one year old, we moved to the brick house our family inhabited for the rest of my parents' lives. The house was in a new, placid neighborhood on the edge of town. An old dairy across the street had been turned into a residence, and I spent hours in my childhood around the now landscaped pond where the cows once drank water.

Betty DeShong Meador, Ph.D., is a Jungian analyst in private practice in the San Francisco area. A member of the San Francisco Institute, she has authored numerous articles on client-centered therapy and on the feminine in Jungian psychology. She has translated the myths and poems of the goddess Inanna, including the work of Sumerian High Priestess and the first known poet, Enheduanna. Her book on Enheduanna is forthcoming.

In those mid-Depression days my parents somehow managed to have a succession of housekeepers. We called them our "nurse-girls." These women were a welcome refuge for me from my mother's anxiety about appearance and form. One of these women I remember in particular was Elizabeth Trimm.

Liz was, in my mother's words, "a big-boned, good German girl," from a nearby predominantly German community. My mother meant that Liz could work hard for long hours without tiring and was not so attractive that she would have suitors to bother us. My parents paid her $5.00 a week.

Liz had been raised in an orphanage and she told wonderful, harrowing tales of her life with the other orphan children. She taught me to thread a needle, to tie a single- or double-strand knot. She could wring water out of the doll clothes I washed until they were nearly dry, twisting the little dresses with her rough, strong hands.

She also taught me a divining method using a Bible and a key, wringing the mystery of the feminine out of that awesome, dry book so dear to my father. We sat on the steps outside the back door. Liz would insert a skeleton key into the pages of the Bible so that it lay right on the passage in the book of Ruth where Ruth speaks to Naomi:

> Entreat me not to leave thee or to return from following after thee; for whither thou goest, I will go, and whither thou lodgest, I will lodge; thy people shall be my people, and thy God, my God.

Liz would then close the Bible on the key and wrap a scarf under the Bible like a sling. Then she would cross the ends of the scarf around the protruding handle of the key, and tie it so that Bible and key were snugly secured together.

Now came the divining. With her fingers pinching the top of the key, Liz turned the key slowly so that its head, tucked between the pages of the Bible, wedged the book open slightly. I placed my index finger under one side of the protruding oval top of the key, and she placed her index finger under the other side. Carefully, we let the Bible-key-scarf contraption dangle between us. One of us would ask a question, burning, important questions such as, "Does Sydney Wagg-horn (my third grade idol) like me?" Or Liz would ask, "Will Billy Piper ask me out?" Or I might ask, "Will I get a bicycle for Christmas?" Then we would repeat together the sacred words from Ruth, "Entreat me not to leave thee. . . ."

If the precariously wedged key held its place, the answer to our question was "NO." If, however, the key moved flat again between the pages, which was of course more likely to happen as the weight of the Bible swung under our fingers, then the book would turn, slowly and mysteriously, bringing the blessed answer from the universe, "YES!" How many magical hours we spent on the back steps with Bible, scarf, and key, probing the One-who-knows-all-things for answers.

Liz was a good mother to me with her earthy practicality. More important, out of her somewhat unsocialized orphan past, she brought to me a glimpse of the hidden world of the feminine. She knew ways other than logic and reason to tease out the truth. She knew intuitive mysterious ways to connect us to an underlying knowing. There on the back steps we huddled together outside the bounds of parental culture. We traveled back in time to that remnant of woman's devotion to woman in the book of Ruth and to hints of a female world beyond imagining in this little Texas town.

The mystery Liz tapped touched a responsive chord in me. I now realize she lived from the feminine, which had not been erased by her orphan-home past or the German peasant farm culture from which she came. The divining she taught derived from our direct female heritage of the dark mysteries of ancient priestesses or seers or witches. Even now I sense the warm opening inside me I felt when we sat over our speaking Bible. I remember the expectant excitement at the hint of worlds beyond the strict confines of Protestant Christianity, worlds I was drawn to and longed to inhabit. Liz carried something which my own mother was lacking.

II

In this paper I want to explore the possibility that this vast world of the feminine, with its particular world view which informs beliefs and actions, with its distinctive forms of initiation and transformation, with its intense bonding between and among women, is a world largely unknown to us that lies waiting in the psyches of women and appears regularly in women's dreams as a call to individuation along a path we as a culture have long since abandoned. This world of the feminine opens in the imagination from a basic core experience of primary relationship to the archetypal feminine.

The idea that a woman's development might rest more authentically on the historical and archetypal matrix of the feminine strongly challenges the Freudian view of the "ultimate normal feminine attitude," in which the goal of normalcy is the girl's attachment in the oedipal phase to her father as love object (Freud 1931, p. 168). Modern women psychoanalysts have criticized Freud's paradigm and offered in its stead a pattern of female development which is based on a girl's pre-oedipal attachment to the mother, a pattern which, they assert, also leads to a woman's healthy autonomous maturity (Irigaray 1985). In this latter view, a woman may remain throughout her development in primary attachment to the mother. Or she may return, after a period of oedipal attachment to the father, to an attachment to the mother. In Jungian terms this second return to the mother signals a profound change. The woman's identity, her sense of self, gradually becomes rooted in the archetypal feminine. This essential self, which had been oriented toward the archetypal masculine in the oedipal phase (an orientation subsequently reinforced by the culture's patriarchal bias), now begins to move to feminine ground.

Thus, Freud noted what he termed "penis envy" in women in that stage of development in which identity is oriented toward the father and upholds patriarchal values of the culture. Euro-American women's experience of being second-class citizens by birth may be in the Freudian sense an experience of loss. While the loss or lack may not be felt directly as a conscious wish for a penis, it can be experienced in the countless ways limits are placed on the woman in the culture. Something is missing. The woman feels deprived. In analysis she names her deprivation, and we analysts concur, "mother did not give me enough" — enough attention, enough nurturing, enough appreciation, enough understanding. However, underlying the woman's personal experience of deprivation is another greater loss. What the mother is missing, and what the culture is missing, is the support of the fully realized power of the archetypal feminine. The lack the woman experiences is not the missing penis. The lack is the absence of the vital symbols of the feminine and its sacred vulva.

III

These feminist psychoanalytic writings emerged during women's recent struggle for redefinition. Synchronistically, archaeologists' discoveries in the last three decades have unearthed Neolithic cultures which were oriented toward and sustained by female deities. These discoveries present historical examples of cultures with archetypal feminine orientation in contrast to the archetypal masculine orientation of cultures in the West. The historical existence of cultures with a feminine base calls for a serious reconsideration of Freud's view.

Surely it is synchronistic that the great Neolithic cultures which oriented toward the feminine were discovered just at the time that the consciousness of women began reaching for autonomous expression. The earliest archaeological discoveries coincided with the beginnings of the women's movement in the late 19th century, but the major Neolithic discoveries came at the same time as the second wave of the women's movement following World War II. The impact of the discoveries did not hit the scientific world until after Jung's death; thus, the full complexity of the archetype as expressed in the Neolithic could not have been taken into account by Jung. The scope and duration of these ancient cultures is astonishing. Those in Anatolia, the Ancient Near East, and Old Europe lie in a continuous line leading to Western civilization, and these are our immediate ancestors. In all of these cultures, figures of the divine female among the artifacts far outnumber figures of males. These societies were based on the energetic wellspring of the archetypal feminine.

The first evidence of the domestication of plants which marks the Neolithic revolution begin to appear around 9000 B.C. Prior to this time humans apparently lived in bands of gatherers and hunters. Archaeologists now believe that the feminine religious orientation reaches from the Neolithic back into the Paleolithic. James Mellaart connects the art of the Upper Paleolithic of Europe with that of Neolithic Çatal Hüyük and Hacilar which he discovered in the Anatolian plain.

> Çatal Hüyük and Hacilar have established a link between these two great schools of art, and a continuity in religion can be demonstrated from Çatal Hüyük to Hacilar and so on till the great "Mother Goddesses" of archaic and classical times, the shadowy figures known as Cybele, Artemis, and Aphrodite . . . . The archeological, anthropological and artistic record of Çatal Hüyük is already strongly suggestive of an important heritage from the Upper Paleolithic . . . . Upper Paleolithic art centered round the theme of complex and female symbolism (in the form of symbols and animals) shows strong similarities to the religious imagery of Çatal Hüyük. (1967, pp. 23, 24)

Archaeologist Marija Gimbutas, in a 1987 seminar in San Francisco, noted that many identical sacred images of the feminine occur from the Paleolithic into the Neolithic. With this evidence we now have a 25,000-year continuous history of a religion based on the archetypal feminine. What is the impact of this long ancestral history on the psyche? The 3,000- or 4,000-year history of masculine religion seems relatively short in comparison and diminishes proportionately in importance. We cannot afford to ignore the weight of both these great archetypal forces and must hold in mind their relative influence on the psyche over time.

Figure 1. Vulture attacking two humans, one of which is crouched in the posture of the dead. From a Çatal Hüyük shrine. (From Mellaart, *Çatal Hüyük*, p. 93.)

As we interpret from the remains of the Neolithic cultures, two facts stand out. Women had their own gender-appropriate place and sacred time. The shrines were women's place. The cyclic ritual was women's time.

All the evidence indicates that women were the priestesses of worship in the elaborate temples and shrine rooms of these cultures. Here women had place, a specific place set apart which held, welcomed, and nourished them. This female place was central to the ongoing life of the community. In the sacred place, worship was in the service of the goddess who reflected perfectly the women's bodies and cyclic development.

Moreover, women had time set apart—a cyclic round of ritual-designated time. Great rituals came to pass at the transition points of the seasons. This was women's time based on a science whose time-keeper was the moon. The surge of the menstrual tides in her body matched the waxing and waning of the moon and matched the coming and going of the seasons. Indeed some of the great rituals required that all the women be menstruating simultaneously; it is likely that they were anyway, living in the close proximity of village life. For these rituals, women whose menses did not synchronize naturally drank an herbal potion to bring on the flow (Meador 1986, p. 35).

Having place and time, women gave birth quite naturally to artistic modes of expression of their creative imagination. Much of the art of the centuries of the Neolithic was created by women. The exquisite and varied art forms reflect the artists' imaginative expression of the archetypal feminine.

What follows is a sampling of the Neolithic cultures which preceded and then developed directly into Western civilization. I would like to ask you to read the descriptions of these societies as you would a series of dreams.

In Turkey, James Mellaart made his first discoveries in 1957. Only one year before, the eminent archaeologist, Seaton Lloyd, wrote:

> The region more correctly described as Anatolia shows no sign whatever of habitation during the Neolithic period. (1956, p. 65)

Mellaart first discovered the mound of Hacilar. A year later he found the spectacular city of Çatal Hüyük, somewhat to the east. Çatal Hüyük is the largest Neolithic settlement discovered so far in the Near East. The culture was active between 6700 B.C. and 5700 B.C. Fourteen building levels have been uncovered, and virgin soil has not yet been reached. The people lived in a large town, perhaps 10,000 in popula-

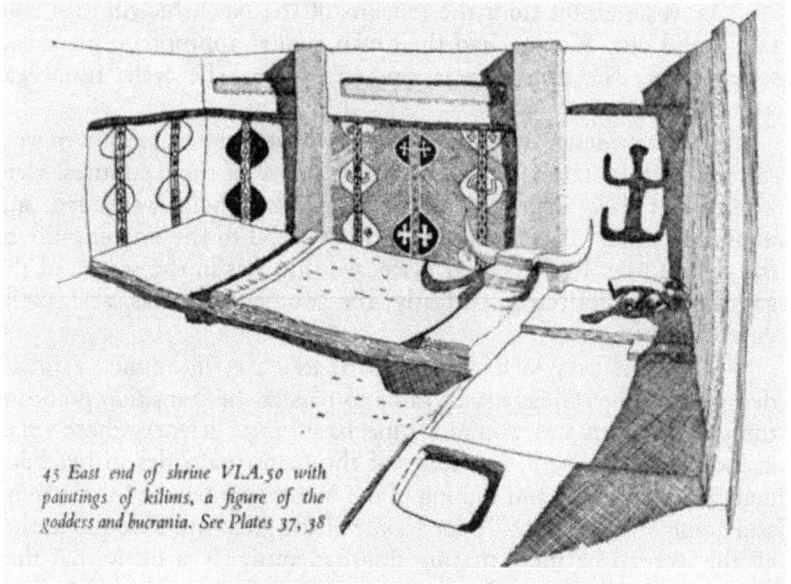

45 East end of shrine VI.A.50 with paintings of kilims, a figure of the goddess and bucrania. See Plates 37, 38

Figure 2. Shrine from Çatal Hüyük with goddess in birth-giving posture and kilim patterns on the walls. (From Mellaart, p. 155.)

tion at its height. Houses were mud brick beehivelike structures with entrances through the roof. The large number of shrines in the housing structures is particularly noteworthy, one for every four or five homes in the portion now excavated.

The many shrines are elaborately decorated, giving us a vivid picture of the religion at Çatal Hüyük. The central figure in the worship is a goddess in many guises. She is the birth-giving goddess, legs spread wide in her earliest image, a bas relief in plaster on a wall. Below her are rows of breasts formed over the beaks of vultures, lower jaws of wild boar, heads of weasel and fox, all scavengers and harbingers of death. Beaks and jaws protrude from the red painted nipple. She is goddess of life and death, nourishment of the breast intimately united with the sharp bite of scarcity, misfortune, and death.

She appears as maiden alone, molded in clay on the shrine wall, dancing or running, her long hair streaming behind her. She appears in another wall sculpture as twin goddess, pregnant mother and pubescent maiden. In one fresco a worshiper with face covered approaches

Figure 3. Kilim pattern painted in red, black, and white
on a shrine wall, Çatal Hüyük. (From Mellaart,
p. 89)

her as a triple goddess figure. Clay figurines of her appear in grain bins, as she is deity of crops. She is a huge figure molded on the wall of another shrine, watching over a scene painted on an adjoining wall of enormous vultures as they strip the bodies of the dead of flesh. She encompasses all, life and death; the vicissitudes of the natural world are held in her embrace.

This society evidently enjoyed a spirit of cooperation between women and men, and perhaps equality, although in excavated burial sites, it is apparent that women were given a more honored status, and that priestesses outnumber priests. Mellaart believes women created the religion at Çatal Hüyük. Women's status was enhanced by their discovery of and control over agriculture. From the sewing and basketry tools found only in women's graves, excavators surmise that women were the artists of weaving. Çatal Hüyük gives us the earliest textiles, pottery, and basketry in the Near East. Elaborate designs of textiles are painted in the first frescoes on the walls of the shrines, paintings of weavings resembling the modern beautiful rugs from this area.

At Hacilar, Mellaart discovered a sizable Neolithic settlement which lasted about 800 years. Hacilar is noted for its exquisite pottery which developed from the style at Çatal Hüyük. A large number of terra-cotta female statuettes have been uncovered, the goddess seated, standing, enthroned, maiden, mature matron, pregnant mother, full-

Figure 4. Goddess figurine giving birth on a throne with two felines as arm rests. From a grain bin of a shrine at Çatal Hüyük. (From Mellaart, p. 157.)

breasted nursing mother, mother with child, and mistress with animals. Many of these figures were found near the hearth in private houses.

South of Turkey in present day Iraq and Iran lie many Neolithic village remains. Between the world wars, excavators made startling discoveries in southern and northern Iraq, and finds in Iran and Iraq since World War II have added substantially to our understanding of prehistoric life in this area. Numerous complex cultures existed side by side distinguished by varying pottery and artifact styles and architectural remains.

In southern Iraq the earliest culture, Jarmo, flourished around 6750 B.C. Here, R. J. Braidwood, working in the 1950s, discovered some 5,000 figurines, animal and human, including goddess figures with large buttocks and thighs (Lloyd 1978, pp. 33–35). Slightly before 5000 B.C., the important cities of Ur and Eridu began to be settled. Leonard Woolley made spectacular finds at Ur in the 1920s. At Eridu archaeologists Seaton Lloyd and F. Safar have uncovered eighteen building levels. The earliest temple is only nine feet square but contains the typical cult niche and offering table characteristic of Mesopotamian temples from this time onwards (ibid., p. 41). Here they found the beautiful examples of the snake-headed goddess alone or nursing her snake-headed baby, her shoulders tattooed or marked with keloid scarring. At another important city, Uruk, German excavators discovered the impressive "White Temple" and the large Inanna Temple, both repeatedly rebuilt and enlarged, the first examples dating back to around 4000 B.C. The earliest examples of precuneiform script are from Uruk, dating about 3250 B.C. (ibid., pp. 48–52).

In northern Iraq the cultures show some influence from those in the south, but develop their own distinctive styles. Near Nineveh at the site of Arpachiyah, excavators discovered a unique temple form, a round building with a rectangular entrance, suggesting womb and birth canal. These buildings date from 4500 B.C. (ibid., p. 67). The Hassuna culture with its distinctive pottery developed skillfully modeled clay "mother-goddess" figures. At Choga Mami, an example of the Samarra culture, archaeologists in 1966 found a new class of terra-cotta figurines. These goddesses are standing with hands at the waist and have exaggerated buttocks and feet. They are elaborately decorated with tattoolike markings on their faces, large slanted eyes, eyelashes and scalloped hair sculpted or painted on. Some have elongated bird-like heads. Choga Mami flourished around 4900 B.C. (ibid., p. 69ff).

In Iran relics of prehistory came to light in 1949. At Tepe Sarab, diggers found the beautifully modeled Sarab Venus seated on her huge dolphin-shaped thighs, her large breasts protruding below an exaggeratedly long, slender neck. Ganj Dareh Tepe, a culture dating from 8400 to 6800 B.C., yielded figurines of a tiny, delicately modeled female with pointed head. At the 1963 excavation of the important site, Tepe Guran, workers found figurines of women and animals made from stone, bone, and shell.

Figure 5. Snake-headed goddess nursing her baby. From Ur.
(From Parrot, *Sumer—The Dawn of Art*, p. 59.)

Figure 6. Mother goddesses painted with red stripes. From Tell Halaf, northern Iraq. (From Parrot, p. 48)

In Iran other sites of the Neolithic from 6000 B.C. to historical time yielded many mother goddess figures and other female figurines. At one particular site, Tepe Yahy (so far the only Neolithic site in southern Iran), excavators in 1967 uncovered a very beautiful female figurine of green soapstone. She was lying on a bed of 63 flints together with three bone tools and three grooved whetstones, suggesting a shrine. A debate arose over this figurine that exemplifies the difficulty of overcoming a cultural bias in order to perceive the reality of a very different culture. Was this a goddess figure, the excavators asked, or a phallus with breasts?

> It has been suggested that it represents the male phallus with the attributes of a female carved over it, but this view has been criticized by Carter who believes that the hole drilled in the top of the head was a purely functional device for fixing the attachment of hair or headdress and it is not the terminus of "the urethra" as suggested by the excavators. (Singh 1974, p. 195)

The third major area of Neolithic discoveries in the continuous line leading to Western civilization is Old Europe, about which archaeologist Marija Gimbutas (1982) has written extensively. This culture stretched from the Black Sea to the Adriatic, reaching its zenith around 5000 B.C. For several thousand years, the culture revolved around its

Figure 7. The Sarab Venus from Tepe Sarab, Iran.
(From the author's collection.)

religious core, the worship of goddesses. Some 30,000 sculptures have been excavated from 3,000 sites, unique representations of a goddess in two primary aspects. One is the goddess as giver of both life and death. In this aspect she controls the length of the life cycle. At death, regeneration begins, so that death and regeneration are interwoven; the good and terrible mother is indivisible. The second aspect is the goddess as ruler of the fertility of nature itself. These two aspects of the goddess contain light and dark naturally and inevitably.

The cultures of Old Europe built elaborate temples to the goddess, some with roof openings through which she might fly, some in the form of her body. On the altars of the temples sat a rounded bread oven not unlike those in pueblo villages of North America. Beside the oven stood a vertical loom. In a room below the sanctuary, the finest

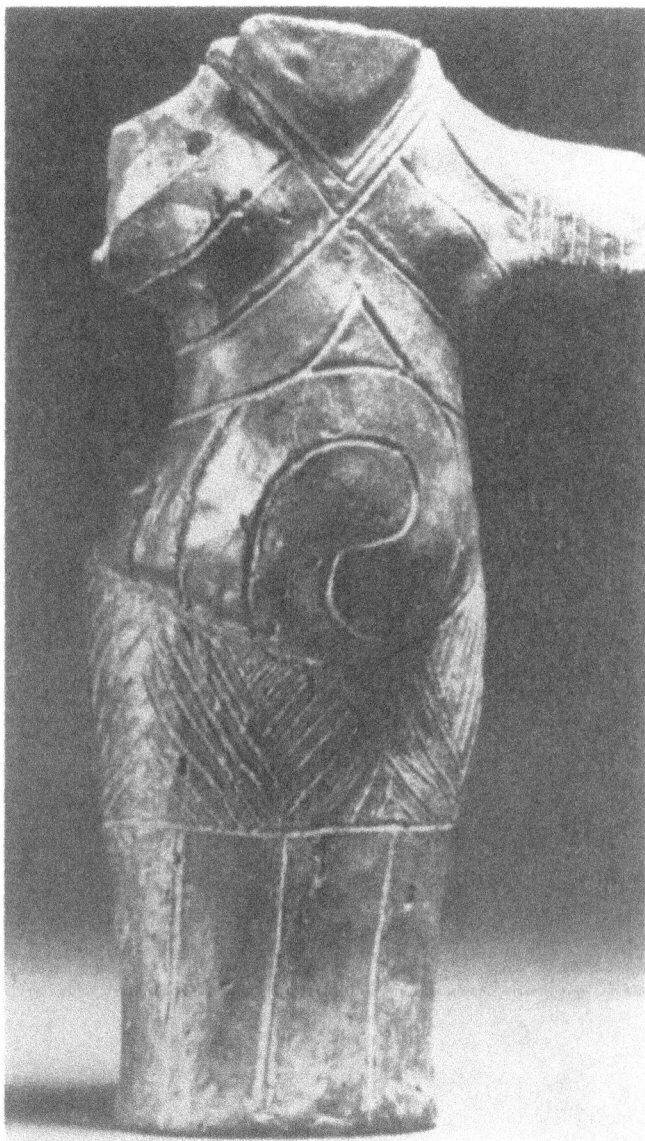

Figure 8. Pregnant goddess with a snake around her belly. Old Europe, 5000-4500 B.C. (From Gimbutas, *The Goddesses and Gods of Old Europe*, p. 202.)

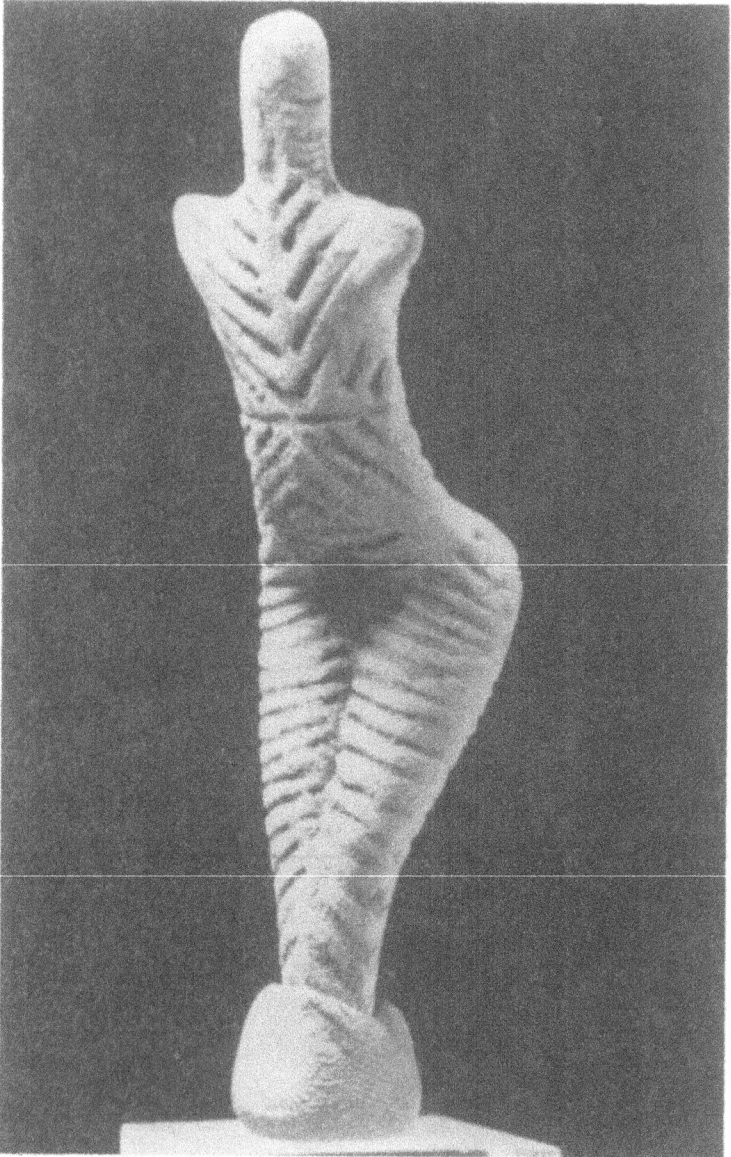

Figure 9. Bird or snake goddess with chevrons on front
and back. Old Europe, fifth millennium B.C.
(From Gimbutas, p. 141.)

Figure 10. Drawing of a cult table with ritual pottery.
Old Europe, fifth millennium B.C.
(From Gimbutas, p. 81.)

women artists created the sacred art of the culture which was dedicated
to the goddess of the temple. As in Çatal Hüyük the tools for making
the exquisite vases and sculptures of Old Europe are found only in
women's graves (Gimbutas 1982, p. 9).

With the discovery of these early societies whose cultures moved
energetically around the worship of goddesses, we begin to piece
together a clear picture of a new pattern, a possibility for the individuation of women which we could only intuit before. The archetypal
feminine begins to take substantial shape with the discovery of these
Neolithic cultures.

A woman whose psychological development takes her back to this
feminine base as the orienting pattern for her ego sees life very differently from a woman grounded in the patriarchal culture's model for her

Figure 11. Bird goddess wearing a duck's mask, ritual skirt. Old Europe, fifth millennium B.C. (From Gimbutas, p. 139.)

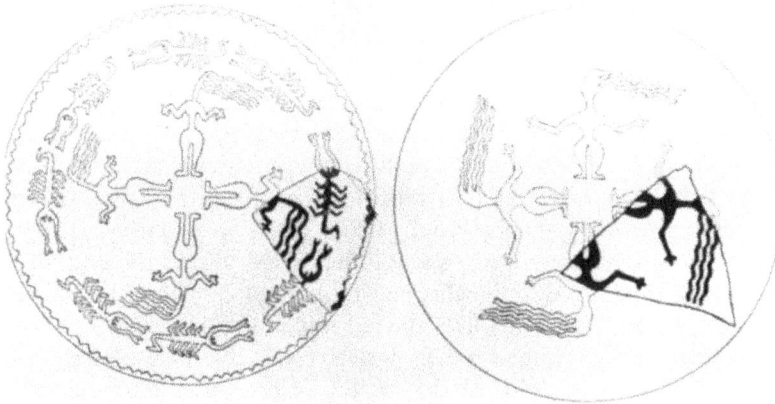

Figure 12. Goddesses with flowing hair and scorpions.
Samarran deep plates. Northern Iraq. (From
Goff, *Symbols of Prehistoric Mesopotamia*,
figures 32, 33.)

sex. Truly this archetypal base is a goddess, not a phallus with breasts.
Standing on this base, a woman no longer need feel, "mother did not
give me the desired genital, did not give me enough." The richness of
these cultures as an expression of the archetypal feminine is a containing matrix for women, an archetypal ancestor to whom we may turn to
inform our development and on whom we may ultimately rely.

This new consciousness presents the possibility that a woman's
individuation process can take place outside Freud's paradigms. Connection to the feminine offers a wholly other source of energetic affirmation, a new/old archetypal pattern of identity. The reality of the
goddess religions gives to woman a fully realized matrix in which her
intuitive searching can come to rest. No longer must she settle for an
adaptation to the father, that identity which is forever secondary, forever unsatisfying. She now stands with the mother on female ground.
Connection to ancient female ancestors gives new meaning to May
Sarton's search for precursors when, in a poem to Virginia Woolf, she
said, "We go forward into the past" (Gilbert and Gubar 1988, p. 167).
Truly women now can go forward under a new sign which flourished in
the very ancient past.

What happened to obliterate this predominantly peaceful tradition of goddess worshipers after so long a history throughout the Paleolithic and Neolithic? Gimbutas records the repeated invasions and final

destruction of Old Europe by the horse-riding, patriarchal pastoralists, the Kurgan (1983, p. 293). Afterwards, remnants of the Old Europe culture appeared in the Aegean and survived on Crete and Cyprus for another 2,000 years. The rise of the patriarchy in Mesopotamia is credited to the destruction of clan kinship relationships as the organizing social principle (Rohrlich-Leavitt 1980), as well as to the military expansion of the state, the taking of captives, the invention of slavery, and the exchange of women (Lerner 1986). Later, in Judaism, the god Yahweh arose who was completely independent of nature, and while vestiges of the Canaanite fertility cult found a place within the Israelite religion, in the 7th century B.C., the last remains of the goddess religion were "mercilessly stamped out by Josiah, especially in his slaughter of the ritual prostitutes and the destruction of the Asheras" (Biale 1978, p. 10).

IV

Since we all grow up in a society with patriarchal values, we find the archetypal feminine primarily in the unconscious. For a woman to return to the archetypal feminine as the matrix of her psyche, she must reorient through a connection to the unconscious feminine. This reorientation requires not only a resocialization into a female-based culture, but also requires a reinitiation through the major stages of female development. Such complete change may scarcely be possible in a lifetime. Nevertheless, many contemporary women have begun this process of reorientation led by strong supporting images from their dreams.

A 40-year-old housewife from a small country town, Barbara came into therapy seeking to adjust to the presence of her mother in her household. Barbara and her husband of 20 years had recently invited her mother to move in with them, since their two sons were now grown and gone. Barbara's smoldering hostility toward her mother was barely below the surface, conflicting with her caretaking self-image.

Barbara's initial dream was of a large house built around a beautiful tree. The tree's growth was beginning to crack the house structure and would soon destroy it altogether. The powerful image of the dream told me that Barbara's problem reached way beyond learning to cope with her mother. The tree as image of the Self and of her own individuation process was pushing her out of the psychological house of her adaptation to the culture, and that familiar house would necessarily come down. Indeed, this proved to be the case. Barbara soon asked her mother to move out. Not long after, with no warning, her husband abruptly left her for another woman, an event I connected to the great disruption Barbara's emerging psyche caused in the status quo of their relationship.

Looking back from the perspective of Barbara's subsequent development, I can see that this initial dream revealed the tendency of her psyche's movement toward an archetypal feminine base. While the tree reaches toward the masculine spirit, it is grounded in the earth of the feminine. Sacred trees abound in the goddess religions. The tree is vegetative life and suggests movement in the psyche at the very deep unconscious level.

Women who are moving into a primary relationship to the feminine frequently bring an initial big dream pointing the direction. Sarah, a middle-aged housewife with three children still in school, was in a 20-year marriage when she came to me. Here is her initial dream:

Dream: *On vacation with my husband and children, we suddenly realize an enormous volcano is erupting, spewing lava, but instead of fire, it spews golden sparks. The sparks fill the air and threaten to fall on us. We seek shelter in a flimsy building. When I come out, my husband and youngest daughter have disappeared.*

From deep within the earth, the realm of the goddess, the golden substance of the Self shows forth, but as with the growing tree, the golden lava threatens to destroy the status quo. The movement of the psyche in both these dreams pictures a powerful inevitable *natural* force which takes the lead in the development of the dreamers, announcing a drastic change. A year into analysis, Sarah's husband also abruptly and unexpectedly left the marriage for another woman.

This view of women's psychological development casts a whole new light on women's dreams as they inform the process of development. As an analyst with a woman client, I open myself as far as I can to the entire continuum of cultures, from the most fully developed woman-centered cultures to the most extreme male-centered cultures. Very soon the woman will tell me, through her dreams and her story, where she sits on this continuum. When dreams of the feminine come, as they inevitably do, I see them not only as a needed compensation to a culturally adapted woman, but also as a beckoning to this woman to begin the long journey back into the matrix of ancestral female orientation.

For all of us, our formative years in a patriarchal culture inevitably shape an adaptation that is oriented toward male values. In addition to this masculine orientation, a woman client usually has at least one foot in paradise and has yet to face the reality of hardship, suffering, and death. Not that she hasn't suffered, sometimes terribly, but she reveals a deep, perhaps unconscious hope or expectation that she will return to a primarily happy life after working out her troubles. Barbara was certain therapy could help her adjust to her mother's presence. This tenaciously held expectation of an idealized life usually covers a drastically wounded and rejected little girl.

In our work we as analysts travel with such women, providing a secure place for each of them to experience the pain and despair of the injury to the child they still carry. With this transition from a patriarchal to a feminine base in mind, I envision the injured child not only being healed, but also discovering the vital, rich, nourishing and sustaining matrix inside, which is the archetypal feminine. With this new feminine matrix, the analyst's hope that the woman may come to mother herself takes on new meaning. The mothering she may discover in herself is not only her image of good mothering within the patriarchal culture, but is the mothering of the matrifocal cultures whose ritual focus from birth to death is on the experience of being female. The archetypal feminine, as expressed in these cultures, holds her and honors her in her very particular female body and its potential for the powerful changes of menstruation, defloration, pregnancy, birth, breast feeding, child rearing, menopause, aging, and death, and all the metaphorical expressions of these states.

The analyst provides a place for the wounded child to be present and to be known. This child has lost contact with her female value as she adapted to a patriarchal-based culture. However, the child still carries female instinctuality, and beneath her wounds, she responds instinctually to the appearance of the feminine Self. This feminine Self appears in countless forms in women's dreams. With the recognition of the new feminine cultural base that is forming for women, I look at these images with a new slant. What does the Self want? Is this dream announcing an opening for the woman to travel out of her masculine orientation into the new world of the feminine?

Some dreams are very specific. The second year of Barbara's analysis she dreamed of a group of women who do not believe in the moon.

Dream: *I am outside at a religious ceremony. A woman leading carries a baby girl. A chorus chants to one side, a chant the baby taught the women. Two men, one black, one white, will teach this*

group, because the group does not believe in the moon. The men
have a film to show, illustrating the reality of the moon. Inadver-
tently, the first of the film shows this group's church burning
down. I am irritated that the men show this part of the film.

This dream is a call from the ancient female religions appearing in
a modern dream as an available orienting matrix in the psyche of the
dreamer. A new religious form is beginning, its liturgy taught by a
baby girl. New animus figures appear, black and white, carrying the
opposites in apparent harmony and unity of purpose. The men will
teach the group of women about the reality of the moon. These new
animus figures relate to the archetypal feminine, not to the patriarchal
masculine of her outer life adaptation. The dreamer, Barbara, shows
her ambivalence to the change by being irritated that the men show in
the film the old church burning down. Barbara, like many women, has
lost her connection to cyclic time, moon time, and finds it hard to
believe the psyche can be held in the waxing and waning, ebb and flow
of the opposites. Moon time presents a new orientation based on her
own lunar periodicity. She is called away from her old animus-
dominated factual orientation to an orientation based on the sway of
the tides. She must learn this new view from supportive, knowledge-
able masculine figures.

The archetypal feminine Self is closely connected to moon time.
Menstruation is the reminder in the woman's body of her belonging to
the moon worshipers, of her deep grounding in cyclic time. For women
out of touch with the feminine, dream images of the blood appear as
dangerous aberrations of the normal flow. She dreams she is hemor-
rhaging or bleeding from her pores or passing large clots of blood. Such
images can announce a readiness in the psyche to correct the imbalance
and call the woman down into the feminine in her body.

One analysand dreamed repeatedly of aberrant menstrual flow.
She had been raised in a strict Catholic family. During her first menses,
she went to mass and fainted. The conflict between the church of the
fathers and the sacred blood of the mothers was too much for her
sensitive psyche. After this incident, she made excuses to her parents to
avoid mass whenever she was menstruating. Her dreams of hemorrhag-
ing dangerously called for a healing of her relationship to the
feminine.

Women moving toward this new female base frequently dream
early in analysis of a devastating calamity destroying the old way of
living. Barbara dreamed a huge tree was growing through her house

and threatened to destroy it. Sarah dreamed of a gold-spewing volcano. Earthquakes may shift the landscape. In one woman's dream, a fierce wind blows a strange tree spiraling into a harbor. Tornados bend and twist toward a dreamer's flimsy house where she cowers. The archetypal feminine announces herself through the elemental forces she controls — wind, storm, flood, hurricane, tornado, earthquake, fire. She destroys the old order, the old church, the old house, the old way of being with a sweep of her powerful hand. These forces of nature and their counterparts in the psyche — furies, rages, passions, intensities of emotion — announce the arrival of the goddess in her primal form.

Such primal natural forces are the familiar powers of the goddess and appear in women's dreams as a reminder of their ancestral heritage. The ancient poetry of Enheduanna, high priestess of Sumer in 2300 B.C., invokes this aspect of the goddess Inanna.

> Lady of elemental forces . . .
> flood-storm-hurricane adorned . . .
> a whirlwind warrior
> bound on a twister . . .
> a ditch of spilling water
> she floods over a road
> engulfs the one she loathes . . .
> fighting is her play
> she never tires of it
> she goes out running
> strapping on her sandals . . .
> (translated by Meador)

Judith Gleason, in her book on the goddess Oya, pleas for further understanding of women's passion.

In being coached by compliant mothers to stifle rather than outride our storms, to dam and conceal our floods, to bank our fires and give tinder over to future husbands, the Oya in ourselves froze in its tracks . . . Thus, in other ways obstructed, Oya strikes us — quirking here, cramping there. Done with our brains, the indefatigable goddess goes jaggedly to work upon our bodies, cutting off circulation, opening sluices, instilling victims who could be votaries with a variety of "female complaints," catching them up in mindless swirls of activity, throwing them down into incapacitating vortices, playing havoc with appetite. Stop, Oya, we beg you! . . . We will strive to know your winds the better to reclaim our part of fire. (1987, pp. 18–19)

Although these elementary forces come early in analysis, they continue to infuse the more developed woman with passion. Analysis calls the forces into livable containers. The raw forces are not lost. They ignite women's creativity. Gleason dares "to wrest women's fire back from Promethean culture-bearers."

> Unfortunately even Jung stereotypically categorizes the elements as active, creative, and masculine—fire and wind—as opposed to passive, submissive, and feminine—earth and water. Such identifications are culturally rather than archetypally determined and can lead to brainwashing in therapeutic situations that promise reclamation of the feminine. (ibid., p. 30)

Feminine fire smolders unrecognized. "After a busy day the floor of the woman's therapy studio is strewn with drawings of incendiary vaginas and uterine cauldrons, burning with culturally imposed shame," says Gleason (ibid., p. 31).

The analyst is challenged to open the door to these passions, to honor the dream images of storm and flood, earthquake and fire as the raw materials of women's individuation. The wounded girl child learned to conform and obey before she could experience the heat of her natural elements. Now the child within the woman is led through her dreams to a primal experience of the feminine in powerful, natural forms. First the woman must experience the intensity of her emotions before her stormy impulses can be transformed into channels of creativity.

This is the goddess. She is violent, randomly capricious, overwhelming, much larger than life. The process of analysis coaxes her energies into manageable expression, allows her fire to cook the wounded flesh of the psyche, transforming it into edible food. Or she allows herself to be impregnated, thus cooling the hot and bloody female force, allowing a softening to show forth. She is transformed, then, into gentle mother, birth-giving goddess, home-center; but as at Çatal Hüyük, the birth-giving goddess is never far from the breasts molded over the vulture's beak, or as in Eridu, the gentle mother has the head of a snake and nurses her snake baby.

As women's individuation reconnects to the female past, women open to the interplay of elemental forces and their transforming containment, not in neat sequential doses, but in unpredictable interaction, point and counterpoint, with which the woman wrestles the rest of her life. The woman who lives from the archetypal feminine base travels expectantly from chaos to form and back to chaos again, just as her ancestors wove patterns out of a mess of threads which might easily unravel at another time. She is no longer the daughter protected from her passionate nature by the father's principles. Rather she is full woman, fully embracing the ebb and flow of her nature, as closely aware of the chaotic elemental forces as she is of their movement into creative containment.

Loosened by such cataclysms from the moorings of the patriarchy, the woman floats free but feels lost and bewildered. Sarah dreamed she was camping with a woman lover on the edge of a snowy wilderness filled with wild animals. Return to the natural world of the feminine can be harsh, cold, and terrifying.

At other times the woman's dreams guide her and reassure her that her disorientation is a necessary part of discovering a meaningful new direction. In analysis this is a time she has big, archetypal dreams. She dreams she digs into the center of the earth or digs up old women's graves. There she finds weird animals or raging harpies. Or she finds strange reed posts on the fresh grave of a patriarchal analyst; the posts turn out to be the ancient symbol of the goddess Inanna. Or a swarm of bees fly spiraling upward out of an old record player. Or in a cave the ancient, decaying body of an old woman begins to move and rise. These archetypal images of the feminine are the ballast which give her stability in a time of confusion. It is important for the analyst to see the dreams as orienting signposts of the woman groping for connection to a feminine-based value system.

Adaptation to our culture imposes on most women a patriarchal orienting frame which gives life meaning and predictability. The frame serves to guide her outer life in the absence of the development of consciousness of the feminine in her formative years. She becomes a phallus with breasts. The patriarchal frame is built over a lack, the absence of the feminine. She is terrified when this frame begins to fall away, for she senses the underlying void. When she becomes aware of the feminine structure which will catch her fall, she first recoils at its alienation from the culture. She dreams of the feminine as outcast, marginal, repulsive. She strongly resists giving up her favored and familiar status as daughter-captive to the fathers.

The analyst has to make a distinction in dream imagery between positive re-emergence of the ancestral feminine and personal shadow issues. Recognition of the shadow is complicated by the fact that in her allegiance to patriarchal values, this woman has repressed natural parts of her healthy instinctual growth such as her full sexual womanhood and her assertive self-supporting voice. The feminine beckoning to this woman may appear shadowy since the woman still has the patriarchal perspective. One analysand dreamed of being seduced by a dark lesbian. Another woman dreamed a sexy blonde in a revealing red dress sat by her in church and made seductive advances. Both these images speak to the awakening in the dreamer's body of a traditionally forbidden sexuality. These images of the outcast or marginal woman reflect the dreamer's ambivalence toward the feminine rather than personal shadow.

These deep shadow issues arise between the values of the patriarchal god, Yahweh, who is wholly spirit and completely free of nature, and the values of the goddess who is in and of nature and sanctifies the material world. The psychological conflict in women centers on the body and its functions which are so intimately a part of their development. The patriarchal value of spirit over nature persists in one segment of the Women's Movement. This view stresses that women are "closer to nature" because of their burdensome bodies and are therefore less creative externally than men (Ortner 1974, p. 67). Basing her argument on Simone de Beauvoir's influential book, *The Second Sex*, Sharon Ortner asserts that women's bodily functions are often the source of discomfort and pain. Breasts are irrelevant; menstruation uncomfortable, involving "bothersome tasks of cleansing and waste disposal." In pregnancy "vitamin and mineral resources are channeled into nourishing the fetus, depleting her own strength and energies," and childbirth is dangerous and painful. Woman is doomed to mere reproduction of transient human beings, while the male creates lasting eternal transcendent objects.

The argument of de Beauvoir and Ortner that women are hampered in their ability to be creative by their bodily functions is the antithesis of the Neolithic goddess religions' belief that creativity issues from the female body. In the ancient religions, matter is the sacred and mysterious expression of the goddess. Women are created in her image, and the birth-giving and nourishing propensities of women's bodies match the goddess's fecundity and abundance. Far from hampering creativity, women's bodily functions are imbued with divine meaning. These functions inspired the exquisite art of the Neolithic and inform its ritual.

Frequent images of shame in women's dreams reflect the basic conflict between nature and spirit in the culture. The wounded child may long for the mother, but the masculine adapted adult feels deep unconscious shame of her female body. This issue is present in dreams in which the female dreamer appears as a man. One analysand dreamed she was a black man in a jail. She is identified with the more glorified masculine but remains an outcast in a prison.

The conventional shadow shifts in meaning as the woman experiments with new behavior. She may be outrageous, spilling over the boundaries of "appropriate" behavior. She must find her voice, as indicated in one woman's dream: she pulls a scream-stifling hand away from her mouth.

The goddess would have her tongue. Silence is tantamount to submission to the status quo. The goddess's insistence becomes more urgent. The woman remembers Inanna's use of her voice in Enheduanna's poetry:

> my Lady
> the blast of your voice
> crushes foreign lands . . .
> in splitting waves
> her shrill cries pierce
> Ebeh's failing heart . . .
> her tongue's poison
> hurls a green-wilting curse
> over forest and fruit-bearing trees . . . .
> (translated by Meador)

The tongue she seeks is not the cleverly adapted animus facility, but woman talk, a new language of women. Woman's new language speaks in the creative inventions of Gertrude Stein, or in the work of the poet H. D., who says she writes from her "womb brain" (1982, p. 22). Contemporary theologian Mary Daly has put forth a new dictionary for women, *Wickedary*, and Judy Grahn calls her lesbian and gay history, *Another Mother Tongue*. In Ursula Le Guin's story, "She Unnames Them," Eve takes away the names from all the animals, then gives back her own name, as she says to Adam:

> You and your father lent me this—gave it to me, actually. It's been really useful, but it doesn't exactly seem to fit very well lately. But thanks very much! It's really been very useful. (1986)

While the woman utters the halting phrases of her new-found woman's language, her facile animus-adapted tongue is silenced. Her animus-inspired activities begin to feel like burdensome requirements. The basis of her way of being in the world is shifting.

Outwardly, the woman may appear highly adapted. Intrapsychically, she lives in an animus prison. She may have fooled even the analyst, because the woman looks entirely successful at work and love. Hidden, however, is the bewildered, injured child who still wonders why her budding female self was abandoned. No female ritual path led this child into the world of women, and somewhere deep inside she knows her true self is missing.

The feminine beckons to this little child, who still possesses a remnant of the female Self. It is this child who responds instinctively to the call of the archetypal feminine, for she longs for validation of her femaleness. She longs for the embrace of the mother, a new mother, not her actual mother who also sleeps in the animus prison. When the injured child begins to respond to the healing approach of the Self, the woman begins to reconcile with her personal mother. One woman dreamed:

> Dream: *I am walking away from a glittering social event with my long-dead mother. I resolve to care for my old mother, take her home with me. I look down and see mother's feet are broken and crippled, bound in the Chinese fashion.*

Only the appearance of the archetypal feminine Self can interrupt the repetitive inheritance of culture-bound adaptation. The analyst carries this healing Self in the transference, enabling the analysand to work with the injured child through her dreams and active imagination. The healing of the child becomes apparent as the child grows older in the analysand's image. Dream images appear that are set in the woman's childhood home, and healing interactions take place where once there was violence, sexual abuse, and abandonment. One woman dreamed she found all of her beloved childhood dolls in a hidden closet. Another woman, after healing from a long series of dark depressions, dreamed the analyst appeared in her childhood home and taught her women's rituals.

The Self, which initiated the woman's long journey of return to female ground, now appears in dreams as priestess or female lover, guiding the woman through female initiation, awakening her deep love for women. The ritual initiations of matrifocal cultures become profoundly meaningful to her. The Indians of San Diego County, California, dug pits for young girls when their periods first began. The women lined the pits with sweet smelling sage, heated the pits with warm rocks. There in the pits lay the naked girls. The women placed a warm crescent-shaped stone between each of the girls' legs. For five days and nights the old women sang ritual songs and danced around the pit, imparting women's tribal wisdom to the young initiates.

Similarly, the woman in analysis dreams her own pubescent girl's initiation, no matter her actual age. The dreams of unnatural bleeding, which marked her alienation from the feminine, now subside, and dreams of bleeding herald a new awakening of love and respect for women's wisdom. One woman dreamed she was dancing with her granddaughter when suddenly she realizes her period has started. The two of them go into the bathroom, and both clean the thick, red blood off her leg. The little girl bends to see where the blood comes from.

During this time of loving connection to the feminine Self, the woman notices a new masculine emerge in her psyche. Not only is the injured child healing and being led to womanhood, but a new animus is growing out of the healed place. He may appear in dreams as a little boy, perhaps her own newly born boy baby. He may appear as an earthy man unlike the old image of hero, king, lawgiver, or father. In one woman's dream he was a cowherd. In Inanna's descent to the underworld, after the sky gods refuse to help her, she is brought back to life by the life-giving waters and the life-giving plant of the earth god Enki.

The new masculine supports her in her reaching out from the feminine, for he, like herself, worships the goddess, and in that respect he is similar to men in matrifocal societies. He understands that she must "unname them," start fresh from a brand new perspective with new words for her experience. In Le Guin's story, Eve leaves Adam, says goodbye:

> "I'm going now. With the —" I hesitated, and finally said, "With them, you know," and went on out. In fact, I had only just then realized how hard it would have been to explain myself. I could not chatter away as I used to do, taking it all for granted. My words now must be as slow, as new, as single, as tentative as the steps I took going down the path away from the house, between the dark-branched, tall dancers motionless against the winter shining. (Ibid., p. 194)

No longer can the woman chatter away. She develops a new way of being in the world. Her awareness is deep and attentive, multilayered, and radiates in a circumference around her. She attends to the physical world through her body, takes the world in through all her senses. She no longer "names them" from her logos: tree, sky; rather she sees "dark-branched, tall dancers motionless against the winter shining." Just as when she is menstruating, she is attuned to her inner world while she goes forth in the outer.

I have watched many women go through this process of healing and self-discovery through reconnection to the archetypal feminine. I believe the energetic movement of the psyche in these women heralds a new opening in the cultural unconscious which is bringing forth a new cultural form particularly relevant to women. Analysis is one of the few places in our culture that can guide a woman on this path, for women still have no truly female place nor time nor institution which fully reflects female nature. Because so many women are pushed from within to develop in this feminine direction, they will undoubtedly create spaces for their new found orientation in the future. But at the present, a woman must search to find companions on the way.

How heartened we women are, then, to discover our ancestors. Reeling under the weight of past pain and present self-examination, we listen as Enheduanna tells us of other women, devotees of Inanna, who bore the struggle of individuation:

> those warrior women
> like a single thread
> come forth from beyond the river
> do common work
> in devotion to you
> whose hands sear them with purifying fire
>
> your many devoted
> who will be burnt
> like sun scorched fire bricks
> pass before your eyes
>   (translated by Meador)

And we join those before us who have sung her praises, understanding at last the poet's impassioned words:

> your torch flames
> heaven's four quarters
> spreads splendorous light in the dark
> you have realized
> the queen of heaven and earth
> to the utmost
> you hold everything
> entirely in your hands

your storm-shot torrents
drench the bare earth
moisten to life
moisture bearing light
floods the dark
O my Lady
my queen
I unfold your splendor in all lands
I extol your glory
I will praise your course
your sweeping grandeur
forever

Queen
Mistress
you are sublime
you are venerable
Inanna
you are sublime
you are venerable
your great deeds
are boundless
may I praise
your eminence
O maiden Inanna
sweet is your praise

(translated by Meador)

References

Biale, David. 1978. The god with breasts: El Shaddai in the Bible. In *History of Religions* 4,3:10.

Daly, Mary. 1987. *Wickedary*. Boston: Beacon Press.

Freud, S. 1931. Female sexuality. In *No Man's Land*, Sandra M. Gilbert and Susan Gubar, eds. New Haven, Conn.: Yale University Press, 1988.

Gilbert, Sandra M. and Gubar, Susan. 1988. *No Man's Land*. New Haven, Conn.: Yale University Press.

Gimbutas, Marija. 1982. *The Goddesses and Gods of Old Europe*. Berkeley, Calif.: University of California Press.

_____. 1982. Old Europe in the fifth millennium B.C. In *The Indo-Europeans in the Fourth and Third Millennia*, Edgar C. Polomé, ed. Ann Arbor, Mich.: Karoma Publishers.

_____. 1983. PIE in 1975. In *Journal of Indo-European Studies* 2:293.

Gleason, Judith. 1987. *Oya*. Boston: Shambhala.

Goff, Beatrice Laura. 1963. *Symbols of Prehistoric Mesopotamia*. New Haven, Conn.: Yale University Press.

Grahn, Judy. 1984. *Another Mother Tongue*. Boston: Beacon Press.

H. D. 1982. *Notes on Thought and Vision*. San Francisco: City Lights Books.

Irigaray, Luce. 1985. *Speculum of the Other Woman*. Ithaca, N.Y.: Cornell University Press.

Le Guin, Ursula K. 1986. She unnames them. In *Hear the Silence*, Irene Zahava, ed. New York: Crossing Press.

Lerner, Gerda. 1986. *The Creation of Patriarchy*. New York: Oxford University Press.

Lloyd, Seton. 1956. Early Anatolia. In *Neolithic Cultures of Western Asia*, Purushottam Singh, ed. London: Seminar Press, 1974.

_____. 1978. *The Archaeology of Mesopotamia*. London: Thames and Hudson.

Meador, Betty De Shong. 1986. The thesmophoria: A women's ritual. In *Psychological Perspectives* 17, 1: 35.

_____. *Three Poems by Enheduanna*. Unpublished translations.

Mellaart, James. 1967. *Çatal Hüyük*. New York: McGraw-Hill.

Ortner, Sherry B. 1974. Is female to male as nature is to culture? In *Women, Culture, and Society*, Michelle Rosaldo and Louise Lamphere, eds. Stanford, Calif. Stanford University Press.

Parrot, André. 1961. *Sumer—The Dawn of Art*. New York: Golden Press.

Rohrlich-Leavitt, Ruby. 1980. State formation in Sumer and the subjugation of women. In *Feminist Studies* 6,1:76–102.

Singh, Purushottam. 1974. *Neolithic Cultures of Western Asia*. London: Seminar Press.

The Archetypal Feminine:
A Response to Betty Meador,
"Forward into the Past"

Lionel Corbett

When Murray Stein asked me to reply to Meador's paper, I was immediately reminded of a psychoanalytic meeting I attended a few years ago, in which, at one point, there were five gray-haired men on the panel discussing female sexuality. I was very aware of how ludicrous this was and I was concerned about being placed in a similar position here. As I wondered about my own connection to the goddess, however, I recalled that one of the most powerful dreams of my life involved a feminine figure of archetypal proportions, which allowed me to connect experientially with this topic. I would like to tell you this dream, and then report dreams of the goddess from various patients, in order to indicate how the goddess seems to manifest herself today, for comparative purposes with her classical imagery as presented by Meador.

Dream: *I see a very old, stooped women. She is extremely hag-*

Lionel Corbett, M.D., graduate of the University of Manchester and the University of Southhampton in England, is Clinical Director of the Inpatient Unit in the Department of Psychiatry at Rush-Presbyterian-St. Luke's Medical Center and a diplomate Jungian analyst at the C. G. Jung Institute of Chicago.

gard and sad, but her face is remarkable in its expression of intense suffering combined with transcendence. It is a dark brown, Asian face, intensely lined. She is dressed in long robes, of a dark white or gray color, reminiscent of a shroud but also a nun's habit. They have a fluted design. I realize that as a child, she had her legs broken by her parents to make her a better beggar for their use. I feel horrified. She has suffered all her life because of this crippling — her legs were permanently damaged — but finally, she has truly transcended her suffering, avoiding none of it. Suddenly, I am holding the actual instrument which was used to break her legs. It looks like a thin, hard, baseball bat; it, too, has a fluted design along its length, exactly like that of her robes.

Now the problem of this figure is quite different from that of the figures in the dreams that Meador mentions. I believe that this kind of feminine dream figure seems to widen the basis of our discussion about the nature of the archetypal feminine as it appears in dreams. My dream addresses the comment of Meador's that what the culture is missing is "the support of the fully realized power of the archetypal feminine" which she suggests means the absence of vital symbols of the feminine, e.g., the sacred vulva. Certainly in the poetry of Inanna, the sexual symbolism is clear:

> As for me, Inanna,
> Who will plow my vulva?
> Who will plow my high field?
> Who will plow my wet ground?
> (Wolkstein and Kramer 1983, p. 37)

—and so on. We are reminded of the comment of Santayana that religion is the poetry we believe in. The numinosity of the vulva is still a psychological fact. It has always inspired awe and fear, and continues to do so.

The imagery of the Neolithic goddess is replete with depictions of genitalia, birth and breasts, nurture and reproduction. I want to suggest that today such imagery, while still relevant, is being broadened in our own era to include issues that are essentially feminine but cannot be simply defined within the traditional cultural stereotype of the feminine as nurturing, passive, receiving, etc. The goddess is now presenting us with much more complex material. She has to do this because we have used our technology to deal with our fear of the feminine — hence, for instance, the abuse of women's bodies by some gynecologists. Synchronistically, as I went back to Kramer's work to read this poetry again, a patient who is a woman gynecologist complained bitterly to me how women with cancer of the vulva and other pelvic cancers were being treated by excessive surgery, by male gynecologists who seemed to have no idea what these unnecessarily radical operations did to women. This, of course, makes one realize that the fear associated with this part of women's anatomy is still alive and well. That the fear of the feminine is still present is evident from imagery such as an early dream of my own, in which under the baleful influence of a woman, I am paralyzed below the waist, so that I can only crawl along the floor using my arms. Because in our hubris we think that through our science we have understood the female body, the mystery of the archetypal feminine now has to assume other forms.

My dream of the suffering woman is a religious dream which depicts part of this mystery. Apparently the goddess still likes a poetic or religious approach rather than a technological one. Meador asks what is the effect of 25,000 years of religion oriented around the archetypal feminine — what imprint has it left on the psyche? This dream helps to answer her question — it is a dream about both embodiment and transcendence, about male Self-images (Christ and Buddha) and the female body. It is also about the abject failure of two major, male-dominated traditions to prevent child abuse. The essence of the dream is a religious problem which includes the problem of exploitation, of the status of women religious, of narcissistic parenting, of transcendence of suffering, and so on. Here we are still dealing with life, death and nurturing, but nowadays, the goddess in the culture is known by or is present within the child's need for mirroring (an anima function), as the good-enough mother, as the empathic selfobject or crudely as the good or bad breast. We should also not forget the idea that dreams point forward, toward future developments of the personality and the culture, so that not only is there "a long journey back into the matrix of ancestral female orientation," there are important dreams which show the way forward, toward the future recognition of the importance of the archetypal feminine within our culture.

In this context, the only dream I recall which speaks to the question of gender and the Self is a complex dream which clearly describes the Self as androgynous (Corbett 1987). However, as Meador's patient's dream indicates, the old church is burning down, and the new dispensation is sure to reveal further such material that may not necessarily be cast in the imagery of ancient religious forms. But it may include such material in modern form. A Catholic woman patient of mine who is conflicted about whether sex and the body are sinful, dreamt that the bread given to her at Mass contained raisins: the Dionysian element also becomes sacramental in her dream. The dream of a woman priest also indicates a radical change in the structure of the Church.

Dream: *I am giving the Eucharist. I come to the word "doubt." I can hardly read it because the light is so dim. I turn the prayer book towards the light and read the word. Then I notice the church stone walls are falling in because a big wind is coming. I turn around because I suddenly am afraid and I see behind me Sophia in her robes. I say to her, "Where shall we stand when the Big Wind comes?" She says, "I don't know, but we shall stand." I see a woman parishioner flee the congregation in fear. I continue with the Eucharist. I look at the windows and see that they have no glass in them and so I know that there will be no blood shed when the wind comes. I continue but I am no longer afraid because Sophia is behind me. But the Big Wind is coming.*

Meador mentions the need to distinguish between re-emergence of the ancestral feminine and the personal shadow. They are not always distinguishable, as the following dream of a woman physician reveals.

Dream: *I enter the room of a woman patient and find her lying on the floor next to her bed in the fetal position. She is weak, emaciated, and two-thirds of her body is covered with bruises where she has been beaten. I understand that she has spent all of her life in jail and has been severely abused. She also has a reputation for being dangerous, combative and out of her head. I lift her frail body into my arms and turn her on her back so that I may listen to her heart. I lay her down gently. I can see the terror in her face and I have the sense that she is like a vicious animal and may attack me at any time. I ask her permission to listen to her heart, then gently lift her gown, revealing no more than is necessary to place the stethoscope so that she will not feel invaded or feel that I do not respect her privacy. Her face and entire body soften with relief and she allows the examination. I come away with the awareness that she is very ill and that she will be my first psychiatric patient—someone I must see through to the end. Her name is Mary and I realize that she is, in fact, the Blessed Virgin Mary.*

Here is a dream in which the mother goddess appears in an abused, beaten form, and the beginning of her redemption is the tender, loving care with which she is received by the dreamer who will attempt to heal her wounds. At the same time, of course, the imagery depicts the kind of treatment that this woman herself received during her childhood, her need to care for this abused aspect of her wounded feminine nature, and the archetypal feminine.

What then *is* this feminine nature? What we call "feminine" is typically related symbolically or by analogy to the female body. The female body is cyclic, gives birth, contains, makes milk, etc., and when a man symbolically or psychologically does these things we call such behavior "feminine." I suggest that one of our future tasks in order to clarify the other meanings of femininity is to look for these processes in subtle forms. Aspects of the archetypal feminine have to be approached in their modern guise, or in subtle manifestations which are not as obvious as in archaic goddess imagery. For example, Meador stresses the cyclicity of women's physiology, and this, of course, is a major factor psychologically and biologically, but it is also true of the feminine in men, especially when we consider cyclic time. The experience of time is quintessentially related to the body — the body experiences time; incarnation means movement into time. Men are also able to experience periodicity, and this is not usually mentioned as an anima function because it is subtle, but there is a connection between the anima and the goddess. For example, to use an astrological metaphor, in my birth chart, I have a Cancer ascendent, so that the moon is the ruler of the chart. I am, in fact, extremely sensitive to lunations — the cycles of new and full moons. Usually, they produce emotional emphasis in different aspects of my life, depending on the position of the lunation itself in relation to my chart. I am very tuned in to these cycles; I find myself waiting for these two- and four-week intervals almost like long gaps between breaths. I do not bleed physically, but I am often moved affectively or somatically. And since in my chart Venus is squared Saturn, I am also fated within my own soul to carry a difficult form of the tension between these two archetypal principals, Saturn/Chronos and Aphrodite. This is simply one example of the well-known fact that we are all predisposed to carry masculine and feminine tensions within us to different degrees and in different relationships to each other. I say all this simply to illustrate how the body may be one sex but the soul must always carry both principals as felt experiences and our dreams reflect this fact. We are incompletely incarnated creatures and our theory suggests that every dream attempts to move us toward incarnating a little more of the Self within a personal self which is incomplete by its nature, since it is embodied, as if the Self is trying to squeeze itself into an impossibly small container. The contrasexual is *experienced*, or carried by psyche, rather that embodied. Embodiment, of course, is necessary for us to differentiate from the archetype. But, because of the intrinsic impossibility of complete incarnation of the Self into a one-sex body, the demand for relationships is inexorable, because the Self can be experienced more fully between two people. (A discussion of homosexual relationship, although relevant, would be beyond the scope of this response.)

Meador stresses the importance of early cultures as a source of ancestor figures for modern women. She stresses that the modern woman must reorient through her connection to the unconscious feminine, and that supporting images from dreams help in this task. These do not always correspond to traditional figures. I often see the goddess present herself in the dreams of wounded women as unknown female figures who do not correspond to anyone in the dreamer's life story but who carry out astonishingly benevolent and helpful acts for the dreamer. These figures are rich, complex, and wise and provide a matrix for the modern woman to ground herself out of her own psyche even in the presence of a negative personal mother. To illustrate how important this is, one relatively healthy analysand of mine began therapy with very irregular menstrual periods. She had a terrible mother and father problem, but over a couple of years wonderfully helpful figures appeared in her dreams — and they were usually either black or Indian, or wise old women. As this material was integrated, her periods became perfectly regular. As she got in touch with her feminine roots via the dreams, her body function normalized synchronistically. However, it is very clear that a great deal of work on the image of the dark side of the goddess must first be undertaken before glimpses of her positive aspect can be seen. She appears, for instance, with modern science-fiction mythologems, as in the dream of a woman early in treatment, in the form of a plant which invades the body of a man, causing him to feel unbearable agony while his gender becomes unstable, so that he painfully and constantly changes from male to female; or, as a devil-woman, who causes such pain that the victim's body feels as if it is erupting and turning inside out. She also has the capacity to make us lose consciousness, even when she presents in a classical form, as in this dream of a severely borderline woman intensely dependent on a hostile mother.

Dream: *I am in a boat at night, floating down a narrow stream.*
There are many stars in the sky. I see the eyes of jackals staring at
me from the shore. Then I see a line in the water ahead of me.
Beyond the line, the water is light. I see the figure of a huge black
woman with six breasts standing knee deep in the water. She is
about 20 feet tall. I cannot see her face — it is above the light. She
is guarding the water. The water is lit with a beautiful white light
and looks like daylight or starlight, having a mysterious quality. I
dive out of the boat as it reaches the beginning of the light. I lose
consciousness; it feels like the right thing to do — I belong in the
light part; the water is inviting and warm and feels safe.

Bearing in mind the number of borderline people we see today, partly
as a result of the cultural neglect of the archetypal feminine, this kind
of material is a very important source of her imagery in modern women.
It is as if the goddess is seeking the transformative possibilities of our
conscious work through our acceptance and understanding in spite of
the fear she inspires. Above all, the consciousness provided by analytic
work seems to have a redeeming power if the therapist and patient can
stand the torment and torture that the dark side of the goddess inflicts
on both participants during intense analytic work. It seems to me that
neither of us can avoid the pain of this encounter, and the goddess
herself seems to provide the matrix within which her own redemption
may occur (the analytic container, dream images of the positive feminine, or the analyst as good-enough mother, for instance). A woman
patient of Jung (1967, par. 70) talks about the need to accept things as
they are, even evil, because although we fear that if we accept things
they will overpower us, this is not in fact true. We can only assume an
attitude to problems if we accept them, instead of trying to force things
to be the way we want them to be.

I want to end by reminding us that the goddess seems to have a
predeliction for announcing her presence in dreams. I think we could
make a case for the fact that, at least from a religious perspective, the
most important dream of Western civilization is the dream in which an
angel appears to Joseph to tell him that Mary's pregnancy is of the Holy
Spirit (Matt. 1:20). Fortunately, Joseph obeyed the dream and took
care of Mary. If he had not done so, the course of Western civilization
would have been different. Eventually, of course, the worship of Isis
was transferred to Mary as an underground current within Christianity,
and then toward the end of the Christian era, in 1950, the dogma of
the assumption of Mary was pronounced. Jung pointed out the impor-

tance of this event. It is of archetypal importance because it finally redeems the body and the feminine after millenia of neglect, reconciles body and spirit, and is a clear replacement of the ancient goddess as Queen of Heaven. Synchronistically, with her return, the body itself is now beginning to attain eternal life: witness the resurgence of interest in ecology and body therapies in the last 30 years. From the viewpoint of the overall mythology, the progression from serpent in the Garden of Eden to Queen of Heaven represents a considerable transformation of the goddess. In fact, this development might be seen as a parallel, if underground, motif within the unconscious history of Christianity.

I think I'm on the right track with these remarks because of a dream I had on the day I finished this writing — I was a woman with x-ray vision, like Superwoman, and with it I looked through several walls of a building, into a woman some distance away, and was able to see what she was really like.

References

Corbett, L. 1987. Transformation of the image of God leading to self initiation into old age. In *Betwixt and Between: Patterns of Masculine and Feminine Initiation*. L. C. Mahdi, ed. Peru, Ill.: Open Court Publishers.

Jung, C. G. 1967. Commentary on the secret of the golden flower. In *Collected Works* 13:47–48. Princeton, N.J.: Princeton University Press.

Wolkstein, D. and Kramer, S. N. 1983. *Inanna Queen of Heaven and Earth*. New York: Harper Colophon Books.

Dream and Psychodrama*

Helmut Barz
Translated by Diana Drachler

With respect to the practice of psychotherapy there are not many
key sentences about which we Jungian analysts display such unanimity
as Sigmund Freud's assertion that the "royal road" into the unconscious
is by means of dreams. Hour after hour we strive to travel this road
together with the patient, impressed ever anew by its sovereign perfec-
tion, which is to be sure not a result of our efforts, but is rather a
natural product of the unconscious.

With further therapeutic experience we become increasingly certain that careful interaction with dreams can bring about expansion of
consciousness, relief of symptoms, even healing. This experience is so
striking that it appears to me completely understandable — though not
praiseworthy — if some Jungian therapists, for instance, lose sight of the
phenomenon of transference to such a degree that they hardly know
how to deal with the patient who does not dream. Such colleagues
often have an outstanding talent for working with dreams, and they

---

Helmut Barz, M.D., is president of the Curatorium of the C. G. Jung Institute in Zürich
and has a private practice in Zürich. He is the author of numerous books and articles in
German and of the forthcoming *For Men, Too* in English translation.

*I dedicate this work to my late psychodrama teacher, Dean Elefthery, in grateful
remembrance.

will in general only be able to hold such patients who are "talented," who are productive dreamers.

Nevertheless the fundamental significance of dreams for our type of therapy should not justify that formula one hears occasionally from outside observers and, fortunately only rarely, even from Jungians: namely, that Jungian psychotherapy = dream interpretation.

This formulation seems false, not only in its narrowness and exclusivity, but still more through the use of the term "dream *interpretation*," which lays a one-sided emphasis on the intellectual, that is, upon the "interpretive" aspect of our work.

Dream interpretation in C. G. Jung's view should thus not be considered only an intellectual exercise in translation; rather, the work should be carried just as much by intuition, sensation, and feeling as by thinking.

Indeed, I must here recall a question that was put to me more that 20 years ago at the Jung Institute in Zürich in the examination subject "dreams" (which I luckily answered correctly). The question was: Which function is the most important for the interpretation of dreams? The answer: All four are equally important.

Regarding this requirement, just as much unanimity should exist as exists regarding our theoretical foundation: as an emanation of the Self, the dream demands total response on the part of the dreamer. Speaking practically, this means that analyst and analysand not only contemplate the dream content, but also take into consideration its "feeling tone," question its perceivable details, and intuitively "circle" around it.

This is how we have learned our craft, this is how we attempt to carry it out, and this is how, *deo condecente*, it works its helpful effects.

I do not mean to imply that this classical type of dream interpretation — dialogue *about* the dream — should be replaced by another type of dream perception, that is, the complete entering *into* the dream in group work. The realization of the dream in psychodrama, which I will introduce briefly, is a *complement* to conventional dream interpretation, a complement which represents an essential enrichment.

In what sense then could the analytical discussion about the dream be enriched? Or, put another way: to what extent is impoverishment inherent in the analytical dialogue?

I will describe a dream. An unmarried woman about 40 years old finds herself in the dream opposite an older, slightly vulgar but nevertheless congenial woman, who apparently is a madam gently urging the dreamer to work in her establishment. In this, she describes in particular the friend relationships that prevail among her employees and which contribute greatly to creating the most pleasant "work climate" imaginable. Already during the dream, the dreamer wonders about the fact that she doesn't feel in any way repelled, and that, in this rather "questionable" old dame, certain characteristics of her physical mother as well as characteristics of her best friend are recognizable.

I have never conducted a discussion with the aim of interpreting this dream. I am acquainted with it only as the object of a psychodrama. But I imagine that even an intensive and clever interpretation of this dream would be a bit impoverished in comparison with what resulted in psychodrama. In the interpretation, one could have collected associations to prostitutes, to the bordello, to the mother, to the friend, to hetero- and homoerotic attitudes of the dreamer, to her understanding of herself as a woman, her fantasies, longings, fears, hopes — and so forth. No doubt both analysand and analyst would have engaged their feelings in this effort, and insights may have resulted in transference and countertransference phenomena. But at the end of the hour, out of a bordello and a madam, would have come words, recognitions, thoughts. One could have spoken in paraphrasing formulations about the accepting of one's own femininity, about the Great Mother or about *hieros gamos*. I don't doubt in the least that this interpretation or one completely different would have been profitable to the dreamer.

But wouldn't she also have lost something? On a different level from the intellectual, an impoverishment may have crept in, namely, the replacement of a shimmering, living symbol by a relatively confining thought.

As mentioned, this dream was not interpreted, but given form by means of psychodrama. We created a somewhat plush, slightly shabby but nevertheless cozy salon, with a corridor from which doors to mysterious rooms branched off. A madam of flesh and blood appeared, and the dreamer finally demanded to see her worthy colleagues. Out came four merry young girls, who attended to the dreamer lovingly and knowingly, chatting with amusement among themselves. They told her how simple, how lucrative and even from time to time enjoyable her employment in the care of the madam would be. The dreamer unmistakably enjoyed being together with the girls, turned finally to face the "mother" of the whole thing and said, "All right, good, then send me a man."

I could (or would like to) imagine that some serious Jungian colleagues will protest at the use of this example. Of course, moral remonstrations — instigation to prostitution! — are presumably not to be expected at this level, but what about respect for the dream? Will it not be arbitrarily altered, instead of being subjected to an expert interpretation? Won't the unconscious material of the dreamer be distorted and almost desecrated in this way, in that others begin to play with it? And, above all, where is the *vas hermeticum* of the analytical relationship? Wouldn't through the participation of an entire group of individuals, a dream proceeding within an individuation process be turned into its opposite, namely, into a backward movement in the direction of something collective?

Before I go into this question by describing the psychodramatic procedure with dreams, I would like once more to emphasize that, with this example, I wish to indicate a possible enrichment of classical dream interpretation, without making a plea to do away with it.

The psychodrama groups with which my wife and I work consist of 10 or 12 persons, more or less half women and half men, and as diverse as possible with respect to age. All group members are, or were, in analysis, either Jungian or another type. The group meets once a week for two and a half hours and generally remains together for a long time, two to three years, as unchanged as possible in its composition.

At the beginning of each session, one person announces his or her wish to be "Protagonist," that is, who would like to give form to his or her psychodrama. The Protagonist is completely free to choose the theme to be performed. It can be an acute problem, a specific fear, or a vague tension. It can be a traumatic childhood experience, an expectation for the future, or a dream. While the Protagonist speaks initially to the remaining members of the group, who are gathered around in a circle on chairs, he or she will be asked after a certain period of time to go around the inside of the circle, accompanied by the director and the co-director. From now on until the end of the psychodrama, the co-director maintains a position behind the Protagonist and strengthens his or her ego through consciously reflected identification, protecting but also — when necessary — calling a point in question. The co-director (in this case, a woman) speaks as "Auxiliary-Ego" in the first person through the Protagonist, and each time she speaks, she lays her hands upon his or her shoulders. Insofar as the Auxiliary-Ego not only draws upon training and experience as an analyst, but also upon a great deal of empathy and intuition, the Auxiliary-Ego becomes a decisive therapeutic agent of the psychodrama. She questions the persona, supports or protects the ego, offers — with great caution — aspects of the shadow to consciousness, and takes over, as a Protagonist once expressed it, the function of guardian angel.

For the director (in this case, a man), the continuous alertness and helpful accompaniment of the Auxiliary-Ego eases his burden considerably. During the phase in which the Protagonist goes around the circle, he can concentrate, by precisely aimed questions, on recognizing the deeper levels of the problem presented by the Protagonist, while simultaneously searching for a suitable scene in which it would be possible to represent this problem dramatically. Occasionally there results for the first time in connection with this search a dream that suddenly comes back to the Protagonist, and which the director selects as the object of the psychodrama to follow.

The director proceeds in this initial phase in a way hardly different from analysis: he gathers information, the ideas and associations of the Protagonist, observing his or her emotions and affects, registers his or her resistances, and tries to conceptualize the unconscious background of the events taking place in the foreground. The only thing he must achieve, in addition to the usual activity of the listening and questioning analyst, is to refrain from making a verbal interpretation. In place of that — entrusting himself to the transcendent function — he seeks out a symbolic scene in which the current problem of the Protagonist can be represented. This scene can be a real, remembered scene or an imagined one. It can have a completely everyday character, but it must offer the possibility of serving not only as an example for the conscious problem, but also as projection carrier for the unconscious background constellation.

If a dream is to be made into the object of a psychodrama, as in my earlier example, the director is relieved of his most difficult task. He can leave unfolding events up to the dream, to the Protagonist supported by the Auxiliary-Ego, and to the participation of the group. I will describe how this takes place using my original example.

The Protagonist had declared right from the start that she wanted to work with this dream. She could already *interpret* it (she had been in Jungian analysis for years), but she felt that it contained more than one could extract by means of interpretation.

As in any psychodrama, the scene is "set" by the Protagonist. She describes in great detail the questionable elegance of the salon, furnishes it with small tables, various chairs and a sofa, describes pictures on the walls, the carpet, the drapes, etc.

In that she does this all concretely, and because she doesn't simply describe from a distance but actually acts in space, the stage for the dream takes on a physical presence that is otherwise not possible. The Auxiliary-Ego asks, "How do I feel here now?" The Protagonist lets herself fall comfortably into an armchair, withdraws into herself for a short time, and finally says, "It's nice here. It's exciting." A little later, "Anyway, it smells a bit too much of perfume."

The director asks if the Protagonist is now ready to meet the madam. She needs still a little more time, but then steps out of the created stage set and chooses a player for the role of the madam. She looks over all the women present and says to one, "I thought actually about you, you are similar to my mother, but . . . ."She chooses then a woman who is considerably younger than herself and "leads" this one "into the role." For this she places herself behind the chosen madam who is seated on a chair, lays her hands on her shoulders and speaks in the first person: "I'm the boss here. I'm 56 years old." And now out of the dream figure is generated a detailed imagination, in which fantasies are mixed about how life would be for a madam who combines characteristics of her own mother and her friend. After a while the Auxiliary-Ego asks, "Why actually have I called this Monica [the name I have given to the dreamer] to this place? What do I want from her?" The Protagonist considers a while, then says, "I think she is really sexy. She would fit in here. We'll see."

Finally the Protagonist will be carefully led out of inducing identification with the dream figure, sits opposite the madam in the salon, and has the discussion with her that she previously had reported as an element of the dream. Astounding in this is the convincing genuineness with which the person playing the madam embodied this role. She reproduces in the finest detail not only the qualities with which she was earlier charged by the Protagonist, but enriches these with convincing, heretofore undiscovered madam characteristics. Thus, one experiences her response not only as a complete taking over of projections (of the Protagonist), but also as a person gripped by the archetype of the Great Matchmaker.

As the Protagonist snaps at the madam, "What do you think you are doing, anyway? I have had a friend for years, I am earning well in my profession—what would I be doing here?" the director then arranges an "exchange of roles." The two women exchange chairs; the Protagonist is now the madam, whose player takes over the place of the Protagonist and repeats the last sentence. The Protagonist as madam smiles in a superior way and says, "My dear child, don't kid yourself. You are looking for adventure just as much as the others—you would like also to get out of your prison sometime." Again an exchange of roles. The Protagonist (again herself) says, "Fresh." Auxiliary-Ego (behind her) says, "Really?" The Protagonist (smiling) admits, "All right. There's a bit of truth in what she says."

The madam now paints the good life among the young girls in her employ, and here the Protagonist departs suddenly from the original dream plot, turns to the director and says, "Please, they should all come!" The director asks, "Who should play them?" The Protagonist responds, "All of them." The director gives the remaining four women a wave and the delightful scene, completely created out of the fantasy of the participating women, which I have already briefly described to you, takes place.

The dream plot, in which the "sisters" or co-workers are only mentioned but had not actually appeared "on stage," is abandoned at this point. But this does not happen in any forced way or by following a conscious intention; rather, it crystallizes out of the intensive feeling-oriented representation of the dream, to a certain extent as an active further dreaming of the dream, or even as active imagination.

As the Protagonist then half impishly, half fearfully, but in any case out of her deepest heart, says, "All right, good, then send me a man," the director brings the staged part of the psychodrama to an end. This was not due to prudery, but out of the feeling (in which the Protagonist and the Auxiliary-Ego concurred) that here a conclusive high point was reached, beyond which the material of this dream would have let itself be played out further only in a forced way.

In any psychodrama the greatest consideration and caution — on the part of all participating — is granted the Protagonist, and this same deferential respect is granted, of course, also to the Protagonist's dream.

Before I turn to the question of whether it is advisable to share something so intimate as a dream with more than one person (thus, before I question the function of the group in psychodrama), I would like to consider briefly dreams in general.

It seems certain that dreaming represents nothing less that a physiological prerequisite for psychic health. I say "dreaming" because, with respect to the basic psychohygienic function of the production of images while asleep, it does not depend on our remembering these products which we call dreams, let alone whether they are processed in consciousness in some way.

But it seems just as certain to us that these dreams, over and beyond their basic health-maintaining function, also contain information and — as we surmise — this is information of great significance that arises out of the unconscious and is apparently addressed to consciousness. In any case, consciousness is able to fashion out of this information "messages," which often prove themselves useful in the highest degree, because they complement the attitude of consciousness, call it in question, or refute it—but in any case challenge it in a fruitful way.

The question regarding the origin of this superior wisdom which manifests itself in dreams is answered in Jungian psychology, as mentioned earlier, with reference to the hypostatized "Self." It remains unexplainable why the messages emanating from the highest psychic authority are, for the most part, formulated in such a coded, sometimes archaic picture language, but the centuries-old practice of dream interpretation (which didn't originate with analysts!) shows that only the effort of the interpretation permits the message to be recognized in all its worth, even that this worth is the more highly esteemed, the more difficult it is to achieve. In this it has, again for centuries, proven useful if the dreamer does not attempt solely on the basis of his own resources to grasp the message of the dreams, but draws upon the help of other, more experienced and wiser individuals. The dream can thus bring about communications, not only between the unconscious and consciousness, but also between the one affected by the dream and other individuals who—precisely because they are not immediately affected—can be helpful with the work of "translation" and interpretation.

The double nature of the dream—the image that can be perceived by the senses on the one hand and the obscure aspect which demands the interpretative discussion on the other hand—in our century has called into being the vocation of the professional dream-interpreter once again. Even Sigmund Freud and C. G. Jung, who were in a position to interpret their own dreams, did not disdain to lay their dreams before one another occasionally.

While Freud was of the opinion that a dream can be completely translated in a comprehensible language, Jung recognized the true symbolic dimension of the dream. It lies in the fact that many dreams evade an unambivalent translation because they, in accordance with the nature of the living symbol, have assumed at least temporarily the best form of expression.

A respectful and careful circumambulation of the dream symbol—calling upon all four functions (intuition, sensation, feeling, thinking)—certainly might be able to arrive in the proximity of its meaning, but there remains an uninterpretable remnant that, perhaps precisely because of its feeling-inducing unfathomability, represents the most important message of the dream.

Not a few of us have associated ourselves with the Jungian school precisely for this reason, because here a space is provided for the unexplainable, to which nevertheless the highest rank is given. One should imagine that we would, for this reason, take care to promote an interaction with our own dreams and the dreams of our patients, characterized by insight into the unexplainable nature of the symbols and by the readiness to permit the symbol its effectiveness, without deadening it with concepts.

But I have the impression that we occasionally stray rather far from this pious respectfulness. In fact it is not only our patients who demand a clear interpretation of their dreams, but also our own theories which not infrequently lead us to set in the place of the living dream symbol, in place of real coin, a worthless halfpenny, which we can easily pull from our pocket with self-satisfied conviction. This is unfortunately also true even when we, in our efforts at interpretation, do our utmost to avoid Jungian jargon. In this we remain true to the Western conviction that concepts and signs are more useful and effective than symbols, because they can be assembled more or less into a system of thought, whereas symbols remain imbedded in the vague and feeling-toned.

Certainly we will make every effort to resist the temptation to intellectualize in dream interpretation, keeping in mind as an example the following passage from C. G. Jung's "Psychology of the Transference."

> Others strive for intellectual understanding and want to skip impatiently the level of mere happening [author's translation]. And when they have understood, they think they have done their full share of realization. That they should also have a *feeling-relationship* to the contents of the unconscious seems strange to them or even ridiculous. Intellectual understanding and aestheticism both produce the deceptive, treacherous sense of liberation and superiority which is liable to collapse if feeling intervenes. Feeling of course binds one to the reality and meaning of symbolic contents, and these in turn impose binding standards of ethical behavior from which aestheticism and intellectualism are only too ready to emancipate themselves. (1946, pp. 279–280)

For this reason we let dreams or individual dream symbols be given form by our patients. We let them draw, paint or model, we encourage some patients to active imagination and are enthusiastic when some patients occasionally feel impelled to give expression to a dream content in dance or pantomime.

I find it astounding for this reason, that a tradition of dramatic representation of dreams in Jungian therapy was not established long ago. Their dramatic structure, discovered by Jung, should have long since invited their dramatic representation, especially in view of Jung's above-quoted warning about the temptation to skip impatiently the "level of mere happening." Where could the "feeling relationship" to the "symbolic contents" of the dream be experienced more intensely than in giving it life once again in dramatic form?

One could imagine that quite a great many Jungian therapists, if they had had the opportunity to experience even a single successful dream enactment, would share in our view that while certainly not a "classical" dream interpretation, it is very much a Jungian mode of respectful and total experience with the symbols of the dream.

Recently I was asked by a Jungian colleague whether the type of dream work that my wife and I attempt in psychodrama could not be carried out in individual analysis. I won't go into a discussion of the experience that one can actually have within a limited frame. Rather, I quote this question as being symptomatic of the reservations of some colleagues: the method of psychodrama seems to them to be completely acceptable, but they glimpse the "fly in the ointment" in the fact that this method is utilized within a group.

The reservations against therapeutic work in groups that exist within the Jungian school can clearly be traced back to C. G. Jung himself, who—scarcely discriminating between formless masses and therapeutic groups—had everything possible of a disdainful nature to say in this connection. He nevertheless conceded, "In my opinion group therapy is only capable of educating the *social* human being" (letter to Hans A. Illing, Jan. 26, 1955).

"Educating the social human being" presumably also takes place in a psychodrama group, as a welcome side effect of working together with a small number of individuals in a creative effort directed toward the individuation process of a single individual. Jung's conviction, rooted in the "group psychology" of the turn of the century, that "when a hundred intelligent heads are united in a group the result is one big fathead," is hardly valid for one hundred heads. For a dozen individuals it most certainly is not valid.

So let us turn to the function and significance of the group in dream drama. The Protagonist lays her dream not before *one* individual, in order to interpret the dream with his support; rather, she shares it with a group—in which there are two professional interpreters as directors—in order to execute the dream completely by performing it.

She probably has already known these individuals for a long time as a result of intensively working with them, and may rely not only upon the absolute discretion of the group, but can also count on the fact that all those present will support her to the best of their abilities. She knows, too, that she will not be forced or talked into anything, and that she herself (or her Auxiliary-Ego) can interrupt or alter the course of the proceeding at any time, should it become too much for her. She knows that all the other members of the group have exposed themselves or will expose themselves in the same way in other sessions, and she has experienced within the group a trusting closeness that is seldom encountered elsewhere.

Should it not be permissible to regard such a group — which I have not represented in an idealized way — with the same right as the *vas hermeticum*, as we do the relationship between analysts and analysands? And if it proves to be the case that the dream challenges communication, is the communication between two in any case more worthwhile than that among several who know each other well and who acknowledge the individuality of the one? In addition, in dream drama the presence of several individuals offers the extraordinary possibility to distribute the symbolic contents of the dream among several projection carriers.

What ensues upon the choice of the role players as a result of unconsciously steered coincidences is in almost every case an astonishing indication of the affinity between the projection carrier and the projected; sometimes it even has the character of a synchronistic phenomenon.

The person to be played stems on the one hand out of the dream of the Protagonist, he or she carries on the other hand characteristics of the real person whom the dream uses — who is nevertheless for his or her part re-formed due to the projections of a dreamer — and, finally, the dream figure is transferred from the Protagonist to the player. Fortunately, these complicated mechanisms are not premeditated on the part of the players; they occur spontaneously within the strictly adhered-to rules of the psychodrama.

As soon as the role players begin to play, they unavoidably bring conscious and unconscious aspects of their personalities to bear, which, given that exactly these people were selected as projection carriers, they were also challenged to do.

The interaction between the Protagonist and the one or several role players takes place on the conscious level according to the text of the dream. Unconsciously this interaction will nevertheless be so strongly affected by the symbolic content of the dream that an expansion of the dream text can result. This is not brought about consciously, but is rather directed by the unconscious, which dreams the dream further as a consequence of the enrichment provided by one or the other co-players.

The co-players thus unconsciously potentiate the functions which the analyst has within analysis: they bring themselves, their ideas, their amplifications and, above all, their feelings, into the proceeding — to be sure not, like the analyst, sitting passively in an armchair, but rather, by actively playing upon the stage of the dream.

It hardly requires mentioning that both directors must register these interactions as sharply and analytically as is possible, in order to prevent an endangering of the Protagonist through the various possibilities which are at the disposal of the psychodrama technique. This could, for example, happen if the Protagonist is pulled unwittingly into the complex of one of the co-players, turning or allowing the dream to be turned in the direction of wish-fulfillment, or that he acts out his transference instead of representing the dream, and so forth.

On the other hand, it is astounding with what certainty the Protagonist in general discriminates the genuine from the false. He or she can, for example, interrupt a role player in the middle of a sentence, exchange roles with her or him, and put right the "false" contribution.

Empathy and a capacity for complete involvement are expected in large measure from the role player, so that frequently he or she is gripped to the same extent and, at the end of the play, is just as exhausted as the Protagonist. For this reason, every group member called upon by the Protagonist to play a role will be asked by the leader if he or she is ready and able to take over a given role, which can, for example, be that of a murderer or the victim of a murder. It very occasionally happens that a chosen group member must refuse to take over a role — which is then always respected. Never, however, will a psychodrama be ended without the respective role players and the Auxiliary-Ego being "changed back" into themselves. This is always accomplished with the same formula: "You are again X or Y," which occasionally needs to be repeated. This ritual is of the utmost importance especially following a dream drama, as the role player was for a period of time the embodiment of a dream symbol of the Protagonist. That it has to do with an experience as potentially dangerous as it is beneficial also to the role player, should be as clear as the extraordinary responsibility which the directors of such a proceeding take upon themselves.

But what happens with those members of the group who do not take an active part in the dramatic action? Do they, as passive observers, introduce an element of voyeurism which does injury to the respect demanded by the confrontation with the dream?

There are, in psychodrama in general and in dream drama in particular, no passive observers. Those who have taken over no role are active witnesses and also contribute to the shaping of the proceeding. Without their emotional and intellectual participation, that physically perceptible tension which charges the psychodrama space in an almost magical way would never come into being. The outer requirements for summoning this *participation mystique* are given by the strict and continuously reenacted rules governing the flow of the psychodrama, which has an almost liturgical, or ritualistic, character. The energy of the content, which draws all present under its spell, is the symbolic power of the dream which we experience and conceive of as a manifestation of the Self.

Thus, in psychodrama the Self is never projected onto the group, as some Jungians have suspected. Rather, in working together to give form to the dream symbol, something of the autonomous dynamic of the Self is experienced, which can never be confused with the dynamic of the group.

Those psychodramas which do not have dreams as objects are able also to exercise a powerful effect on *all* members of the group for the same reason, because, insofar as they are well led, they always lead back in the final analysis to archetypal situations. In dream dramas the archetypal dimension is already given by the dream text, and the participation of several group members makes it completely clear that here not only personal, but also collective, archetypal motifs are represented and experienced. This feeling of *tua res agitur* ("this pertains to you") that the dream drama also conveys to the outwardly passive group members is the basis for the so-called "doubling," to which all members who have no role to play are summoned at all times. This doubling consists of the fact that everyone who has no role to play can step behind the Protagonist or one of the figures of the dream at any time, place hands upon the shoulders of this one or that one, and can then speak through him or her. The sense of the doubling does not lie in giving an intellectual commentary on the situation. Rather, the doubling provides a possibility, out of this identification with the Protagonist or with a dream figure, to offer one's own feelings or associations. Whether these are accepted or rejected, the Protagonist alone decides with surprising assurance.

Thus the supposed "on-lookers" also work very concretely in the circumambulation of the dream and often enough make astonishing contributions, which are a further indication of the shared deep emotional effect of the Protagonist's dream upon the group.

This shared effect is then in the last part of the psychodrama — in the "sharing" — expressly made into a topic. After the Protagonist, who has built up the scene alone, "builds it down" again and has dismissed the role players from the scene, the group sits again in a circle, as in the beginning. The individual players then report to the Protagonist, who now only listens without comment, what they have experienced and felt in the roles. Only after this will they be "changed back" into themselves by the director.

The communications which the Protagonist receives from the players can be of the greatest value. Individuals who have gone into the forming of the dream mirror the Protagonist; they have experienced the dream figures as if "from the inside." This develops on the one hand out of the greatest possible objectivity — each one made a great effort to enter the inner world of the dream to the fullest. On the other hand, the subjectivity of all players is obviously also a factor in what they report, precisely because *they* were chosen by the Protagonist to submerge themselves in these roles.

The last one to report is the Auxiliary-Ego, who — still speaking out of her identification with the Protagonist — describes how she felt, thought, and experienced while in the condition of identification. This sharing places especially high demands on the director who embodies the Auxiliary-Ego. On the one hand, she now puts into words feelings that hardly reached the consciousness of the Protagonist during the dream drama, but which the Auxiliary-Ego, because of precise observation and empathy, could record. On the other hand, she sets some accents during her recapitulation of the most prominent events of the drama from the standpoint of the Protagonist. These spring from her analytic understanding of the proceeding, and for this reason these represent an indirect interpretation.

It is clear that a deficit either in talent or in the conscious assuming of responsibility on the part of the Auxiliary-Ego in this position can lead to the same harmful manipulations to which the analyst in an individual analysis also might be prone. But I have seen this danger avoided and the masterpiece realized many times.

At the conclusion of her sharing through the Auxiliary-Ego, the co-director is also "changed back" into herself, and one can imagine that it is often a relief to be returned to her own being.

The sharing now continues in a form in which each member of the group reports what the dream drama signified for him or her, what sort of effects it evoked. In this, the laying of psychological commentary or instruction on the Protagonist is strictly avoided. Here, all share with the Protagonist the ways in which they were most personally affected, reporting similar dreams of their own, comparable conflicts, or related patterns of experience.

The exhausted Protagonist now learns more about the archetypal commonalities and obligations of his or her dreams than the analyst could ever communicate in discussion. The fact that fundamental patterns of human existence are touched by every dream need not be discussed at the end of a dream drama, because it becomes evident through the sharing of all those involved.

The dream drama is distinguished by the fact that this comes about without any theoretical discussion. Psychological terms are not only forbidden, but actually superfluous. For example, the important and difficult understanding of discrimination between subject figure and object figure in dream interpretation is not required at all in the dream drama. The Protagonist *experiences* that, on the one hand, he draws the forms and spaces of his dream out of himself, in order, on the other hand, to stand opposite them, personified.

At the beginning of the next psychodrama session the Protagonist is given an opportunity to report his or her feedback. At this point, he or she is free to interpret, using psychological language if desired, what the working-through of the dream has shown him or her. Sometimes, the Protagonist prefers simply to share with the group a new dream which has occurred since the last meeting or to show the others a picture which he or she has painted. Only the two directors will attempt to form an impression, on the basis of the feedback, of how much the Protagonist could accept into consciousness from what was experienced directly in the psychodrama, and they will take it into consideration in further psychodramas.

I would like once more to repeat that both directors reflect to the best of their analytical abilities upon all the details of the drama, as well as on the total developmental process of the Protagonist and the group. Although a lowering of the Protagonist's level of consciousness begins already in the first phase of going around the circle, deepening more and more during the course of the work, and although the remaining participants are much more involved with their feelings than with their intellects, the directors must (despite all empathy on the part of the Auxiliary-Ego) maintain the highest measure of consciously reflective and distanced presence. In addition to this, my wife and I have always remained true to the rule that was instilled in us in our training: after every psychodrama we sit together for a detailed evaluation, not only in order to analyze the event, but also to provide each other with mutual critical supervision.

I don't think that the use of psychodrama as a means of dealing with dreams is a tool that is simple and undangerous to use. On the contrary, I consider it very demanding and at least as dangerous as is intensive individual analysis. But I have become convinced that it is rewarding to employ this tool as a complement to individual analysis, because it makes possible something which all too often in analysis receives short shrift: the experience of total effect through the symbol. The valid work of analysis is in making conscious the symbol to be interpreted in it finest ramifications, using speech as the essential tool. Moreno, the brilliant founder of psychodrama, tried to find precisely a way out of the "logical and syntactical form of communication," as he formulated it.

We have him to thank for making possible the visualization of symbolic images personified, to experience them directly in bearing, mimicry, gesture and voice, and to convince ourselves that they are not a product of a private dream analysis, but are, rather, present and effective in us all.

In conclusion, I would like to describe very briefly another dream drama that will perhaps shed some light on the positive significance of a group for the individual confrontation with a dream.

A young man, a loner, withdrawn, shy and sensitive, wanted to work through a dream which he had already dreamt several times. In this dream he took leave of his parents and undertook, alone, an expedition to the South Pole. Each time the dream ended with him sitting before a glacier crevice with the certain feeling that he must venture to jump into it, in order to reach something unknown but supremely important. Nevertheless, he is always unable to find the courage to do this, waking up tormented instead.

The dream was played out in psychodrama. Both parents were led in, the dreamer bade them farewell extremely coolly and arrived at the glacier crevice at the South Pole. Both directors and most certainly all group members are conscious of the enormous danger inherent in the situation, and the Auxiliary-Ego is—wordlessly—concerned to the utmost with lending the Protagonist warmth and support.

After sitting for a long time, the Protagonist says very quietly, "It won't work. I have to go home." He goes back, stands silently before his parents, then he says suddenly, "I will try again, but not alone."

He now chooses for himself two male companions for the new expedition, the one whom he liked the most in the group and another, with whom he was least sympathetic. He addresses them with their real names and asks them if they are prepared to come with him. The two agree. They play the trip to the South Pole essentially more realistically than he had done previously, taking sleds, provisions, and furs along with them, and finally they sit with him before the crevice.

The scene is enormously dense and naturalistic. All three tremble from the cold and wrap themselves in blankets, although in external reality, it is a hot summer day. Now the Protagonist says, "Wait. I will make a fire." His pantomime is so perfect that soon all three sit before a crackling fire holding their outstretched hands to the flames. A long silence ensues.

Then the Protagonist gets up very quietly, grasps the other two by the hands and they stand in a circle around the fire. Finally he says quietly but firmly, "It's good now. That was it. I did it. Thank you."

Whoever has shared in such a dream drama will never doubt that it can be a healing thing to share a dream with a group.

Reference

Jung, C. G. 1946. The psychology of the transference. In *Collected Works* 16:163–323. Princeton, N.J.: Princeton University Press, 1966.

Dreams of Nuclear Warfare: Does Avoiding the Intrapsychic Clash of Opposites Contribute to the Concrete Danger of World Destruction?

J. W. T. Redfearn

In therapy we often strive with clients to help them become more mindful of their behavior, whether their behavior is instinctive or conditioned. We hope that to a certain extent mindless, choiceless behavior, whether instinctual or learned, will be modified and enriched by archetypal and personal mental experience and by moral choice.

In this sense we can say that the unconscious is our behavior—reflex, instinctive, and conditioned—not much of which can become fully experienced in the psyche, certainly not when it is simply being enacted without internal or external holding, frustration, or inhibition.

If we envisage in this way a gradient between mindless enactment and physical experience, the dream, particularly if remembered, can help both client and therapist to move along this gradient toward mindfulness.

J. W. T. Redfearn, M.D., is a training analyst at the Society of Analytical Psychology, London, and has a private practice in London. He is the author of *My Self, My Many Selves*.

Obviously we can only integrate small quantities of the Self at a time. For many years I have been aware of the overwhelming, shattering, and unfaceable impact of the Self on the "I" and have often thought of the epileptogenic power of the experience of the Divine. The invention of the atomic bomb naturally reminds us of the dark, awesome, destructive aspects of the God image (Adler 1946).

When I was learning psychiatry, fantasies of world destruction were taken to be suggestive of a diagnosis of schizophrenia. Today it seems probable that a majority of schoolchildren do not think they will reach adulthood because the world will be destroyed before them. Most of us know with our minds that this is a fairly realistic assessment of the facts. But knowledge with our minds alone about how we are actually behaving does not, of course, mean that we are in effective emotional contact with what we are in fact doing. This seems even more true of people in power than of others, judging by behavioral criteria. Wishing to avoid disaster while at the same time edging inexorably toward it, is the sort of behavior with which we as therapists are very familiar. We cannot even regard such a state of affairs as unusual or pathological, so typical is it of ourselves and our clients. Such a contrast, between conscious intentions and actual behavior, is characteristic of social behavior and sociohistorical movements. At the present time in history, however, it does seem likely that some of us may be more aware of the unconscious psychological forces underlying historical movements than we have been before. It is certain that the dangers for mankind are incomparably greater than at any other time in history. But we do not know whether the awareness of the danger will be a factor for good or evil, such is the magnetic quality of danger.

In psychotherapy we come to a partial understanding of the dreams and fantasies which provide the leading motifs of our lives, and we realize after a time how we are continually acting out these prevailing fantasy themes without ever having been aware of the fact. In this paper I am pondering, as thousands of others have pondered, whether the same may be true now of civilized mankind as a whole. The fantasy or the vision of apocalyptic universal destruction has been part of the mythology of mankind for many thousands of years, and we are all familiar with the Judeo-Christian versions of this. Is it possible that if we no longer believe in hellfire, or the apocalyptic triumph of good over evil, the myth may simply have been pushed into the unconscious? If that were the case, there would be grave danger of it taking over behavior and being acted out concretely.

In the Judeo-Christian type of apocalyptic vision, there is com-

monly a titanic world clash between the forces of good and the forces of
evil, in which the world as we at present know it is destroyed. The forces
of good triumph, the forces of evil are destroyed. The evil perish and a
new world rises from the ashes of destruction, in which the good inherit
the blessings of a new earth. The present nuclear catastrophe, as it is
being enacted in history, is such that most sane people do not foresee a
triumph of good over evil, but a cold and largely dead world of no
triumph, no survival. This could be the most hopeful aspect of the
present highly dangerous situation. It would surely be the end if one or
the other side omnipotently believed they would win such a war.

On the other hand, as opposed to the mass apocalyptic fantasy, I
hope to show in this paper that the *personal* apocalyptic experience of
the individual, in which the subjectively titanic conflicts and clashes of
opposing psychic forces are fought out consciously, results in a strengthening and an enrichment of the person concerned. It is part of the
point of this paper to emphasize that the conflicts seen from the outsider's position seem quite personal and ordinary, and not at all world-
shattering.

There is a very real sense in which the defenses of our inner world
need to be periodically shattered and disrupted by the awareness of the
conflict of opposing forces within ourselves. But this entails taking
one's share of responsibility in moral conflict where right and wrong are
not black and white, not cut and dried. Failure to feel morally conflicted means clinging to a blind and delusory feeling of wholeness and
oneness of the self.

In so far as each one of us clings to a hope of conflict-free wholeness and harmony in ourselves, I believe we are contributing, albeit
minutely, to the catastrophic enactment of its opposite. We are inviting
God's thunderbolt in concrete form.

The enormity of the reality that confronts us is characteristic of the
omnipotent destructive fantasies of the psychotic level in ourselves and
our patients, and of the visions and fantasies sometimes produced by
hallucinogenic drugs in normal people. Dreams of world destruction,
of titanic struggles between great armies, of wars between light and
darkness, good and evil, etc., occur in analysis when such levels of the
psyche are being reached.

In the "wars of the opposites," the important opposites in therapy
are love and hate, good and evil, light and darkness, inner and outer,
large and small, omnipotence and impotence, and so on—we could all
make up our own lists. Out of the awareness of the essentially con-

flicted and paradoxical nature of the psyche, a stronger yet more tolerant and responsible self may emerge.

In the *religious* apocalyptic vision, on the other hand, good often seems to triumph over evil, for example in the Christian version of the apocalypse, when the second coming of Christ will wipe away all tears. In my view this would not represent a higher synthesis but a mere reversal or turning of the tables either in the present or the next world. As therapists we know that the worst always seems to happen when one side triumphs over another in the unconscious lives of our patients.

Stanislav Grof, in his book *Realms of the Human Unconscious*, ascribes the apocalyptic visions of his LSD therapy subjects to memories of birth experience, of passage through the birth canal, when the fetus is experiencing a struggle to survive, with mechanical crushing pressures and frequently a degree of suffocation. Grof says:

> The most important characteristic of this pattern [i.e., this phase of the birth experience] is the atmosphere of titanic struggle frequently attaining catastrophic proportions. . . . The visions typically accompanying these experiences involve scenes of natural disasters and the unleashing of elemental forces, such as exploding volcanoes, raging hurricanes . . . and various cosmic cataclysms. Equally frequent are images of similar events related to human activities . . . explosions of atomic bombs, thermonuclear reactions. . . . Some individuals describe complex catastrophic events such as . . . the destruction of Sodom and Gomorrah, the Biblical Armageddon. . . . (1976, 124)

Apart from analysis, meditation, and drug experience, religious and mythological experience can take us to these levels of the psyche. Christians are familiar with the apocalyptic visions of St. John described in the Book of Revelation. Here Christ, the sacrificial Lamb of God, is transformed into the Sword of the triumph of good over evil, the bridegroom of the mysterious marriage with the New Jerusalem, when God shall wipe away all tears, but the fearful, the unbelieving, the abominable, the murderers, the whoremongers, the sorcerers, the idolaters, the liars, shall be cast in the lake of burning brimstone (Rev. 21).

But the apocalyptic vision, at first interpreted concretely by the early Christians, was not at all confined to Christianity. Indeed we now have to see Christianity as arising out of a powerful current of Jewish apocalyptic movements of the century or two before the Christian era. The Book of Daniel is an apocalyptic vision. The prophet Elijah is surrounded by apocalyptic mythology (Mal. 4:1–5). The Apocrypha has several references to a prophesied apocalypse. And the first Dead Sea Scroll is in an important sense a war manual for the apocalyptic army of the Essenes, the Sons of Light, in their vanquishing of the Sons of

Darkness and bringing about a world ruled by the Righteous. It is a 40-year war plan whereby the Essenes were to conquer the world in three military campaigns. The second scroll is a doctrine of the two spirits, truth and error, light and darkness, good and evil, purity and impurity, together with a statement as to how the sect is to be organized and disciplined along the lines of this doctrine. The third scroll uses passages from the Old Testament Book of Habakkuk and re-reads them to refer to the Maccabean Age in which the scrolls were written (Campbell 1964, 282–285).

But whereas the Essenes were looking forward to the Messiah, the early Christians believed that the Messiah was come, and the Good News was interpreted literally in apocalyptic terms (e.g., Paul, Rom. 13:11–12, "Salvation is nearer to us than when we first believed: the night is far gone, the day is at hand").

The emphasis on light and dark may derive from Mithraic influences, where we encounter the divine fiery thunderbolt of illumination which features also in the aspect of Buddhahood known as Vajradhana, "bearing the bolt." Vajra means both "thunderbolt" and "diamond." Zeus's thunderbolt and the thunder god of the Aryans and the men of the North reflect the psychological profundity of the image of the shattering and (we hope) delusion-dispelling shock of God's illumination. The atom bomb image is closely allied. If enacted objectively, literally, and concretely, this image can destroy mankind. If interpreted subjectively and as a psychological truth, mankind might not merely survive but take a step forward in awareness and vitality.

In my patients I find that the atom bomb *image* (not to be confused with the *actual* world-destroying *use* of the atom bomb *in fact*) can represent an unfaceable psychic situation or confrontation which, when actually faced, leads on to further development of the personality. In this sense the atom bomb image functions like the shattering aspects of the divine which may be to great moral and spiritual effect. It is the epileptic experience of the divine that St. Paul encountered on the road to Damascus. The danger seems to me to be that because of the religious value of the image, an irreligious humanity may be in danger of acting the image out in a concrete way, just as the psychotic patient acts out fragments of these deep religious and mythological themes in a broken-up, concrete (i.e., nonmetaphorical) manner.

The Atom Bomb Image in Psychotherapy

For many years I have been mindful of clinical material from analytical patients in which explosions, particularly atomic ones, figured prominently. This material seems to confirm that, in analysis, an atom bomb dream image signifies a conflict or confrontation of opposing drives or parts of the self which, in the context of a containing analytical situation, tends to lead to resolution of the conflict and a higher synthesis. First I would like to describe typical examples of this synthesis. Following this I will speculate about the significance of these findings for a psychotherapeutic approach to the real social situation.

The first case history illustrates my thesis simply, indeed it puts it in a nutshell. Here the atom bomb image represents an unfaceable yet magnetic primal scene in a broad sense. It concerns a young man for whom marriage meant a *coniunctio* or a primal scene that was both exciting and fearful to the point of being unfaceable. His dream of an atom bomb coincided with having to face this primal scene, and this led to a resolution of his fear.

The young man, Peter, had had a close and loving relationship with his mother and a much more distant one with his weak and unsuccessful father. He had had many girlfriends and these included close and affectionate relationships, but he had always avoided marriage when it became an issue, and two relationships had foundered on this particular hurdle, which he had not been able to surmount. He had an elder brother whose first marriage had been unsuccessful but who was now marrying for a second time. The night before his brother was to marry, Peter dreamt of an atom bomb exploding and destroying everything around, and he awoke in a state of some anxiety, which he associated with the dream rather than his brother's wedding. But it seems reasonable, in view of his own history of anxiety preventing marriage, to assume a connection between the unfaceability of the atomic explosion and the unfaceability of marriage now being embarked upon by the brother. Peter's anxiety must however have proved faceable on this occasion, because within three months Peter was himself able to marry his current girlfriend, with whom he had been very much in love in any case. The marriage proved as happy and successful as he could have wished.

Peter loved this elder brother, in whose shadow he had on the whole lived, except for the fact that Peter was the one preferred by the mother. How much identification and how much rivalry there was in connection with the marriage cannot here be assessed. The brother's successful second marriage clearly helped Peter to face marriage and it is clear that this marriage was symbolized, before the event, by the explosion of an atom bomb. We cannot know whether the brother's marriage, and the marriage he himself both feared and wanted, represented the forbidden incestuous union with his mother, or the unfaceable union of his parents, or whether the jealousy of his brother or even of his future sister-in-law were the most important factors. All these formulations or interpretations are no doubt valid, but in a sense they are mere words attempting to describe something mightier, more explosive, less consciously faceable than any of these emotions.

For the psychoanalyst, the term "primal scene excitement" seems to convey something of the unfaceable violence with which we are dealing. For me this violence is the violence with which we are confronted when the opposites are being brought together at a deep level of the personality. If our splitting defenses, whereby the opposites are kept apart, are being abandoned, the conflict between love and hate, perhaps the mightiest conflict of all, produces energies of the appropriate order of magnitude to be symbolized by world catastrophe. A few years ago I wrote a short paper called "The Energy of Warring and Combining Opposites" (Redfearn 1978). It was about the practical problems of containing these immense psychic forces, particularly for the psychotic patient and his or her therapist, and thereby achieving a creative resolution. For the analytical psychologist, the notion of the union or the clash of opposites seems to be one that deals with the same psychic level as the psychoanalytical concepts of schizoid splitting and of the primal scene but which also acknowledges other opposing forces in the psyche of all degrees of energy and at all levels. I refer to the union and clashing of the opposites as a notion, but to the analytical psychologist it is a profound experiential truth. It was apparently the goal of alchemists to harness this energy with continence and skill, but I note that explosions were a by-product of the alchemical art. My edition of Chamber's Encyclopaedia (1959) ascribes the invention of explosives in the Western world to the irascible alchemist Roger Bacon. In Peter's case, the opposites concerned were not the male and female *coniunctio*, but his opposing feelings about the primal scene.

When we think of cosmic clashes of the gods and the titans, or the nightmare horrors of the wars of history, we can no longer thoughtlessly say that images and actions of such immensity could not possibly have to do with the child's anger or excitement. We know, for instance, that for the timid and frightened child the quarreling or violently copulating parents assume monstrous imagined forms. We know that at an early psychic level the mother seems to be experienced as a Great Mother, or as the whole world, with immense power and energy for good or evil. Thus, if we talk about the conflict between the forces of good and evil, or of light and darkness, the clash of the titans, the image of world destruction by nuclear conflict, and the conflict between the good and bad Kleinian breasts all in the same breath, we must remember that we are referring to an early and archaic psychic level where things are what they seem at that level, rather than what they seem to an adult outsider.

For my second patient, whom I call Henry, the atom bomb symbolized the imagined ego-shattering effect of confronting his unconscious murderous impulses toward the mother figure — the idealized, dominating mother figure of his childhood and as projected onto his wife and onto me as mother/analyst.

I saw Henry for about three years when he was in his late 30s. He had been referred by an older female colleague who had become exhausted by him. He suffered from severe depressions and self-destructiveness. He had made several suicide attempts and had had horrifying motorcycle accidents in one of which he had lost a foot. Two of his children had died from sudden infant death syndrome (SIDS). As I said, he idealized and was dominated by his wife and suffered form uncontrollable rages and moods. He was the most gentle and the most violent man imaginable.

At that time, I was working in a town some distance from London, and it was becoming clear that for various reasons I and my family should move to London. Three or four months before this was to take place, I told him of my decision. He came about 30 miles each way to see me at the time, and seeing me in London would have meant a round trip of about 120 miles instead of 60. He said he would discuss the matter of continuing or terminating analysis with his wife and after doing so he told me he had decided to bring our work to a close when I moved.

A few days later he dreamt of two adolescent boys manufacturing an atom bomb. In another scene of the dream, his wife was shopping in London. This dream ushered in a phase of intensely angry, murderous dreams. The chief target for murder in these dreams was the mother figure, and the murderer was himself or a shadow aspect of himself. During the ensuing weeks, he became more in touch with his anger, both in the past toward his mother and in the present situation toward his wife and toward me as the mother person who was failing him. An important observation was that his depressions improved dramatically at this time. Ten years afterward, I learned that he had decided to divorce his wife.

In Henry's case we could say that the atom bomb symbolized the dreaded confrontation with the unconsciously hated aspects of the consciously idealized, dominating mother (with the restitution, incidentally, of the undervalued and despised father). The unfaceability of this confrontation could only be appreciated if one knew him and knew how gentle and polite (and underneath how violent and angry) he was, so I will not labor the point. It may help convey the energy involved if I again stress the violence and murderousness in both his dreams and his feelings in the weeks following this atom bomb dream occurring when his wife persuaded him to terminate his analysis with me, for I was the father who was despised and ineffective as well as the abandoning mother in that situation. The atom bomb dream ushered in this intense phase of consciousness of anger and murderousness associated with the murder dreams and the lifting of his chronic depression.

Both of these very brief case histories illustrate the existence of a confrontation, even a clash, which at a deep level was felt to be destructive and indeed perhaps unthinkable; but when the emotions involved were actually confronted and felt, a forward movement was possible, marriage in the first instance, confrontation with a dominating, idealized partner in the second.

In my third example the unfaceable, as symbolized in the atom bomb dream, seemed to be confrontation with me, the analyst, and that meant facing both homosexual feelings and aggressive phallic impulses toward me.

In the transference in this example, I represented mostly the young man's father but also partly a brother figure. The patient was a young professional man who had married after several years of analysis and had had his first baby, a boy. He had come from a family of several brothers and had had close and mostly affectionate relationships both with his brothers and with his father. We had worked well together in this analysis. He had used the couch most of the time, lying supine and never looking at me although he could easily have done so. He had had an occasional dream in which I had made romping, homosexual advances toward him which he had repulsed, but there was no conscious homosexual feeling. Just before his baby was born his father died, and although he was able to do some mourning, he was disappointed at not experiencing more grief than he did.

By the time his child was a toddler and becoming more independent, he himself started talking of ending his analysis, although I felt aware of our relative failure to confront each other in aggressive posture or really work through the homosexual transference. At this time he had a dream of atomic warfare, and very shortly afterward he dreamt of shooting an elderly man in the face. When he came the next time after this shooting dream, he said he wanted to sit in a chair so that we could talk to each other man-to-man in the normal way and confront each other. When he did this, he found himself able to feel both the clashing and disagreeing, and the warm feelings toward me that had been avoided before in his rather impersonal and workmanlike approach to analyzing before he was able to sit up and face me. The final phase of the analysis was begun and a more satisfactory ending was achieved.

In my next example, an atom bomb dream again seemed to symbolize a feared confrontation, but this time with a shadow aspect of the analysand's own personality. This instance occurred in the analysis of a single woman in her 50s who worked very successfully in a therapeutic profession. Her profession and her philosophy dealt with caring for others, although she had never been able to marry or to be really close to anyone, man or woman. Perhaps partly for this reason, we had never been able to have more than one session a week. For several years of our work we had talked a great deal about her hated, selfish, and sadistic father and her rather feckless mother and about negative authority figures in her everyday working life. Her feelings toward me were mostly positive and rather the opposite of her very negative feelings toward her late and unlamented father, although there was not perhaps much warmth or closeness between us. She had several dreams of extreme cold; in one of these, she was in a group of people who were dying from the cold in Russia. One day she brought me a dream in which the world nuclear war that we all dread, between America and Russia, had begun.

At this point I would like to mention the surprising distance that all of these dreamers experienced in relation to the atomic explosion and the nightmarish horror of the actual event. So far, of the dozens of atom bomb dreams I have noted in analysands, I cannot think of any that had the horror, the hideous mutilations, the searing flames, the acute or chronic suffering and dying that radioactivity can bring, or the darkness and death of nuclear winter. A distant explosion which is known to be nuclear, the bombing raid which is known to be nuclear, the declaration of nuclear war, the black cloud carrying radioactive poison which is looming, these are the usual images in the series of dreams I am reporting. This distancing of affect is obviously important, if only because it is similar to the distancing, the denial, and the other defenses we all seem to erect against the real nuclear threat.

To resume my patient's story, like the other atom bomb dreamers she did not experience any great anxiety in the dream or on waking. When we tried to discuss the dream, the only association she produced was that, for her, the Russian political system used people for its own ends and that the conflict between the world powers might mean for her a conflict between treating other people as persons and using them for one's own political or ideological purposes, so that people become statistics or the recipients of one's "do-gooding" impulses and wishes. This cold, impersonal aspect of her personality was *the* important element in her shadow and disturbed her greatly in view of her conscious, completely opposite persona and ideals. So the dream ushered in an important confrontation with the shadow in her case.

In all the examples I have given so far, the atom bomb dream seemed to represent a momentous coming-together or clashing of important opposites in the personality. In the first case it was the primal scene, in the second it was a conflict between love and hatred toward the mother/anima, in the third it was the conflict between love and hatred toward the father/brother, and in the fourth it was the conflict between persona/ideal and shadow.

Perhaps for all of us, certainly for most of us, our death, the end of our world, the end of the whole world maybe, symbolizes *the* moment of truth when our false hopes, our pretenses and self-deceptions have to be finally shed. It often symbolizes having at last to abandon our illusions and wishful dreams and face the truth about ourselves and others. My fifth patient exemplifies this. She was a woman in love who had harbored unrealistic wishful fantasies and plans in connection with herself and the man she loved. One day she dared to express some of these hopes to him, and his reply was brutally honest and disillusioning. That night she dreamt of a distant atomic explosion with a plume of smoke that reminded her of an ejaculation. In a second dream the same night there was a reference to death and mourning. Again the dream seemed to usher in a positive development in which she was able to experience and face her anger about being left out and rejected, and about the gap between wish and reality. We must not forget, then, that in a very real sense the atom bomb image, like the image of one's death, may signify the moment of truth, analogous with God's thunderbolt of revelation or illumination.

Discussion

The vast and monstrous scale of the nuclear threat is a concrete projection of the feelings of powerlessness and the annihilation fears of the early and powerless infantile "I." What is projected and projected in a concrete, factual form, is our omnipotence and destructiveness. What is done is done in our name, for us, and yet we are not responsible.

I have shown that, at least in the context of a successful ongoing analysis, the atom bomb image may *stand for* things that are *potentially* therapeutic, i.e.,

confrontation with the "bad mother" or the "bad father,"
confrontation with latent homosexual feelings,
confrontation with the shadow side of one's personality,
the loss of cozy delusions of oneness, and
the working through of attitudes toward primal scene material.

In short, the atom bomb image may represent the bringing-together of opposites that is one of the attributes or functions of the Jungian Self and the way toward individuation. The corollary of this finding, it seems to me, is that in so far as each of us seeks to deny internal conflict and to promote harmony, integrity, and perhaps even "goodness" in our subjective state, each of us is guilty of helping the concrete acting out in projected form of the opposite intrapsychic forces. These intrapsychic forces of schism and conflict *may* be destructive but often in a good sense, with a potential for the enrichment of life.

If we try to make a rounded, well-defended whole of ourselves, we avoid the healthy shattering of our narcissistic defenses and this might encourage the birth of material explosive forces, which are to be seen as outward projections of the internal need for conflict. The idealization of bliss, harmony, and feelings of wholeness may constitute a major social sin, for which we may be beginning to pay dearly if the present state of the world is anything to go by.

The demagogic and shoddily entrepreneurial boosting of individuality, the dethronement of God and of the Devil as psychically real figures, while of potential long-term benefit, may in the short term be contributing to this concrete enactment of omnipotent destructiveness.

This is not meant to absolve psychoanalysts from interpreting as helpfully as possible these psychotic or archaic "defense mechanisms" where and when they occur. But it should teach us to listen to others, including our patients, when they accuse us of such psychoticlike defenses, for our defenses themselves preclude self-diagnosis.

Of course it has to be said that the direct interpretation of paranoid defenses is more often counterproductive that therapeutic and tends to strengthen them rather than help in their resolution. Paradoxically, the more truly secure one feels or is allowed to feel, the more effectively these defenses can be looked at and worked through. Strident accusations of paranoid defensiveness, even if disguised as interpretations, are not necessarily the way we should proceed on a social scale any more than in individual therapy. We are in an area where psychotherapy impinges on peoples' morality, religion, and on what is held most dear in life. So to be useful, one's own integrity, morality, and philosophy must be thrown into the melting pot.

In a recent paper entitled "Original Morality in a Depressed Culture," Andrew Samuels distinguishes between what he calls original morality on the one hand, with its ideas of black and white, superiority and inferiority, and moral imagination on the other, characterized by plurality of viewpoint, forgiveness, humor, and conflict. Here we see analogies with the Kleinian paranoid-schizoid position and the depressive position.

In depression, elevated to a moral philosophy, argues Samuels, aggression is condemned and suppressed. Then we are faced with an injury to moral imagination. The positive value of ambivalence and of aggressive fantasy is lost. There is prompted a conflation between aggressive fantasy and destructive fantasy, and a conflation between fantasy and action. Samuels points out the value of aggressive feelings and aggressive fantasy in ego development, ego-self interaction, and separation from the maternal matrix. It is indispensable for consciousness as such. The perversity and horror of aggressive fantasy may give it its creative capacity to nourish the soul. In the nuclear situation, aggressive fantasy has become fact. We can destroy them. Depression is thus increased, aggressive feelings further suppressed.

In any acting-out situation the individual concerned is operating in a Winnicottian no-space environment, a boundaryless situation where mental activity is not possible. Only behavior is possible. The movements of history, including those of politics and sometimes of religion, are largely of this sort. As therapists, we struggle to give people the space to think, symbolize, and imagine. Concrete and, especially, provocative actions may reduce this space. The use of force may sometimes work in the short term by depressing one's adversary, but the destruction of his or her mental space is a price we are at last beginning to understand.

The archetypal motif of death-and-rebirth can be used defensively by individuals and whole groups and nations when fear and despair are near to being overwhelming. It can be concretized to such an extent that an actual apocalypse can be thought purifying or desirable, even something to be hastened.

The concretization and acting-out in the history of sociopolitical movements, of largely unconscious conflicts, seems to be the story of the human race so far. There seems to be little ground for believing that this is about to change. Depth psychology provides the way forward for a relatively small number of individuals. The way forward concerns the facing of moral conflict in oneself. Adopting mass solutions is a spurious, dishonest, and probably in the long run unsuccessful way of trying to heal one's split nature. Yet paradoxically, it seems obvious that only mass movements of a psychologically and philosophically unbalanced nature, such as peace movements and visions of the positive *coniunctio*, for example the vision of John Lennon, seems to provide a hope of substantial weight and mass support. Again, history does not teach us to be very optimistic about any peaceful philosophy or way of life prevailing over a warlike one, but in the present case the arguments for peace are unprecedentedly powerful.

The danger of committing mass suicide in the hope of rebirth into a better existence is a real one. The clashing combination of opposites is such a potentially valuable intrapsychic event that enactment in a concrete form must be a very real possibility. This danger is, I believe, greater in the present state of history than dreams of victory and world domination, which are now seen to be dangerous. However, in this latter connection I should like to mention the only atom bomb in my recollection which appeared to be positive to the dreamer.

This dreamer was a highly successful professional man in his 40s whose meteoric rise had been interrupted by a heart attack and radical heart surgery. He became depressed and was advised to change his way of life. He decided to try psychotherapy. He had a medical model of psychotherapy in mind, i.e., reduction of harmful stresses.

Having reached the top of his profession, he was hoping to go into politics. He dreamt that he was the head of state and that his country—our country—was engaged in nuclear conflict with an enemy who was eventually defeated.

Shortly after this dream he felt much better and pronounced himself cured of his depression. He felt he had no need for psychotherapy and that he had won his personal battle against adversity just as he had vanquished the enemy in his dream. He broke off contact with me and a year later I learned that he had committed suicide a few months after his dream, his depression presumably having returned in overwhelming degree.

It is hard to believe nowadays that manic fantasies of survival, rebirth, or even victory motivate our own people or the rulers of this world. But if the splitting off and projection of evil is our greatest danger, the manic defense of triumph and victory runs a close second and, moreover, is easy to recognize in our own politicians and military leaders. In a paper entitled "The Phantasy of Nuclear Survivability," Jerome Radin (1985) provides some documentary evidence for the thesis that the military men of the United States, unable to admit their helplessness in the face of a lack of rational defense against nuclear weapons, produce one spurious military solution after another to convince themselves and their employers that they are *not* helpless. The fantasy of survivability emerges as one way of denying one's helplessness, bolstered by the various "deep rivers of denial and hypocrisy" with which we are now familiar, described in detail by Radin and also by Segal (1986).

Conscious awareness of the opposites at war within ourselves is the first step toward healing the deep split in ourselves, with its concomitant need of denial and projection. Such splitting and projection produce *behavior* that is explosive and disintegrative. There is in humankind a reciprocal or inverse relationship between awareness and behavior. Our behavior is our unconscious; our unconscious is, in fact, our behavior. To the extent that we become aware of and manage to work through our schizoid defenses, we shall cease to need the real atom bomb, and we shall have become aware of our atomic, i.e., disintegrative, behavior.

The withdrawal of the paranoid projection of the evil in ourselves is the same thing as integrating the split-off and projected opposite. This healing is feared by all of us as a personal catastrophe to be avoided at all costs. It is a fear of the shattering of the ego, in the sense of a fear of the shattering of the feeling of integrity, honor, a threat to one's person and loved ones, a threat to one's sanity, and finally a threat to one's existence. So the healing of our own schizoid splitting and projection is not something we are at all enthusiastic about in practice. The shattering of the ego *feels* like the end of the world, but it is something that should be happening to each of us all the time to a containable degree if we are to stop *enacting* the end of the world. The face of God is too shattering and too intense to be faced without risk of blindness, convulsions, or death. And the more unconsciously omnipotent we are, the more this is the case.

The abandoning of splitting and projective defenses, the healing of social splinterings and schisms, the coming-together of opposites within a containing boundary, and the facing and working-through of subjectively cataclysmic conflict—whichever way you like to look at this fundamentally most human task of individuation, of living together and of living with oneself, is at last something on which we can begin to make real headway. Bringing together parts of the self which we have learned to keep apart, or have never brought together, is a function of the Jungian Self working is some ways against the gradient of our omnipotent narcissistic defenses, the defenses that are absolutely necessary in the first instance but which prevent our reaching the goals of the second half of life.

If behavior and awareness are opposites, we have an even more distant opposite of awareness in the shape of *matter*. If behavior is an alienated part of the personality, then once behavior has material effects, the material effect behaves still more as an alienated and autonomous bit of Self. Actual, material atom bombs dictate behavior and people's minds as alien forces. They need and get their own millions of slaves and beneficiaries whose livelihoods depend on them. By contrast peace and reconciliation are immaterial and command very few slaves. Relatively few people earn their livelihood by peacemaking. Therapists and industrial conciliators and arbitrators are very important exceptions to this. Dare we include artists of all kinds with their courageous visions of the gruesome reality of our minds and our behavior? Perhaps we sorrowfully now have to exclude some religious fundamentalists with their one-sided "goodness" and their shortcuts to rebirth. If the atom bombs have their slaves, do beautiful, good, and nourishing material objects have their slaves, too? Undoubtedly! There are more friends of the earth than that small band of believers who actually call themselves the Friends of the Earth. It is very tempting to see the situation in terms of a struggle between the Forces of Good and the Forces of Evil! But this illustrates how difficult it is even for psychologists to avoid the very splitting which may be responsible for the explosive behavior of society.

In the world of mutually assured destruction, it is those who have the more powerful schizoid-paranoid defenses who will perforce prevail in an ultimate confrontation. They are the madder ones, more sure that they are right and have God on their side. They are the ones who therefore would be the more prepared to sacrifice everything for their beliefs. Being cut off from affect, they would be the better bluffer in the mad poker of international relations. The efforts of the sane must therefore be directed at avoiding the confrontative situation, and this is where the Europeans and the Third World countries may be able to help (unless the nuclear bomb were to be deployed as part of a Muslim or Muslim/Israeli religious war).

Awareness is the only weapon against the unconscious enactment of the final war of the opposites, and awareness is what we as therapists peddle. There are many people whose business is selling materials and behavior as opposed to awareness, but fortunately or unfortunately, they don't know what they are doing. The historical process is largely a story of the concrete enactment on a large scale of archetypal fantasies. The archetypal motif of death/rebirth and of the war of the opposites is now being enacted: the stakes are unprecedentedly high and this may favor a shift toward awareness, although if panic sets in, suicidal apocalyptic acting-out is more likely to happen on the social or mass scale, because of the magnetic pull of the unconscious. When trying to coax the would-be suicide down off the parapet, one does not try to increase the state of fear and panic.

To summarize, then. The atom bomb dream image is the latest of a long line of apocalyptic images. For the individual, it seems to represent the conflict of important opposing emotional forces within the personality, with the fear of bringing together parts of the psyche previously kept apart. If faced as such in terms of moral conflict, without either of the opposing tendencies being allowed to triumph over the other, an enrichment of the person occurs. However, if the conflict is avoided, there exists the danger that these forces may seek unconscious expression, and this must contribute to the collective enactment of these conflicts and to the danger of their attaining material form in actual world catastrophe.

References

Adler, G. 1946. Psychology and the atom bomb. Guild of Pastoral Psychology Lecture No. 43, London. Reprinted in *Psychological Perspectives*, Spring 1985.
Campbell, J. 1964. *Occidental Mythology*. New York: Viking Press; Penguin Books, 1985.
Chamber's Encyclopaedia. 1959. Explosives, 5:532. London: George Newnes.
Grof, S. 1976. *Realms of the Human Unconscious*. New York: E. P. Dutton.
Radin, J. 1985. The phantasy of nuclear survivability. *Psychological Perspectives* 16/1.
Redfearn, J. W. T. 1978. The energy of warring and combining opposites. *Journal of Analytical Psychology* 23:231–241.

Samuels, A. 1986. Original morality in a depressed culture. Paper given at I.A.A.P. Congress, Berlin, September 1986.

Segal, H. 1986. Silence is the real crime. Paper delivered to the British Association of Psychotherapists, London, November 1986.

Book Reviews

Dream Interpretation in Review

August J. Cwik

Webster's New World Dictionary (1968) defines *interpret* as follows: "1. to explain the meaning of; make understandable, as by translating; elucidate. 2. to have or show *one's own* understanding of the meaning of; . . . 3. to bring out the meaning of, especially to give *one's own* conception of, in performing, criticizing, or producing a work of art . . ." (pp. 764–765, emphasis mine). It is this "one's own-ness" that should by emphasized in the "art" of dream interpretation. When we interpret we are translating the imagery of a dream into some other more understandable system. This system is clearly the interpreter's preferred belief system.

Jung suggested that we learn everything that we can about symbolism and imagery and then forget it all when we approach the dream. Of course he meant that we always need to approach the mystery of the dream anew and not to impose circumscribed meanings onto it. But perhaps it would be more honest to stay cognizant of our frameworks because, as we know, forgetting is an act of unconsciousness, and those "lost" items are not gone at all, but function indirectly in the background of consciousness.

Perhaps the stance that we might seek to establish in interpreting is best expressed by Joseph in the Old Testament story, when he answered the chief butler and baker who asked him to interpret their dreams, "Do not interpretations belong to God?" (Genesis 41:16). This would remind us of the power of, and source of the authority for, interpretations. In an article titled after Joseph's quote, Kahn (1975) argued that all interpretation is tentative and a technique which, at

---

August Cwik is a diploma candidate in the Analyst Training Program of the C. G. Jung Institute of Chicago. He conducts a private practice in Chicago.

best, allows for additional shades of meaning to be explored; it can help to provide the individual with a new viewpoint or perspective. He emphasized that "an interpretation is at its best when it is capped by a better one from the patient" (p. 234). With this attitude in mind, let us take a brief overview of dream interpretation with an eye on contrasting developments in the field with the Jungian orientation.

Freud's monumental *The Interpretation of Dreams* (1900/1965) established the viability of using dreams in modern psychotherapy. In this book he not only elaborated a method of dream interpretation, but outlined his whole psychoanalytic system: dream formation became the paradigm for symptom formation in general. So great was its impact that every school of interpretation that followed had to either incorporate many of Freud's tenets regarding the nature of dreams, or have some pretty good reasons for not doing so. Jung himself regarded Freud's method as a valid approach when reductive analysis, uncovering the childhood roots of the problem, was necessary.

Originally Freud's method, based on the topographical model, consisted of an analysis of the contents of the unconscious: hence, the now famous statement, *"The interpretation of dreams is the royal road to a knowledge of the unconscious activities of the mind"* (p. 647, Freud's italics). The unconscious was the repository for repressed traumatic memories and infantile sexual and aggressive wishes and drives; these would be the underlying dream thoughts or latent content of a dream. Some emotional experience in the dreamer's waking life, the day residue, resonates with these old thoughts and feelings and produces the dream. Since these thoughts would be so upsetting to the individual and disrupt his sleep if he became conscious of them, Freud postulated the presence of a psychic censor which disguised and distorted the original contents in order to make them more acceptable to the sleeper. The function of dreams for Freud was then to preserve the sleep of the dreamer: dreams as the guardian of sleep.

The censor accomplished this task of disguise through the "dreamwork" which consisted of mechanisms such as displacement, reversal, condensation, and symbolization. The result was the manifest content—the dream as remembered.

Dream interpretation was then an attempt to reverse the dreamwork process by unraveling the distortions in the manifest content in order to return to the latent content. The technique involved free association to the individual images of the dream to provide the raw material for the connections to the repressed contents. The process has been likened to deciphering a ransom note which has been pieced together with words from different sources. The message itself is less important than tracing the individual components back to their origin.

As the structural/tripartite model of id, ego and superego was developed, the emphasis in dream interpretation became the elaboration of the conflict between the three agencies. Therapy shifted to a focus of analyzing the transference and defenses rather than the original "id analysis." Every dream was approached as a transference dream having something directly to do with the analytic process itself. With theory becoming more ego psychologically oriented, there was a shift away from the importance of dream analysis altogether; the dream became another communication, like any other—the royal road became just another street.

By 1970, Greenson obviously felt the need to argue for the special importance of the dream in his classic article, aptly titled, "The Exceptional Position of the Dream in Psychoanalytic Practice." Aside from the changes in theory noted above, one of the reasons he gave for the declining interest in the use of dreams was that many analysts themselves may not have had the personal experience of having their own dreams properly analyzed in any kind of depth. He stated, "It is my belief, after many years of psychoanalytic therapy with private patients and candidates in psychoanalytic training, that one cannot carry out genuine analysis in sufficient depth if one does not understand the structure of dream formation *as well as the patient's and the analyst's contribution to the technique of dream interpretation*" (p. 521, author's italics). Only in this experiential sense can true understanding exist.

He went on to describe the dream as the "freest of free associations" and emphasized the uniqueness of the dream in reaching material that was otherwise inaccessible. The article portrayed a sensitive clinician working in the classical model as he demonstrated the use of dreams to elaborate transference reactions and to reconstruct childhood memories. But one is struck by the associative activity on the part of the analyst and the rich use of the metaphors of the manifest content of the dream. It is changes in these areas which epitomize the latest developments in psychoanalytic theory regarding dreams.

Generally the movement has been away from a wish-fulfillment and disguise/censorship model to one that is more problem-solving, synthetic, and integrative. Fosshage (1987) has gone the farthest in delineating a revised psychoanalytic model. In this model, there is a clear attempt to remain within the phenomenology of the dream itself.

The most radical departure from classical theory can be heard in: "Dream figures and images are typically seen not as the product of disguise, but rather as poignant organizational nodal points for particular affective reactions or thematic experiences" (p. 31). Also, the analyst is not considered to be present in every dream unless he is actually imaged in the dream.

Clearly, Jung anticipated these developments and Fosshage does reference Jungian views as impacting on his model. This movement toward a greater appreciation of the manifest content is a very interesting development in dream interpretation.

Warner (1987) noted the increasing use of manifest content in dream interpretations found in a number of psychoanalytic journals. To him, it seemed that "unofficially" analysts often interpreted dreams entirely, or in part, on the manifest appearance alone. "Officially" the party-line was adhered to in treating manifest content as something to be discarded in order to get to the real core of the dream, the latent content.

Since the Freudian unconscious, Jung's personal unconscious, consists of only repressed material and derivatives of the sexual/aggressive instinctual urges, one can never explain a creative or problem-solving function of dreams; all is disguise or the product of some infantile wish. So one is necessarily drawn reductively back to the thoughts and feelings of childhood.

Outside of the traditional psychoanalytic movement, various schools of interpretation abound, and many claim the dream as an extremely useful tool. One of the best ways to get the flavor of these orientations in comparison to one another is in the "anthologies" that are published every so often. One of the more current collections is Natterson's *The Dream in Clinical Practice* (1980). Besides the series of papers on the dream in various psychotherapeutic modalities, one can find papers updating relevant changes in theory; on the use of dreams in sundry pathological states, i.e., schizophrenia, obsessive states, dissociative states, psychosomatic problems; detailing dream use in special therapeutic situations, as with suicidal patients or in handling nightmares. One personal favorite paper is the account of an analysis utilizing dreams, contrasting the analyst's view of what happened and why, with that of the patient's own description of the experience (Anonymous 1980).

The interested reader is directed to other notable collections and historic overviews such as the encyclopedic, *The Dream: 4000 Years of Theory and Practice* by Parcifal-Charles (1986); Hall's (1977) comprehensive review in *Clinical Uses of Dreams*; Ullman and Limmer's (1987) *The Variety of Dream Experience*; and Wolman's (1979) *Handbook of Dreams: Research, Theories and Applications*. These books allow for comparisons between disparate orientations and truly demonstrate the richness of how the dreaming experience can be used therapeutically.

But nowhere is this seen as clearly as in *Dream Interpretation: A Comparative Study* (Fosshage and Loew 1978, rev. ed., 1987). In this book, eight major schools of dream interpretation are compared by having a theorist from each present the basic premises of their orientation; they then demonstrate how they might work with dream material by responding to the same series of dreams. Most notable is exactly how each therapist's belief system affected what they did and the type of interpretations they made, as suggested earlier in this paper. Each approach yielded different nuances of meaning and, at times, even very contradictory understandings.

Angel Garma covered the Freudian approach and pretty much held the classical line discussed earlier. He added the notion that the regressive activation of conflicts probably goes back to the birth trauma in almost all dreams. The general attitude toward dreams can be felt in his rather strong statement that "only a person who reacts masochistically (although without realizing it consciously) and derives pleasure from self-deceit can enjoy his dreams" (Fosshage and Loew 1987, p. 28, author's parentheses).

Whitmont had the honor of presenting the Jungian approach which will be discussed at greater length later. He did acknowledge that interpretation will be colored by the interpreter's attitudes, feelings, and intuitive capacities. He stressed the importance that the therapist be related to his own inner world of images in order to be able to do justice to the patient's. This certainly echoes Greenson's statement quoted above and emphasizes that dream interpretation can never be a purely intellectual affair.

Walter and Florence Bonime cover the Culturalist approach to dreams. This orientation emphasizes interpersonal experience as the dominant force in personality development. Dream work is highly valued because it lends itself well to associative activity and, most importantly, because it helps the patient become involved in a collaborative effort. It is almost as if the dream is used as a projective technique, like a TAT in motion, to which both analyst and patient associate. Collaboration is seen as a curative process in itself.

The Bonimes stress the tentative nature of interpretations by suggesting that we present "interpretive hypotheses" rather than interpretations *per se*. Another interesting notion here is the concept of "personal glossaries." They feel that individual dreams repeat certain terms, phrases, or symbols of intricate but established dynamics that become powerful communications within the analytic relationship. I think we all have experienced how a particular metaphor or image is able to capture a sense of very deep experience which cannot otherwise be put into words. Jung's notion is that the true symbol expresses something relatively unknown but which the individual has a great need to express somehow.

Parallels with Jungian thought can easily be heard in statements such as the dream being "an unguarded expression of self" and "the dream is not a disguise, but probably the most authentic presentation of personality" (Fosshage and Loew 1987, p. 81). And while the Bonimes feel that the majority of associations to dreams are highly subjective and idiosyncratic, they allow that there are a number of referents that are shared by members of the same culture; the "symbolism of dreams cannot be universal, even though some of it may refer coincidently to a common heritage and experience" (p. 88). So while denying a collective unconscious and any movement toward a universal symbolism, the culturalist approach speaks more to the reality of a cultural unconscious similar to that proposed by Henderson in the Jungian school.

The object relational approach, as described by Padel, is not a unified orientation but draws on the writings of such theorists as Balint, Fairbairn, Winnicott, Sutherland, and Khan. The emphasis in this approach is on the nature of the psychological bonds between people. Padel states that "the relationships actually lived in the family and the personalities of the adults present in the child's formative years accounted for all the personality structure that was not the outcome of his own creativeness and his own refusals" (Fosshage and Loew 1987, p. 126). Notice that in the possibility of personality development from "creativeness," the object relational approach takes a giant step from the classical Freudian approach. This emphasis on creativeness and the ability to play is one of the hallmarks of this approach. Winnicott (1971), in discussing the goal of psychotherapy, states:

> Psychotherapy takes place in the overlap of two areas of playing, that of the patient and that of the therapist. Psychotherapy has to do with two people playing together. The corollary of this is that where playing is not possible the work done by the therapist is directed towards bringing the patient from a state of not being able to play into a state of being able to play. (p. 38)

It is the task of the analyst to get the patient working or, better yet, playing with the ideas and images that preoccupy him or her. Here again dreams are especially useful in this endeavor especially because individuals attach special importance to them as their own productions. Free association becomes less of a technique to be acquired than a capacity to play in thought with words and images. Dreams are taken to be statements about the present life of the dreamer, situations from the past, and the "state of affairs" of the inner object relations. Analysts look less for underlying infantile wishes in the associative material than for attempts to deal with bad or threatening object relations; the dream illuminates the fixation points and may often suggest solutions to past relationship problems. Padel states that often what is looked for is the *transitional* component in dreams. He defines this as "any element which has a markedly ambiguous quality, an ambiguity in its status of existence: it is at one moment part of the self, at another part of the central figure in the world beyond the self" (Fosshage and Loew 1987, p. 134). This figure "beyond the self" is the personal mother in the object relations view, but it is quite suggestive when heard from a Jungian perspective.

Analysts belonging to the Society of Analytical Psychology in England have gone the furthest in incorporating the object relational approach with a Jungian perspective. The English School utilizes the similarities of internal objects and complexes in their interpretive approach (Lambert 1979). Certainly one can hear the parallel in the dream describing the internal object relationships with Jung's emphasis on the revelation, not only of the complexes, but more importantly knowledge of how they are interacting within dream material. The ability of the dream to depict the internal "state of affairs" is also echoed in Kohut's (1977) description of "self state" dreams. Here again the manifest content is accepted as relating an undisguised picture of the inner situation; for Kohut, this would be a phenomenological description of the current state of the self.

"Playing" in the Jungian modality is probably most powerfully experienced in active imagination. Utilizing this technique can help many individuals to find that certain playfulness described so well by Winnicott (1971).

This description of looking for the transitional in dreams would seem to correspond with Jung's notion of the true symbol as being able to unite opposites. Whether in dreams or imaginal work, both the object relational and Jungian analyst are seeking to help the individual to develop the transcendent function; only in this manner can the stuckness or fixations of the past be overcome.

The remaining two schools compared by Fosshage and Loew are the Phenomenological and Gestalt approaches. At first blush they would not seem to have much in common with the Jungian approach as both eschew the concept of the unconscious altogether. Much of what is normally considered unconscious contents in other orientations is described as just being outside of ordinary awareness. Since both schools are existentially oriented and thus promote human nature as being active and emphasize the necessity of making choices, it is not surprising that the conceptualization of an unconscious which can and will work outside of human awareness might well be frowned upon.

In the Phenomenological or Daseinsanalytic approach covered by Boss and Kenny, dreaming is considered another mode of existence of the human being—just a different way of "being-in-the-world," the individual's Da-sein. The basic character of the dream state appears more open, more free and less constricted than when we are awake; it is more chimerical in nature. Yet it is the waking state where one can freely choose; it is thus the waking mode of existence which assumes the highest rank.

Material in the dreaming state is never considered to be "symbolic" of anything else; all phenomena appearing in dreams are "nothing but what they reveal themselves to be" (Fosshage and Loew 1987, p. 157). Rather it is the "significances and references of meaningfulness" which make up the essence of any particular image that the dreamer needs to become more aware of in the waking state. Very often we need to be "shaken to our roots" in order to be able to break up rigid and stagnant ways of seeing and being. The dream is particularly useful in this endeavor as it allows the therapist to lead the dreamer toward clarification of his existential waking state. Along the way, any signs of courage or freedom expressed in the dream can be encouraged by the analyst.

One might wonder if a knowledge of the imagery of alchemy wouldn't be helpful in informing this process of "shaking an individual to the roots"—of course, in the Jungian perspective, the "shaking" emanates from the Self and not from the analyst. Here the deintegration process could be placed in a context of transformation and renewal.

In the phenomenological model the dreaming state is continuous with the waking state—there is only one being, one dasein, encountering different forms of existence. In comparison, Jung's model is a balance theory in that the unconscious, and hence the dream, is thought to be in a compensatory relationship to the conscious view-point (see Dallett 1973, for further elaboration on the function of dreams). In many ways the phenomenological perspective presents a more complementary view, a milder form of compensation. This can often be observed in borderline patients whose dreams often don't compensate the tremendous affect states of the waking world but present the conflict in a slightly different form. Sometimes these differences are useful in helping patients to begin to see their part in the conflict. And any indications of strength can be encouraged by the analyst so as to facilitate the assimilation of these qualities by the individual's ego.

To some extent Hillman's (1979) views of the dream can be seen as a parallel to the phenomenological approach in his emphasis on the "underworld" as a unique existence unto itself, although he places this existence higher on the hierarchy than the waking state: the mythos of the underworld is more highly valued than the logos of the waking world. Hillman's approach appears to be a mirror image of the phenomenological way; he comes from the bottom up instead of the top down. But the existential emphasis on will and choice would seem to be the epitome of Hillman's complaints against the "heroic-ego." The ego of the dream should then be held in the same regard — contempt? — as the waking ego, in that ego motives are always held as suspect and resistant to "dying" to the underworld perspective of mythos. Clearly Hillman's "significances and references of meaningfulness" come from archetypal understandings rather than the outer world. He emphasizes the need to stay at the descriptive and metaphorical level rather than interpretation *per se* and clearly recognizes that some contents of the psyche require submission, rather than dominance.

Shelburne (1984) argues that in giving primacy to mythos over logos we lose the tension between the two worlds and the value of Jung's point that logos, the rational approach needs *compensation* from a nonrational mythos, rather than a simple replacement of one for the other. Also Shelburne emphasizes the need for a reality-oriented ego before the wealth of the depths can be used and appreciated; totally devaluing the importance of adaptation to the outer world places the entire personality in jeopardy.

The Gestalt approach as presented by Fantz emphasizes that the personality is composed of polar or opposing traits. The goal of therapy is to integrate these traits by first separating them out, recognizing that they belong to oneself, and assimilating them in a way that allows the individual to use them in appropriate life situations. The dream is particularly useful in this endeavor because it is "an existential message from the dreamer, a means of creative expression, much as a painting, a poem or a choreographic fantasy is a creative expression, which allows the dreamer to come into touch with the very personal, idiosyncratic parts of his being" (Fosshage and Loew 1987, p. 192). The dream is considered an existential message which presents the dreamer with the "holes" of the personality.

The method involves reclaiming these lost, rejected parts by identifying with them. The dreamer is asked to *become* the images of the dream and thus to become aware of the feelings and body states attached to these images. Dialogues between these different parts of the personality are encouraged; these inner discussions help to elaborate the conflicting relationships and resistances to the various alienated parts and, hopefully, promote wholeness and self-actualizaiton.

Of all the orientations presented thus far, the Gestalt approach to the dream could almost be considered a subset of Jungian theory. Although the philosophical underpinnings are radically different, the parallel with subjective interpretation of the dream and the use of active imagination is almost identical. From the subjective level of interpretation, all the images of the dream are aspects or qualities of the dreamer. From a Jungian perspective the focus is more on developing a relationship to, rather than necessarily identifying with, these "shadow holes" in oneself. Certainly in Jung's perspective there are powerful archetypal images one would never identify with for fear of inflation, or worse, possession. Approaching the dream entirely on the subjective level also dissipates the tension between inner and outer — everything is *not* always oneself, especially in real world interactions — we lose the dream's ability to help us understand the role of others in our lives. Plus, exclusive focus on the separate elements of the dream might draw one away from seeing what the unconscious is saying about the relationship of the complexes to one another, similar to what can happen in a Freudian reductive approach which focuses solely on causes.

But the Gestalt emphasis reminds us that many a patient may need to *become* a certain element before it truly can be experienced as real and ownership taken. Talking *to* something is quite different than *being* it!

This short overview of the major schools of dream interpretation finds the Jungian approach in relatively good standing regarding the varied ways of approaching the mystery of dreaming experience. As we focus on the Jungian approach, one is already aware of the great diversity that this view allows in working with dreams: Jung always emphasized that no one theory could ever do justice to the dream.

In Jung's view pathology is due to a separation of the conscious from the unconscious mind; the goal of treatment is to heal this split and dreams are the directors of the process. Dreams are natural productions of the psyche and not disguised material, and Jung was more concerned with their *purpose* than their source in the past. This is a synthetic, teleological, and prospective approach as compared to Freud's reductive and casual view. Dreams can reveal not only the complexes, but how they are interacting with one another and what the unconscious has to say about the eventual outcome. Jung also posited a deeper layer of the unconscious, the collective unconscious or objective psyche, which contains an archaic wisdom in the form of the archetypes that can eventually help lead the dreamer out of the dilemma and to an experience of the Self, the central ordering archetype or god-image in the psyche.

The importance of the dream in analysis has never flagged in the Jungian approach — it remains the chief therapeutic modality. Lambert (1979) spoke of a softening of this view by the London School's valid reminder that it is the *individual* that is the subject of the analysis and not just the dreams. The concern here is that the transference/countertransference situation takes primacy in the analytic endeavor and that it is this relationship which mediates the healing processes of the Self.

This discrimination can easily be signaled by whether a particular analyst will initially ask for dreams from the patient or not. If yes, then the dream is held as more important than risking an immediate strain or resistance in the relationship. It would seem that if one truly trusts dreams to reveal what needs to be analytically addressed, then the dreams themselves will reveal whether compliant or rebellious motives are involved in response to the request. If there are no dreams forthcoming, then one can always move to an analysis of the transference treating the request as a "real" disruption and not just as part of the patient's neurotic system. But Lambert does well in reminding us that "archetypal themes may be discovered in the patient's material in many forms other than in dreams, i.e., in his reports of actions and events, in his descriptions of people, in slips of the tongue, in non-verbal communications and in the transference/countertransference situation" (p. 132).

As important as dreams are in the Jungian approach, Jung himself never drew together a formal presentation of how to work with dreams;

references to dream analysis are scattered throughout the collected works. In the category of "everything you always wanted to know of what Jung said about dreams—but were afraid to look up yourself," Mattoon (1977) has given us *Understanding Dreams*. This penultimate reference book presents in a methodical and articulate manner the major steps that Jung suggested in approaching dream interpretation. Summed up, they are as follows:

1. State the dream text in terms of *structure*; examine for completeness.
2. Establish the dream context, the situational material in which the dream is embedded, the context it is composed of:
   a. *amplifications* of the dream images which may include:
      (1) *personal associations,*
      (2) *information from the dreamer's environment,* and/or
      (3) *archetypal parallels;*
   b. *themes interconnecting* the amplifications;
   c. the immediate and long-term conscious situation of the dreamer; and
   d. the dream *series* in which the dream occurs.
3. Review the appropriate attitudes to bring to dream interpretation.
   a. Nothing can be assumed regarding the meaning of the dream or of the specific images.
   b. The dream is not a disguise but a set of psychic facts.
   c. The dream probably does not tell the dreamer what to do.
   d. Awareness of the personality characteristics of the dreamer and the interpreter.
4. Characterize the dream images as *objective or subjective*.
5. Consider the dream's *compensatory* function.
   a. Identify the problem or complex with which the dream is concerned.
   b. Ascertain the relevant conscious situation of the dreamer.
   c. Consider whether the dream images and the psychic development of the dreamer require a *reductive or constructive* characterization.
   d. Consider whether the dream compensates by opposing, modifying, or confirming the relevant conscious situation;

  e. Whether the dream is noncompensatory; *prospective, trau-matic, telepathic, or prophetic.*
6. Hypothesize an interpretation by translating the dream language in relation to the relevant conscious situation of the dreamer, test it against the dream facts, modify where necessary, and state the interpretation briefly.
7. Verify the interpretation. (pp. 48–49, author's italics)

The dream is first addressed in terms of its dramatic structure: the exposition, the setting or context, and the characters; the development, the initial situation and the beginning of the main plot; the culmination or peripeteia, where the action reaches a climax, either for the better or worse; and, the solution or lysis, where some kind of meaningful conclusion or result is reached. In this manner the essential theme of the dream is acknowledged, although any particular dream may not contain all of the elements.

In place of the free association of Freud we have the amplification process, starting with the dreamer's own responses and resonances to the images, but always keeping mind the central image rather than linearly moving from thought to thought. The analyst may add additional associations especially as the analysis proceeds and the individual is better known — the "personal glossaries" of the Bonimes, and cultural or functional references. Archetypal themes may be added by the analyst, if appropriate, usually to images which didn't constellate associations from the patient.

Instead of the day residue of Freud, there is more of a focus on the overall conscious situation of the dreamer. This may bring in reflections on the previous day but are not limited to what has actually occurred. Meier (1987) has elaborated the various recognizable sources for a dream and divided them into two main categories: constellations occasioned indirectly by conscious contents, and constellations occasioned directly by unconscious contents. Once again, the autonomy of the unconscious is emphasized by allowing that the nonrational sphere may instigate a dream by itself — it is purposive.

At the objective level, figures that are actually known to the dreamer are assumed to be just who they purport to be. This approach allows the dream to literally comment on and add additional information about the outer world. Unknown figures or known figures which deviate in any way from their outer world equivalents draw one to the subjective level where every image is thought to portray qualities and attributes of the dreamer.

Jung's notion of the compensatory function of the unconscious, and hence of dreams, is the closest he comes to a fixed theory of dreams. This function allows for a balance point to be sought by understanding and digesting the message of the dream. And yet, as seen above, noncompensatory functions are allowed and should be considered. Some dreams can be prospective in that they may portray future possibilities given the current psychic circumstances. This should not be considered prophetic in the sense that the situation is unchangeable; Jung allowed for truly prophetic dreams, but these are quite rare. Other noncompensatory dreams are the repetitive traumatic dream and the genuinely telepathic dream.

The interpretation pieced together by taking all these variables into account is held up for verification by the dreamer—note Mattoon's wording of "hypothesize an interpretation," again reminiscent of the Bonimes' *interpretive hypotheses*. She focuses on several responses to look for. Does the interpretation "click" for the dreamer, the old "ah-ha" experience? (Hillman (1979) questions this response as belonging to the ego world of the dreamer; it could just be confirming some old ego-supportive stance.) An interpretation may "act" for the dreamer adding additional energy to the life of the individual. Other dreams may confirm, or question, the interpretation reached. Events in the dreamer's life may occur which are anticipated by the interpretation. I would add that there may simply be the release of more unconscious material from the patient—remembering more of the dream, a connection to another dream, or the constellation of an old forgotten memory. Or perhaps there is a deepening, or loosening, of the transferential relationship as related by the derivative communications surrounding the interpretation.

Almost any Jungian-oriented book is going to have something to say about dreams, so intrinsic is the dream in this approach. But a few specific ones are currently providing the foundation for deepening our understanding of dreams.

Hall's books, *Clinical Uses of Dreams* (1977) and *Jungian Dream Interpretation* (1983) are two such foundation works. As noted above, the former book contains a detailed historical retrospective and an overview of other theories of dream interpretation. It fits into the category of "What most everybody else has had to say about dreams." Besides a quite competent detailing of the Jungian approach, it covers such diverse areas as laboratory studies of sleep and dreams; a wonderful section on neglected uses of dreams demonstrating applications in diagnosis and prognosis, anxiety, physical problems, marriage problems, and alcoholism; the use of dreams as indicators of past and current conflicts, and of the transference-countertransference situation; dream recall; related phenomena such as hypnogagic imagery, déjà vu, daydreaming, lucid dreams, and hypnotic dreams; and different types of dreams, such as traumatic, adolescent, alchemical, mirror dreams, and dreams of falling.

One of Hall's particular contributions is in the area of delineating the relationship between the dream ego and the waking ego. Observations in this sphere emphasize the relativity of the ego by comparing past to present ego states and present to future ego states. The latter brings in the relationship to the Self, the central archetype and regulating center of the psyche, and considerations of the individuation process itself. Hall states:

> Individuation might be described in terms of the complex theory as the gradual reshaping of the ego, under the pressure of the Self, so that it becomes more inclusive and comprehensive. There is a loosening of the ego's transient identification with any particular ego image, so that it becomes increasingly able to reflect, with decreasing distortion, those contents of the total psyche that are focused and coordinated by the Self and given expression . . . in the growth of the individuating ego. (1977, p. 173)

Using Polanyi's nomenclature of tacit and focal knowing, Hall states "that the waking-ego relies in a tacit manner upon contents of the psyche that would appear to the dream-ego as focal" (Hall 1983, p. 110). In other words, our waking sense of I-ness in actuality depends on underlying assumptions and connections that can be more clearly revealed by the activities of the dream ego. The dream is a type of snapshot of a specific complex structure on which the waking ego has been tacitly depending.

Hall's distinctions in this area aid in creating a structural approach to the contents of the psyche rather than emphasizing topological considerations, i.e., what has been repressed into the unconscious and why. He wants to stay clear of making value judgments of whether the dream ego is inferior, superior, or equivalent to the waking ego. But I wonder if taking a more quantitative stance may not add to our understanding of the tacit underpinnings of the waking ego. There are often dreams where the dream ego moves in the direction of having greater knowledge or emotional stability than that of the waking ego, those instances where self approaches Self, in a particular interaction. Could these shifts indicate a greater and/or more focused compensation of the conscious attitude and a readiness for the waking ego to assume more responsibility vis-á-vis the constellated situation?

In the section on enactments, Hall reminds us that ideas and images are not the only possible carriers of symbols: the symbolic vehicle can have concrete form and dreams can provide the basis for enactments rather than only interpretations. Like Jung's paintings, stone carvings, and the Bollingen building itself, it may be necessary to objectify and concretize images in order to facilitate their "realness." To *enact*, "acting in," rather than to *act out* is the goal here. "Fantasy is play, but it can also be harnessed to carry the contents of the mind and allow them to develop symbolically, to seek their existence in the outer world as symbols rather than as compulsions, neuroses, fears and fearful forms" (Hall 1977, pp. 331–332). In physical form, this can take the form of paintings, sandplay, poetry, or writing; imaginal forms may include hypnoanalysis, active imagination, and guided fantasy.

Under the "care and nurturing of symbolic forms," Hall rightly warns that one should avoid overburdening the symbol by attempting to force it to carry the tension of the opposites; in other words, it cannot be used defensively or it becomes a type of fetish rather than a symbol. The actual symbol arises naturally through the transcendent function and the ego cannot ensure that it will retain its symbolic effect. It needs to be nurtured with care and attention like a developing child or puppy.

Hall's second book is to the first as a crystalline precipitate is to the mother solution. He hones in on the structural aspects of the Jungian psyche as being composed of, but not limited to, the ego, persona, shadow, animus and anima, and Self. Approaching these components as structures parallels the structural theory of Freud's division into id, ego, and superego. Hall discriminates further by describing the ego and shadow as identity structures; shadow being an alter-ego image of unacceptable traits and qualities split off from the ego-identity, the perceived sense of I-ness, in childhood. Animus/anima and persona are relational structures in that both enlarge the personal sphere of the ego; the persona bridges to the outer world and animus/anima to the inner world of the collective unconscious. Hall describes the use of dreams in analysis as particularly helpful in integrating these aspects of the personality and thus increasing the range of consciousness.

In place of the often used ego-Self axis, Hall suggests the term ego-Self spiration. He feels this is more phenomenologically descriptive of the varied and shifting relationship of the ego to the Self rather than the static quality implied by the word "axis."

There is an excellent section on transference and countertransference dreams discriminating the nuances of when the analyst is in the associations of the patient, when the analyst actually appears in the dream, when the patient appears in the analyst's dream, and when there are sexual dreams involving either of the participants. There is also a short section on alchemical symbolism appearing in dreams which gives a good sense of how to approach these arcane processes. Hall makes an interesting generalization suggesting that conflict dreams often occur early in an analysis associated with a differentiation of the ego from the unconscious. More developed individuation images, such as alchemical imagery, occur only later after some ego autonomy has been achieved. I have observed this general progression although images of "lesser *coniunctios*," combinations of contents leading to "defective" productions, eg., deformed or dead babies and monsters, which occur quite regularly in the dreams of borderline patients. It is almost as if the psyche of these individuals attempts the final stage of union before purifying processes are performed on the initial contents. In Hall's terminology, particular complexes are still contaminated by deeper tacit structures and their combination results in distorted end products.

Meier's (1987) *The Meaning and Significance of Dreams* is itself a scholarly amplification of dream interpretation focusing on different methods of dream research and ancient dream theories. A short series of dreams from a patient is used to demonstrate the amplificatory method since the patient was too severely depressed to present personal associations to the material. Meier reminds us that the Jungian approach does not aim at providing a universally valid "key" for dream interpretation, nor is there any attempt to achieve completeness in interpretation, emphasizing that the dream should only be approached with the greatest possible openness.

He suggests an interesting hypothesis for approaching dreams from which the dreamer is rudely awakened and in which no lysis (solution or answer) has been presented within the dream itself. Perhaps this sequence of events is pointing out to the individual that no solution to the particular problem can be found in the unconscious and that consideration needs to be given over to waking consciousness; the dreamer needs to be "shocked" into this realization. Here waking up itself is the "solution" that is imperative and the much needed compensation.

Interestingly, Meier wants to temper the notion of the creativity of the unconscious. There is no doubt of the ability of the unconscious to produce powerful symbols, but he reminds us that Nature, although highly productive, never creates anything entirely new (barring the exception of the rare mutation). Even symbols themselves are basically all "known" in their essence, even though they are always "individual" as their variants depend on the individual history of the bearer. Only in *confrontation* with the conscious mind does the creative aspect appear: consciousness is required to incarnate the collective archetypal contents. Or as it has been said, "God needs us as much as we need God." Living this principle is the truly creative life.

In *Inner Work*, Johnson (1986) demonstrates his knack for putting the technically obscure into digestible components for Everyman. For example, in his explanation of the archetypes and why Jung felt that the Greek heroes and gods were actually such excellent symbols for them, he states:

> The gods, as the Greeks conceived them, were forces that interacted with individual human lives. These forces were present in every life, yet were universal, timeless, and lived outside the limits of a particular life or time. "The gods" could as well have been described as "fields of energy" acting on the human race. Yet their images presented *integrated personalities* that are similar to the "persons" in our dreams who carry an aura of great power and fit some great type in human nature. (p. 33, author's emphasis)

Johnson presents a very workable and structured approach to the dream utilizing a four-step approach: making associations, connecting the dream images to inner dynamics, interpreting, and doing rituals to make the dream concrete. He takes an interesting tack in dealing with the quite common occurrence of deciding between competing interpretations of the same dream. He suggests arguing from the opposites until the lesson of the dream becomes clearer. Often we begin to realize that there is some truth to different interpretations and that the final understanding is often a synthesis of different viewpoints.

This echoes an approach presented by Gendlin (1986) that he calls "bias control." Here he *encourages* us to find the opposite interpretation so that we are not simply confirming our usual attitudes and understanding of what is going on. This is the standard complaint of Hillman, although Gendlin does not assume that the usual attitudes are necessarily wrong. Gendlin's approach to the dream is atheoretical, in that he has amassed a series of questions gathered through various theoretical approaches to the dream and "validates" the correctness of an interpretation through the body. He details how a vague or fuzzy body sense and any subsequent change in it can be useful to guide an interpretation toward what he calls the growth-direction. In this manner an interpretation and its opposite can be examined, and any resistances can be illuminated.

Under the care and feeding of symbols, Johnson encourages the use of ritual as the last step in any interpretation. The message of the dream needs to be brought into the real world, in a physical act, in order to ground the psychological work in the body and to help prevent it from remaining purely an intellectual understanding of the head. He suggests that sometimes it is just this symbolic act that deepens the meaning of the dream in a powerful way. He gives numerous examples of how this might occur, the least of which is just giving it some form of acknowledgment. Once again this "child or puppy" of the psyche needs attention and tender loving care.

The last half of Johnson's book is dedicated to describing the technique of active imagination and it is arguably one of the best accounts of the process in the literature. In this manner the imagery of the dream becomes the starting point for imaginal dialogues that deepen the relationship to the unconscious and provide the foundations for the establishment of the transcendent function. For Jung, active imagination is the royal road to the transcendent function while dreams and, more specifically, their "architects," the complexes, are the royal road to the unconscious itself.

Bosnak (1988) extends this imaginal approach to dream as underscored in his statement, "a central principle in dreamwork . . . [is] that *the training of the imagination is a discipline*, just as important as the training of the mind" (p. 73, author's italics). Body awareness is emphasized to a high degree and very much parallels Gendlin's approach noted above. The dreamer is instructed on how to enter an altered state of consciousness by focusing on the remembered details of the dream; this is similar to many hypnotic inductions. As a matter of fact, the night after reading his description, I experienced a lucid dream as I began to focus on the phenomenal detail within the dream itself—an altered state within an altered state.

Bosnak's book is filled with exercises to sharpen the imagination, especially regarding ways to reflect upon alchemical imagery. These skills, once refined, can then be utilized in approaching the dream. Here active imagination is the primary modality used in understanding the dream. In his approach there is less talk of interpretations *per se*, and more emphasis on the need to return to the reality of the dream: the dream, and the feeling responses surrounding it, is its own best interpretation.

One might argue that active imagination, as described by Jung, is an activity that is best performed where there can be no influence by the analyst. The nature of an ego that can approach the unconscious

alone might be significantly different from one that does it in supportive situation. Many of the examples given by Bosnak are of dreams
approached in a group context; members share with one another their
own experiences in interacting with a particular dream. But without
getting caught in pedantics, Bosnak's book is a powerful demonstration
of what can be accomplished by addressing the dream through and
with the imagination.

The last book to be discussed is an old book that has just been
republished, Layard's (1944/1988) *The Lady and the Hare*. The first
half of the book is a description of a short analysis with a devout
Christian woman whose overly strict and rigid belief system is
"challenged" — compensated — by her dreams. The account is especially
fascinating because of Layard's attempt to record in detail his own part
in the process as well as the patient's. At times it almost feels as if the
religious function itself is the subject under analysis. This is reflected in
the powerful statement: "To serve Him, not by opposing nature, but by
transforming it in obedience to its own hidden laws which it is the
purpose of psychology as the handmaiden of religion to reveal" (p. 95).
Also, the impact of the analysis upon the woman's family, especially
her daughter, is dramatically portrayed, anticipating a family systems
perspective by many years.

The turning point in the woman's analysis hinged around a dream
depicting the sacrifice of a hare. At the time Layard amplified the
image in terms of Christ's sacrifice of himself for redemption. But
drawn to the question of why it might specifically be imaged as a
rabbit, he began looking into the mythological underpinnings of the
motif. The second half of the book is the result of this survey and
reveals the theme of self-sacrifice associated with the hare across numerous and diverse cultures — the most familiar probably being the connection of the rabbit with Easter.

It is interesting to note that although both analyst and patient
were totally ignorant of the worldwide mythology associated with the
hare, the appearance of the image in her dream still exerted, or her-
alded, a radical change in the woman's psyche. Yet Layard stated,

> The fact that the dream of sacrificing the hare had no effect on her till enough
> of its meaning was explained, and that it then produced this great effect,
> demonstrates clearly . . . not only the power of the archetype but also the part
> it plays in the redemptive process that lies latent within us all, though it
> remains comparatively inoperative till joined to consciousness, but becomes so
> potent a force for good when activated by being recognized and honoured. (p.
> 229)

Without a doubt, the archetypal approach, concomitant with the technique of amplification, is Jung's unique contribution to dream understanding and appreciation. At the subjective level of amplification the individual's own associations illuminate the structure of the personal complexes tacitly involved in an emotional response or conscious attitude. Techniques such as those described by Bosnak allow deeper subjective amplifications to be elicited through the complexes themselves. At the objective level of amplification universal motifs can be added by either analysand or analyst which reinforce an image and widen its emotional tone and nuances. Both subjective and objective amplifications do not interpret meanings as much as enlarge the image to include personal and universal connections. In between the two emerges the transcendent, for example, when Jung's inner dialogues with Philemon become more than just an interaction with a split-off ego personality and truly reach down into an archaic wisdom of the unconscious (see Hobson 1971, for an excellent discussion of amplification).

When it works well, archetypal amplification can lead the dreamer out of feelings of isolation to an awareness of the universality of the problems encountered. Analysis of archetypal dreams can facilitate the wholeness of the dreamer as "consciousness can once more be brought into harmony with the law of nature from which it all too easily departs, and the patient can be led back to the natural law of his own being" (Jung 1934, p. 160).

Yet so often we find in the literature that archetypal motifs are simply noted and not amplified to the dreamer: the series of dreams sighted above by Meier were never amplified or interpreted and yet they are presented as demonstrating archetypal effects; Layard's minor comments on an archetypal image only to learn later of the deeper implications of the image; even Jung (1984), in *Dream Analysis*, an extended seminar that could be considered one large amplification on a middle-aged man's series of dreams, states how little was actually said to the patient regarding the archetypal motifs of his dreams. Naturally, much of this work is to provide the empirical validation of the reality of archetypes. But perhaps a large part of the task of those following the Jungian orientation is to just "hold" and recognize the archetypal, whether as divine or lowest common denominator. We perform this labor in the historical, anthropological and sociological researches that are currently being published and which provide the material for the actual amplification of imagery in analysis. We provide the space, the *temenos*, for them in the analytic situation. And most of all, we honor them in our researches into our own psyches every night. Perhaps this is our greatest contribution to dream interpretation and to the collective consciousness of our time.

Ullman (1987) has stated that:

> dream theories are no more than waking metaphors for expressing, in highly condensed language, the therapist's preferred way of seeing the patient's predicament. When there is a good fit between the therapist's metaphorical construct and the metaphors of the dream imagery, there is a sense of contact between the dreamer and the therapist and the exchange has a liberating impact on the dreamer. The therapist's theoretical position is relevant only to the extent that it stimulate this dual response. (In the Foreword to *Dream Interpretation*)

This "liberating impact" could well be understood from the Jungian perspective as the activation of an archetype which leads to the healing of a wounded psyche through the mediation of the analytic relationship. This paper has been an exploration of the various methods for facilitating this experience through the use and appreciation of the dream in psychotherapy. Perhaps the goal of all approaches utilizing dream-work is to establish what Khan (1974) calls the *dream-space*. Although coming from an object relational emphasis, his conceptualization can be useful to us all. He states:

> [I]t is my clinical experience that when patients cannot establish a dream-space in their inner reality they tend to exploit their social space and object relations to act out their dreams. I am here proposing that a dream that actualizes in the dream-space curtails acting out of dreams in social space. The dream that actualizes in the dream-space of a given patient leads to personalization of the dream experience and all that is entailed in it by way of instinct and object-relating. (p. 314)

Here the dream becomes its own enactment and a potential space for finding *self* as separate from, and in relation to, *Self*.

In conclusion, it is well known that the "royal road" can certainly become a dead-end street. Personal glossaries can be used to conceal meaning and dreams can be reported in the service of resistance, as a bribe or seduction of the therapist, indicative of narcissistic aims or archaic object attachments, and approached so intellectually as to avoid emotional experiencing. And yet they offer something, an opportunity, so truly unique that we would be quite remiss in dismissing them out of fear or ignorance. It should be remembered that even after Joseph invoked God as the ultimate authority regarding interpretation, he went on to give quite adequate interpretations of the dreams. The paradoxical nature of dreams is nicely stated by Whitman (1974):

"[D]reams seek as they hide, reveal as they conceal, unify as they mystify, play as they work—much as the marriage of poetry and language do. One must learn how to savor one's dreams" (p. 648). And the interpreters who approach these complex phenomena of the night are no less paradoxical in the "sureness of their tentativeness."

References

Anonymous. 1980. A collaborative account of a psychoanalysis through dreams. In *The Dream in Clinical Practice*, J. Natterson, ed. New York: Jason Aronson.

Bosnak R. 1988. *A Little Course in Dreams*. Boston: Shambhala.

Dallett, J. 1973. Theories of dream function. *Psychological Bulletin* 79(6): 408–416.

Fosshage, J. 1987. New vistas in dream interpretation. In *Dreams in New Perspective: The Royal Road Revisited*, M. Glucksman and S. Warner, eds. New York: Human Sciences Press.

Fosshage, J. and Loew, C., eds. 1978/1987. *Dream Interpretation: A Comparative Study*. New York: Spectrum, 1978; rev. ed. New York: PMA.

Freud, S. 1900/1965. *The Interpretation of Dreams*. J. Strachey, ed. and trans. New York: Avon, 1965.

Gendlin, E. 1986. *Let Your Body Interpret Your Dreams*. Wilmette, Ill.: Chiron Publications.

Greenson, R. 1970. The exceptional position of the dream in psychoanalytic practice. *Psychoanalytic Quarterly* 39:519–549.

Hall, J. 1977. *Clinical Uses of Dreams: Jungian Interpretations and Enactments*. New York: Grune and Stratton.

———. 1983. *Jungian Dream Interpretation: A Handbook of Theory and Practice*. Toronto: Inner City Books.

Hillman, J. 1979. *The Dream and the Underworld*. New York: Harper and Row.

Hobson, R. 1971. Imagination and amplification in psychotherapy. *Journal of Analytical Psychology* 16:79–105.

Johnson, R. 1986. *Inner Work: Using Dreams and Active Imagination for Personal Growth*. San Francisco: Harper and Row.

Jung, C. 1934. The practical use of dream-analysis. In *Collected Works* 16:139–161. Princeton, N.J.: Princeton University Press, 1954.

———. 1984. *Dream Analysis: Notes of the Seminar Given in 1928–1930*. W. McGuire, ed. New York: Princeton University.

Kahn, J. 1975. "Do not interpretations belong to God?" The validity of interpretations in psychotherapy and in literature. *British Journal of Medical Psychology* 48:227–236.

Kahn, M. 1974. The use and abuse of dream in psychic experience. In *The Privacy of the Self*. London: Hogarth Press.

Kohut, H. 1977. *The Restoration of the Self*. New York: International Universities Press.

Lambert, K. 1979. The use of the dream in contemporary analysis. *Journal of Analytical Psychology* 24:127–143.

Layard, J. 1944/1988. *The Lady and the Hare: A Study in the Healing Power of Dreams*. Boston: Shambhala, 1988.

Mattoon, M. 1977. *Understanding Dreams*. (Previously published as *Applied Dream Analysis: A Jungian Approach*.) New York: John Wiley and Sons.

Meier, C. 1987. *The Meaning and Significance of Dreams*. Vol. 2 of *The Psychology of C. G. Jung*. Boston: Sigo Press.

Natterson, J., ed. 1980. *The Dream in Clinical Practice*. New York: Jason Aronson.

Parsifal-Charles, N. 1986. *The Dream: 4,000 Years of Theory and Practice*, 2 vols. Conn.: Locust Hill.

Shelburne, W. 1984. A critique of James Hillman's approach to the dream. *Journal of Analytical Psychology* 29:35–56.

Ullman, M. 1987. Forward. In *Dream Interpretation: A Comparative Study*, J. Fosshage and C. Loew, eds. rev. ed. New York: PMA.

Ullman, M. and Limmer, C., eds. 1987. *The Variety of Dream Experience*. New York: Continuum.

Warner, S. 1987. Manifest dream analysis in contemporary practice. In *Dreams in New Perspective: The Royal Road Revisited*, M. Glucksman and S. Warner, eds. New York: Human Sciences Press.

Whitman, R. 1974. Dreams and dreaming. *Journal of the American Psychoanalytic Association* 22:643–650.

Winnicott, D. 1971. *Playing and Reality*. New York: Basic Books.

Wolman, B. ed. 1979. *Handbook of Dreams: Research, Theories and Applications*. New York: Van Nostram.

Nietzsche's Zarathustra

C. G. Jung. Edited by James L. Jarrett. Princeton, N.J.: Princeton University Press, Bollingen Series XCIX, 1988. 1,578 pages. $130.00

Reviewed by Ross L. Hainline

Jung opened his five-year seminar on Nietzsche's "Thus Spake Zarathustra" in 1934 with these words:

> Ladies and Gentlemen: I made up my mind to give you a seminar about Zarathustra, as you wished, but the responsibility is on your heads. If you think that Zarathustra is easier than those visions (the previous seminar), you are badly mistaken, it is a hell of a confusion and extraordinarily difficult. I broke my head over certain problems; it will be very hard to elucidate this work from a psychological angle. However, we will try to do our best, but you must cooperate.

From the above, one gets the impression that those attending the seminar selected the topic, but I suspect Jung put the idea in their heads. Jung's interest in Nietzsche went back to his early years. Both Nietzsche and Jung attended the University of Basel; Jung was a student from 1895 to 1900, Nietzsche taught Philology from 1869 to 1879 and became a full professor in the 1870s. During Jung's student days there were still people around who knew Nietzsche, including

---

Ross L. Hainline, M.D., is an analyst in private practice in New York City and West Nyack, N.Y., and is a psychiatric consultant to the New York Institute's Jungian clinic.

his reserved friend Jacob Burkhardt, whom Jung also knew. It was during these days that Jung, hearing gossip and rumor about Nietzsche, first became attracted to him.

Barbara Hannah, who was among the group of analysts, candidates-in-training, and a few lay people attending this seminar, said in her biography of Jung that he did give them a choice but that they voted for Zarathustra, hoping to get a view of what was happening in Germany just prior to World War II.

> Jung had often reminded us that, although we were still able to live our ordinary lives, we should never forget the storm clouds hanging over Europe. He also mentioned that he thought Nietzsche's idea of the Superman was the direct forerunner of the German idea that they were the *Herrenmenschen* (the Masters or Supermen), so it is possible that the vote of the class was swayed by the hope that we would get more understanding of and insight into the strange events that were taking place so near us, just over the German border. (Hannah 1976, p. 227)

A measure of Jung's interest and attraction to Nietzsche is a list compiled by Henrietta Bancroft, an elder member of the Analytical Psychology Club of New York, entitled, "References to Nietzsche — Taken from the Writings of Prof. C. G. Jung." The references, some long, some brief, appear throughout the eighteen volumes of Jung's Collected Works, and without a doubt Jung was especially well acquainted with Zarathustra. In this seminar, he stated, "I read Zarathustra for the first time *with consciousness* in the first year of the war, in November, 1914" (1988, p. 259). Later he said, "I read Zarathustra for the first time when I was only twenty-three, and then later, in the winter of 1914–15, I studied it very carefully and made a lot of annotations" (1988, p. 391). It would seem Jung read it at least two times, not including the page-by-page analysis during the seminar.

There are many factors and similarities that explain Jung's early fascination with Nietzsche and his later objective study of Nietzsche's psychology. Both Nietzsche and Jung were sons of Protestant parsons and both had strong feminine influences in their early life. Nietzsche's father died when he was four years old and the boy was raised by his mother, two aunts, and a grandmother. Although Jung was twenty when his father died, he was closer to his mother. Both Nietzsche and Jung reflected on religion differently than their fathers who were caught in the conventional rules of a rather decadent late Christianity. Both men were introverts and very similar as regards their superior and auxiliary functions — Nietzsche an intuitive thinker, Jung a thinking intuitive, at least early on — later he developed other functions.

In my view the greatest attraction Nietzsche held for Jung was that Nietzsche, perhaps more aware of the opposites in life than any of his contemporaries, came up with the concept of the self as a way of transcending the opposites. Liliane Frey-Rohn, who was among those who attended Jung's seminar, states in her recent book, "Jung once made the interesting remark that he originally came upon the concept of the self when reading Zarathustra for the first time at the age of 17. He adopted it and went on to pursue the concept in Hindu writings" (1984, p. 96ff). As Self is so often confused with ego, I regret that Jung didn't choose one of Nietzsche's other terms, such as "god image" or "greater personality," as a way to differentiate the concepts more completely. My sole criticism of this excellent new edition is that "self" is not capitalized as it is capitalized in the privately printed seminar notes.

In approaching the content of this seminar one must first ask, Just what is this work which Nietzsche saw as his magnum opus? Is "Thus Spake Zarathustra" a metaphorical poem, an epic, a dream series, or a visionary experience? Jung considered it a bit of all these things and he approached it very systematically, chapter by chapter, reflecting on each image and its relation to the image that preceded it and to the image that followed, much as one would follow a dream series in an ordinary analysis. In the latter, one would work through a lot of personal unconscious material, with perhaps at some point an archetypal theme emerging. By contrast, "Thus Spake Zarathustra" is largely archetypal from beginning to end. Jung often found it difficult to discern when and if Nietzsche's ego was speaking within the archetypal chorus of voices and images.

Throughout the seminar, Jung's "method of amplification" of the various images and motifs, bit by bit, shed light and meaning on Nietzsche's abstruse hymn to the superman. Archetypal images change very slowly over the centuries, and so it was the arduous task of Jung and his students to search for parallel imagery from past civilizations and religions that corresponded to Nietzsche's imagery until the feeling and the meaning became clearer. Without this important method it is doubtful whether Jung could have analyzed "Thus Spake Zarathustra," for Nietzsche himself did not understand the power that overcame and possessed him.

Jung explains in the first seminar lecture the origin of Nietzsche's interest in Zarathustra. He reports that Nietzsche's sister, Elisabeth, had said that Nietzsche dreamt of Zarathustra as a boy. Historically Zarathustra is the semi-legendary Persian old wise man who is believed to have lived between the seventh and ninth centuries B.C. He, supposedly, was the first to draw the distinction between good and evil, in that he encountered the god of light and the god of darkness, later called Ormazd and Ahriman, the opposites.

In the very first chapter of Nietzsche's puzzling drama, we find Zarathustra, age 30, leaving his home by the lake and going to the mountains, taking with him his eagle and his serpent. Jung points out the parallel of Christ starting his teaching at the same "legendary age" and observes that Nietzsche, in spite of his aversion to Christianity, wanted to teach a morality much higher than the Christian morality (Jung 1988, p. 13). And so Zarathustra leaves his home by the lake, the personal unconscious, and ascends to the mountain top where he accumulates his wisdom, a kind of superconsciousness, from the sun. He remains there for 10 years, after which time he descends to give his message to common men. Jung along with his students evaluates the eagle and the serpent in detail. They conclude that the eagle corresponds to spirit and the serpent to body, instinct, and the sympathetic nervous system, and that these can work for or against Zarathustra depending on his ego's relation to these archetypal realities.

Partway down the mountain Zarathustra encounters an old man in the forest, an anchorite, representing the old Christian spirit that did not know of Nietzsche's pronouncement that "God is dead." Nietzsche, alias Zarathustra, for he is totally identified with Zarathustra as Jung proves many times in this seminar, finally descends to a village where he will preach the superman to the common man. It is here the calamity occurs which forecasts Nietzsche's tragic end. A rope-dancer is performing in the village square. As he crosses his rope bridge, a fool or buffoon emerges and jumps over the rope-dancer causing him to fall to his death. The rope-dancer living dangerously on his rope bridge is an aspect of Nietzsche-Zarathustra as is the fool who corresponds to the other pole, the folly of Nietzsche-Zarathustra's inflated wisdom. Zarathustra says to the rope-dancer just before he dies, "Thy soul will be dead even sooner than thy body" (Jung 1988, p. 130). Jung says, "This is the prophetic word, it prophesies Nietzsche's fate. His soul died in 1889 when his general paralysis began but he lived on for eleven more years" (ibid., p. 115).

Nietzsche was invaded by archetypal contents and although he was aware of the extreme opposites, being an intense idealist, he identified with the spiritual pole almost completely. The unconscious compensated, trying to get him off his lofty throne by bringing up earthy images, each of which Jung discusses in detail (notable examples are the serpent, toad, spider, dog, and the ugliest man). Nietzsche could not accept what he himself preached. He preached the body, but he didn't live the body, for he was plagued with migraines, sleeplessness, stomach troubles, and loneliness, and avoided banality and common men like the plague.

Edinger in a 1984 address for the Jung Foundation of New York entitled "Encounter with the Greater Personality," in which he used Nietzsche as one example, expressed the view that it was Jung's knowledge of Nietzsche that prevented him from suffering the same fate. In other words, Jung was able to discriminate ego from Self and not identify with the Self as Nietzsche had done.

Anyone who reads this seminar can discern that, in spite of the rumors about both, neither Nietzsche nor Jung were anti-Semitic. More to the point would be the fact that Nietzsche's sister Elisabeth was married to a blatant anti-Semite, Dr. Bernhard Forster. Later, when Nietzsche was unable to defend himself because of his psychosis, Elisabeth tried to make it seem that Nietzsche's teaching was in accord with the views of the National Socialist party; it could be seen that way if totally misunderstood. H. F. Peters in his book, "Zarathustra's Sister," gives the history of Elisabeth and comments, "By vulgarizing her brother's ideals, Elisabeth had perverted them into their opposites—superhuman had become sub human" (1977, p. 227). In his book is a picture of Elisabeth at age 88 receiving Hitler at the Nietzsche Archive. Hitler also came to her theater box on two occasions and attended her funeral.

In writing this review, I realized early on that I could only give but a sample of the seminar's contents. The seminar went on week after week, until World War II forced its participants to go on about their business elsewhere. I can only direct the reader to the source. When one reads Jung's seminar notes, many surprises are in store. The conversational style with humor, wit, and anger interspersed, makes one feel present along with the other students. Jung comes across as a great teacher. Ideas of other books he had yet to write are seen here in germinal form. For example, in the Nov. 27, 1935, lecture (p. 724), there is one paragraph that contains the essence of his later work, "Answer to Job." One never knows what will emerge next, for in answering students he sometimes goes into comparative religion, ancient and modern, or again talks of current happenings in America and Europe or then again about the great puzzle of what would emerge in Germany.

Even though it was given half a century ago, this seminar is highly pertinent in today's climate, perhaps even more so than when it took place. The collective mind is still present, but in greater numbers; the world has shrunk even more, and prejudice is rife. As technology has grown, religion has weakened, morality and ethics have lost ground. These happenings were stimuli for Jung writing that small gem, "The Undiscovered Self" in 1957. As a twentieth-century man, Jung discovered more of the undiscovered Self than did other contemporaries; he fulfilled his individuation process as much as was humanly possible to do so. The proof is the energy and learning this one individual contained, its source, the Self, with Jung its human instrument. In the five years of this seminar, Jung was at a peak of energy, for how else could he have accomplished what Jarrett, in his excellent introduction to the seminar, lists—the many publications of this period, a trip to India, Eranos lectures at Ascona, Switzerland, lectures in London and the United Sates, plus his ongoing private practice and the start of his alchemical research.

I would highly recommend this seminar, a five-year voyage through Nietzsche's magnum opus, as a study in analytical psychology in action with its founder at the helm. In a few words, its real essence is, Don't look for God in extragalactic space, for it's quite cold out there; rather look within, where the God image and the archetypes reside.

Sources Cited

Bancroft, Henrietta. n.d. References to Nietzsche: Taken from the writings of Prof. C. G. Jung. New York: Kristine Mann Library.

Edinger, Edward. 1984. Encounters with the Great Personality. On tape.

Frey-Rohn, Liliane. 1984. *Frederich Nietzsche: A Psychological Approach to His Life and Work*. Zurich: Daimon-Verlag.

Hannah, Barbara. 1976. *Jung: His Life and Work: A Biographical Memoir*. New York: G. P. Putnam's Sons.

Jung, C. G. 1988. *Nietzsche's Zarathustra*. Bollingen Series XCIX, vol. 1. Princeton, N.J.: Princeton University Press.

Peter, H. F. 1977. *Zarathustra's Sister: The Case of Elisabeth and Frederich Nietzsche*. New York: Crown Publishers Inc.

Female Authority: Empowering Women Through Psychotherapy
Polly Young-Eisendrath and Florence Wiedemann. New York: The Guilford Press, 1987. 242 pages. $25.00

Reviewed by Marilyn L. Matthews

Female Authority, by Wiedemann and Young-Eisendrath, is a scholarly work that is well researched and documented. The authors wrote it because they were distressed that women clients are most often assessed in terms of deficits measured by the usually accepted standards of psychopathology and behavioral norms. Evalu-

Marilyn Matthews, M.D., is a Jungian analyst who lives and practices in Santa Fe, N.M.

ation from these traditional perspectives upholds and reinforces women's internalized sense of inferiority. Because they wished to focus on women's strengths rather than deficits, the authors chose to emphasize two critical issues: the first, how women claim the validity of their own truths in a patriarchal society, and the second, to define a "competence assessment" model which systematizes women's strengths in the contexts of stress and vulnerability. In other words, the authors look for qualities which are effective and adaptive rather than deficient. Young-Eisendrath and Wiedemann combine their knowledge of Jungian analysis, fairy tales, mythology, feminist literature, and Loevinger's research on ego development as the mainstay of the book.

They have solidly grounded each stage of animus development with research from ego psychology and feminist literature as well as giving detailed observations of the kind of problems and characteristics that a therapist might see in women in transition through each stage. Their clinical assessments of three patients demonstrated the personal style from which they work and provided detailed pictures of the process of the women's developments. Their care and consideration both to protect these clients and to have them share in the process of the writing of the case exemplifies the cooperation of their therapeutic work.

The authors write in detail about the dilemma of American women whose process of socialization allows few ways to evaluate themselves in positive terms. Psychology tends to reinforce the negative self-concept. When women fight these feelings of inferiority by identifying their competencies, strengths, and capabilities, they are told they are either compensating or too masculine. If women identify with the traditional role of passivity and submission, the other side of the double bind here becomes one of being seen as childlike or dependent. The authors observe again and again that when women are assessed by standard male norms for autonomous behavior, they are often judged as overly dependent or insecure instead of being seen as connected to basic human needs for interpersonal contact.

The authors emphasize the imprecision of the psychopathological model and the damage that deficit labeling causes, especially when psychotropic drugs are used to limit consciousness and activity. Even so, on behalf of the "medical" model I have to reaffirm the necessity of recognizing certain kinds of "dis-ease" states, which if not recognized by the therapist, could lead to serious trouble. Most psychiatrists use psychotropic medications wisely. However, the caveat remains that we must pay attention to our own reactions when prescribing, especially to women who have learned a "victim" stance to bring the yearned-for attention.

In defining *female authority* as the "ability of a woman to validate her own convictions of truth, beauty, and goodness in regard to her self-concept and self-interest," (p.8) the authors include a woman's occupational and social functioning, her personal agency and self-confidence, her body image and sexual pleasure as well as her subjective self-assessment. The feminine strengths of intuition, emotional expressiveness, and regard for her personal beauty underly the authors' proposed model for female development of identity evolving through relationship of self and other.

The Jungian concept of animus describes the masculine aspects excluded from a woman's consciousness. Women who grow up socialized by patriarchal norms have to exclude authority from their concept of self. In order to regain that sense of authority, women must retrieve it from its masculine form and convert it into positive experiences of self. The double-bind conflict about female authority is inherent in all stages of female development from birth to old age. In order to foster greater self-appreciation and self-validation in women, therapists and educators must recognize this conflict. Retrieving personal authority from being only reflections of the men in women's personal as well as collective lives and actualizing it leads to authenticity and flexibility. Conscious dialogue with others as well as with one's own psyche is the authors' aim for psychotherapy with women.

The book provides a detailed examination of the stages of ego development, animus awareness and integration, as well as the use of several myths and fairy tales to help the therapist recognize each stage and its pitfalls. The authors emphasize the need for an accurate language in assessing emotional interdependence. For example, they indicate that for some people dependency means passive dependence on others and vicarious identification with others' successes rather than living from one's own authentic needs. If we are to recognize emotional dependence as basic for human interaction, the authors believe that the term *empathy* more accurately describes that ideal. In order for empathy to be present one must have a well-defined sense of self as well as being attuned to both differences and similarities with others.

I found myself in a dilemma in reading this work. I know and respect both authors and wish to praise them for the depth of knowledge and careful consideration they have provided in their work. However, their style is dry, scholarly, dense, and wordy, and although it is quite well organized, I found the book difficult to read. The authors write as if they know best. The book provides much information which feels force-fed and leaves little room for me to think for myself. The writing did not enliven me nor did it hold my interest. There was little evidence of eros, of relationship, or of the Feminine, except in the chapter that Dr. Wiedemann wrote about her analysand. It seems to me that the authors are not really listening to the feminine psyche, but rather are trying to fit women's processes into a model of development to help us out of a culturally created conflict.

While I agree that praise and positive assessment are important to help us regain our self-esteem, I believe the therapist must listen carefully to the woman's story and not try to fit her into some preconceived mold. There is something too male or perhaps too Athena-like in the image they paint of woman's authority. It feels like the animus wrote the book.

Woman's authority is ultimately more than animus. Woman's power and authority come from being embodied, from female values, from being nurturing as well as having strength. It is as if any feminine softness, any possibility for reverie or reflection, any invitation to the imagination was erased from the writing. What is left I find hard to digest and equally hard to apply.

The Dreaming Brain: How the Brain Creates Both the Sense and the Nonsense of Dreams
J. Allan Hobson. New York: Basic Books, 1988. 319 pages. $22.95

Reviewed by James A. Hall

This is both a fascinating and a disappointing book. It is fascinating because of what it says and disappointing in that it is not responsibly concerned with Jung's theory of dreams or with the problem of parapsychological dreams.

Hobson, a professor of psychiatry at Harvard Medical School, presents a clear, readable, and articulate review of a "brain-based approach to dreaming." He deftly reviews nineteenth-century studies of dreaming, relates them to the early twentieth-century studies and to the exciting unfoldment of the understanding of brain activity that led to the epochal discovery in 1953 by Eugene Aserinsky and Nathaniel Kleitman of the relation of REM (rapid eye movement) sleep to dreaming.

It is this understanding of REM sleep that led to what Hobson presents as a new model of the dreaming brain. In clear prose he traces the newer understanding of the brain during dreaming: the aminergic neurons of the brain stem, related to attention and memory, rest during sleep (particularly REM sleep) and permit the disinhibition of the sensorimotor neurons that fire, both to maintain and perhaps to creatively transform brain circuits. Consolidation of memory traces and transformation of old and new information may be facilitated.

Hobson's "brain-based" theory of dreaming seems to rest on a tacit assumption of the usual epiphenomenalistic bias of science — that physical reality is primary and that mental activity is secondary. He thus explains that the hybrid term *brain-mind* is used "to signal my conviction that a complete description of either (brain or mind) will be a complete description of the other (mind or brain)" (p. 16). Hobson does not explicitly state, but strongly suggests, that the "mind" can eventually be reduced to the brain.

Despite a pious hope that "at some future time, the two words may well be replaced by one" (p. 16), Hobson's choice leaves no room for the possibility that mind and brain might refer to actually separate realities. Why is it important to keep open the option of mind and brain being separate? Simply because the phenomena that Jung called *synchronicity* (ESP, telepathy, clairvoyance, and precognition) are difficult if not impossible to imagine in the epiphenomenalistic model that "mind" is simply a term for brain-in-action. Since Hobson does not really concern himself with the problems of synchronicity (there is only one scant reference to ESP), he neatly side-steps the central problem posed by precognitive dreams, for which Jung gives several striking examples in his essay *On Synchronicity*.

James A. Hall, M.D., is clinical associate professor of psychiatry, University of Texas Health Science Center, Dallas, and a founding member of the Inter-Regional Society of Jungian Analysts.

Part IV is an intellectual tour de force that relates the phenomenology of dreams of "The Engine Man" with possible neurophysiological "causes." Hobson discusses the dream journal of the Engine Man in terms of the form of dream drama, the form of dream sensation and movement, the bizarreness of dreams, and the interpretation of dream form. In an authoritative critique of Freudian dream theory, which lays the basis for comparisons throughout the book, Hobson suggests that many of Freud's assumptions can best be explained in terms of brain functioning during REM sleep. The "repressed dream wish," for example, may relate to the inhibited motor impulses that are suppressed in the brain stem during REM sleep.

I read with anticipation and interest the section on "The Transparency Hypothesis of Carl Jung" (p. 65). Hobson correctly notes that Jung saw dreams as "not necessarily serving the purpose of disguise." Hobson clearly appreciates Jung's view that dreams are "transparent" — they say *in symbolic form* what they mean. Hobson finds Jung more scientific in his approach to dreams than was Freud.

And yet, this brief section on Jung is highly disappointing for a Jungian analyst. Most of the three-and-a-half pages are devoted to discussion of Jung's relation to Freud, not to exposition of Jung's own radically different understanding of dreams. There is no presentation, for example, of the central Jungian concept of the compensatory nature of dreams.

In short, Hobson presents an authoritative and impressive understanding of the development of current laboratory research in sleep and dreams and relates it in a masterful way with nineteenth- and early twentieth-century precursors. From this base, he effectively demolishes the Freudian theory of dreams although explicitly stating that "I do not mean to imply that I disagree with its psychodynamic spirit" in spite of proposing "alternative explanations for all of its important claims" (p. 12).

In his basic synthetic and hopeful tone, Hobson is very close to Jung. For example:

> In shifting the emphasis from the opaque to the transparent aspects of dreaming, activation synthesis [Hobson's theory] regards the dream process as more progressive than regressive; as more positive than negative; as more creative than destructive. In sum, as more healthy than neurotic. (p. 16)

While Hobson seems so close to Jung in his synthetic emphasis of the purpose of dreaming, he has not understood nor adequately critiqued Jung's theory of dreams in relation to the findings of laboratory dream research. Should he write another book, I hope that he will extend his comparisons into the actual field of Jungian dream interpretation.

This book can be highly recommended as a basic and reliable presentation of laboratory dream research and as a beginning dialogue between the relevance of such studies and the psychoanalytic uses of dreaming.

The Japanese Psyche
Hayao Kawaii. Dallas: Spring Publications, 1988. 227 pages. $17.50

Reviewed by Josip Pasic

The author of this brilliantly written, lucid book simply says the ego in
Western fairy tales is represented by a man and in the Japanese ones by a woman.
In the nine chapters of the book, he tries to explain the deeper psychological
significance and relevance of these facts for depth psychology. Throughout the
book he juxtaposes Western and Japanese fairy tales, making obvious their fundamental differences.

Western tales are seen as clearly developmental in their nature and Neumann's
stages of development fit accurately as their psychological explanations. The hero,
almost always a man, strives to gain the maiden and the treasure, and the complexity of that near superhuman striving is depicted in the overcoming of a series of
obstacles (dragon, monster, the inhuman elements).

In a nutshell, the Western fairy tales consist in gaining through striving.
Japanese fairy tales, on the other hand, consist in losing, in having less than they
had when they started. The Western hero finds a treasure and a maiden in the
secret chamber, while the main character of the Japanese tale finds a bird to let go,
or a branch, or a flower. He simply finds basically nothing. Finding something and
finding nothing correlates to the notion of the psyche as thing (as something) and
the psyche as nothing, the psyche as breath. One can also view psyche as a clutter of
things, of psychological notions, and the psyche as stillness, as a vacancy in which
everything is. Fundamentally speaking, the Western stories insist above all else on
their sense of continuity. The Japanese insist on their ending. Hero myth and
phoenix myth are two absolutely extreme examples of the essential attitude of these
fairy tales.

In order to understand this polarity more deeply, one must understand the
nature of the psychological masculine and psychological feminine. It is a well-
known fact in depth psychology, art, and religion that the psychological masculine
principle is that which is divisive, defining, limiting, directive, deliberate, differentiating, discerning. These are the *visible* attributes of the masculine attitude, but
what lies behind them? What is it that actually creates the psychological masculine
knowledge if not psychological knowledge itself, that which is stored up in the
brain as memory, thought, and image with their personal and collective ramifications? The whole of consciousness that includes even the unconscious consciousness
is actually a masculine psychological phenomenon. Interestingly enough the ety-
mology of the word "consciousness" comes from the composite Latin word, "con"
meaning "with" and "scientia" meaning "knowledge," pointing toward looking
through an intricate network of knowledge. The words "thought" and "thing"

Josip Pasic, M.D., is a Jungian analyst and faculty member of the C. G. Jung Institute of
Chicago. He conducts a private practice in Chicago and Evanston, Ill.

come from the same Latin word "res," which means both thought and thing simultaneously. Thought, being knowledge, points in the same direction.

Psychological knowledge, being essentially limited, isolates and manifests itself psychologically as loneliness and constriction. It breeds a self-perpetuating development that eludes and distorts new realities. Psychological knowledge, being limited, as any knowledge is no matter how much wisdom it contains, divides, and that division is felt psychologically as conflict. This is not to say that psychological knowledge has no place in life, it does, but only if it is in the right place. And it is only in the right place if it emerges out of the depth of the true psychological feminine. If it is on its own and fixed as a rigid psychological identity, as is usually the case, then it has no true and creative place.

But now what is the feminine psychological principle? Is it another principle at all? If it is a principle, then it is nothing but a variation of the masculine. Even in asking, What is feminine? one expects definition and so by that expectation we must realize we are back in the realm of the masculine. On these terms the feminine is nothing but another form of knowledge and so inherently masculine. One sees this phenomenon clearly in Western fairy tales and in Western psychology as well. The feminine, then, is nothing but a result of (masculine) discrimination demonstrated in notions of the "feminine" that divide it into stages of categories (four stages of anima, etc.). That which has stages has boundaries and is therefore masculine. Isn't the feminine that which can only be negatively defined, that which one can come upon only through the negation of fixed masculine psychological structure?

The atmosphere of openness, wherein there are no boundaries, no fixed notions, is the space that describes the true feminine. After all, intellectually speaking we are correct when we use negative terms for the description of the feminine psychological attitude as that which is receptive and yielding, but in actuality we are talking about the receptive that is more or less receptive and the yielding that is more or less yielding. All that is then quasi-feminine, not a true feminine. The essence of the masculine is in the gradation, in the measurement; it can't also be an essential attribute of the feminine. This surrogate or quasi-feminine is nothing but a disguised masculine protecting itself, pretending to be something other than itself and so remains essentially the same masculine perpetually. Examples of this quasi-feminine are seen in Western fairy tales where it stands as a projection, expectation of the hero (masculine). It has no validity in itself except as it serves the hero's needs and so can be pursued, possessed, married.

The example of the true feminine is seen in the Japanese fairy tales where it stands on its own essential nature as other-worldliness, meaning not of the same order of the masculine divisibility and so not as its product and consequently serving its needs. This true feminine cannot be pursued by the masculine but can contain and marry and even give birth to the masculine. Being an actuality of a fundamentally different order (other-worldliness, a term explicitly used), the true feminine is not and cannot be opposite nor even complementary to the masculine. The true feminine, providing the atmosphere for wholeness, and so being of the wholeness itself, neither has nor needs an opposite.

When masculine dominates, reigns, there is no feminine. Whenever there is a tendency for the psychological masculine to take over areas where it has no rightful place, the feminine just disappears, dies, or goes away politely. An example of that attitude is seen in the Japanese fairy tale, "The Crane Wife." The woman, who was a crane, forbade her husband to look into the closet during the three days she spent inside it, and while he obeyed everything was fine. Once he succumbed to curiosity to know who she was while in the closet, she left. That impulse to violate her request, born of the desire to know and therefore to limit, was a degenerative tendency to capture her nature and imprison it in knowledge. That very tendency to know, to box the feminine into the limitation of knowledge, is what drives it away. It is only in the very death, ending, dissolving of the masculine as we know it, that there is a coming upon that stillness and inwardness, the necessary feminine. From that stillness and inwardness all things are born, including the true, accurate masculine. As in many ancient myths, primordial reality is feminine; by her very nature the feminine carries within herself the masculine potential and even its actual unfoldment.

Inwardness, actually named in these fairy tales as other-worldliness and usually represented by a woman, is often also an animal, bird, or some other aspect of nature, and it transcends both the so-called inner and outer. That inwardness is nothing other than wholeness and the feminine, the true feminine, the necessary ground in which wholeness manifests itself.

Jungian Child Psychotherapy: Individuation in Childhood
Mara Sidoli and Miranda Davies, editors. London: Karnac Books, 1988. 286 pages $29.00

Reviewed by John Allen

This book is the sixth in the series of the Library of Analytical Psychology, published for the Society of Analytical Psychology of London. It consists of a collection of 15 articles, some reprinted from the *Journal of Analytical Psychology*, and is largely a product of the child analysis training division under the supervision of Dr. Michael Fordham. Three papers are by Fordham, nine by others of this London group and three by members of the International Workshop on Analytical Psychology in Childhood and Adolescence.

The book begins with a useful preface by Sidoli and Davies and an introduction by Astor. These papers set the scene for the book describing it in part as a tribute to Michael Fordham and as a means to introduce the reader to the practice of Jungian child psychotherapy based on the theoretical formulations of Fordham.

John Allan, Ph.D., is an associate professor of counseling psychology at the University of British Columbia and a member of the Pacific Northwest Society of Jungian Analysts. His private practice focuses on children and families and he is author of *Inscapes of the Child's World: Jungian Counseling in Schools and Clinics*.

The papers are grouped into five parts: History and Theoretical Basis; Individuation, Analysis and Symbolic Play; Management Problems; Children with Autistic Features; and Working with Adolescents. Of all of the sections, I found the most stimulating to be those involved with theoretical formulations as opposed to the descriptions of the actual practice of child psychotherapy.

I have very strong mixed feelings about this book. In many ways it is an exceedingly complex, if somewhat disjointed, selection of readings, many of which offer some profound insights into the origins of mental life and the nature of emotional development and relationships. It is slow, challenging reading as the material makes one pause to think about various issues. Many times I had to go back and forth rereading the material to fully comprehend some of the concepts. It was well worth the effort. I felt my theoretical understanding of early developmental issues was greatly deepened. Particularly notable for me were the articles by Sidoli and Davidson and the way they handled such issues as the process of deintegration and reintegration; the quality of absoluteness; playing and imaging; mourning and re-creating; giving experience form, space and individuation; and defenses of the Self. Also there is a very good integration of Jungian ideas with concepts from Bion, Meltzer, Klein, and Winnicott.

The theory section is an excellent source for Fordham's seminal ideas of the Self and individuation in childhood and on how archetypes function in a similar way in children as in adults. Much attention is given to insights gained from mother–infant observations and the model of primary Self, deintegration and reintegration, and defenses of the Self. Fordham ties together Klein's concepts of unconscious phantasies and good and bad objects with Jung's work in the *Psychology of the Unconscious* (later revised in *CW* 5). He also examines fusion, attachment to mother, analysis of children, the analytic attitude, the frame, transference, and interpretation.

My concern with this section is a lack of focus on what is healthy development during the first three years of life. Fordham criticizes Neumann for "lack of real evidence" (p. 27) based on infant observation but fails to mention the excellent research by Mahler, Ainsworth, or Main, which identifies stages of separation, the achievement of object constancy, and the formulation of a viable ego, and also lends support to several of Neumann's ideas.

Now we come to my more strident concerns. As a whole I think the book is inappropriately titled. The contents seem to me more like Freudian-Kleinian child analysis than Jungian child psychotherapy. The treatment techniques seem to center around the analysis of defenses through constant interpretation. Little attention is paid to creating a therapeutic alliance or a safe and protected space with appropriate toys or materials. The language of children is the language of play and yet for the most part, these London analysts use adult consulting rooms for seeing children and "adult" language and concepts for interpreting their actions. Apparently Fordham stopped using play as a healing approach in and of itself in the mid 1940s because he did not want to clean up the sand and water! I think his therapeutic effect greatly deteriorated at that point. The whole Jungian notion that, given the alliance and protected space, the psyche knows how to heal itself seems very alien to many of these analysts. Indeed, there seems to be a distinct distrust of the child's own abilities as if the child's behavior is *all* defensive or compensatory in nature as opposed to including its healing and reconstructive aspects.

Many children referred for play psychotherapy are already suffering from profound internal and external persecution anxiety. I see many of the interpretations used in this book as increasing persecutory feelings and actually isolating the child. As opposed to the therapist commenting on what is occurring (i.e., reflection of feeling), these interpretations frequently stab the child and shift him or her out of enactment experience into cognitive processes. In doing so, the analyst has disrupted and devalued the natural healing process embedded in the psyche. Many of these analysts focus exclusively on pain and seem to believe that growth occurs only through cognitive analysis of painful areas. I think this is a very erroneous premise — not only with children but also with adults.

The book is riddled with the kind of interpretation that Jung would call "adultomorphic speculations." I find many of them intrusive and destructive, as for example this one:

> And you want a big pooh in your bottom like a big cock that tells you you have power . . . . You want to make us mummy and daddy when they make love, which gives us together the good feelings they must have, when you feel like only a little baby with a little cock. (p. 151)

There are many more simple and effective ways of helping this boy with the emotions (and ambivalences) that he is experiencing in his play and in the transference. Obviously, interpretations can and do play a very important role in play psychotherapy but I find the timing and language of many in this book to be inappropriate and lacking in sensitivity to the child as a person and to the child's developmental level. From my perspective, many of the interpretations actually entrench ego defenses, narrow the ego–Self axis, and cut the child off from natural, symbolic healing potentials that are embedded in his or her psyche.

Another concern is the issue of "analytical attitude." Of course this is one of our most critically important tools, but my experience is that the London authors use it as a distancing device that keeps them aloof and unable to act (i.e., to be emotionally involved with the child, to play with the child, and to set effective limits). Involvement and analytical attitude are not mutually exclusive. In fact, involvement often heightens transference and countertransference issues and can yield deeper insights, provide more effective containment, and thus facilitate growth. Once again by not setting limits and providing safe outlets for aggressive and murderous impulses, I see these analysts as increasing the child's guilt and suffering. Fordham allows John to burn insects with matches but then stops him when he attacks his desk with a knife (p. 134)! No attempt is made by Fordham to help John understand his desire to hurt, his own feelings of being hurt and to have permission to redirect his rage to an object that is okay to burn, attack, or destroy.

From my perspective, the British authors generally seem to lack an understanding of how children heal and grow. Specifically, I am referring to creating a free and protected space and providing a relationship that is significantly more than "an analytical attitude." The therapeutic style is definitely patriarchal and Logos rules. It is very hard to imagine how a successful therapeutic alliance is formed and maintained when there is so much detachment, inadequate play materials, a failure to set basic limits and boundaries, and an excessive reliance on the use of complicated interpretations which frequently confuse and wound the child.

How can children be free to express their traumas symbolically and safely through play, resolve paranoid-schizoid splits, internalize the "good enough" feeling, and develop object constancy with this approach? Generally, I believe it is not possible. Where is the archetype of the Good Mother whose warm and yet firm presence creates the facilitative environment for healing and who uses interpretation sparingly and judiciously? Many of the analytical techniques mentioned in this book talk at the child's head and ego and miss the earth and the Self. With the exception of the treatment sessions described by Feldman, Bovensiepen, and Gabriellini and Nissim (whose therapy I found sensitive and excellent), I don't see this treatment style as Jungian and I think Jung would have been horrified by it. However, two Kleinian words aptly sum up my views of much of it: Bad Breast.

www.ingramcontent.com/pod-product-compliance
Lightning Source LLC
Chambersburg PA
CBHW050223270326
41914CB00003BA/547